E. L. Doctorow's Skeptical Commitment

Twentieth-Century American Jewish Writers

Daniel Walden
General Editor

Vol. 13

PETER LANG
New York • Washington, D.C./Baltimore • Boston • Bern
Frankfurt am Main • Berlin • Brussels • Vienna • Oxford

Michelle M. Tokarczyk

E. L. Doctorow's Skeptical Commitment

PETER LANG
New York • Washington, D.C./Baltimore • Boston • Bern
Frankfurt am Main • Berlin • Brussels • Vienna • Oxford

Library of Congress Cataloging-in-Publication Data

Tokarczyk, Michelle M.
E. L. Doctorow's skeptical commitment / Michelle M. Tokarczyk.
p. cm. — (Twentieth-century American Jewish writers; vol. 13)
Includes bibliographical references (p.   ) and index.
1. Doctorow, E. L., 1931–   —Criticism and interpretation. 2. Politics and literature—United States—History—20th century. 3. Doctorow, E. L., 1931– —Political and social views. 4. Political fiction, American—History and criticism. I. Title. II. Title: Political fiction of Edgar Lawrence Doctorow. III. Series.
PS3554.O3Z89   813'.54—dc21   99-19886
ISBN 0-8204-4470-7
ISSN 0897-7844

Die Deutsche Bibliothek-CIP-Einheitsaufnahme

Tokarczyk, Michelle M.:
E. L. Doctorow's skeptical commitment / Michelle M. Tokarczyk.
–New York; Washington, D.C./Baltimore; Boston; Bern;
Frankfurt am Main; Berlin; Brussels; Vienna; Oxford: Lang.
(Twentieth-century American Jewish writers; Vol. 13)
ISBN 0-8204-4470-7

Cover design by Nona Reuter

The paper in this book meets the guidelines for permanence and durability
of the Committee on Production Guidelines for Book Longevity
of the Council of Library Resources.

© 2000 Peter Lang Publishing, Inc., New York

All rights reserved.
Reprint or reproduction, even partially, in all forms such as microfilm,
xerography, microfiche, microcard, and offset strictly prohibited.

Printed in the United States of America

Table of Contents

Preface   vii

Acknowledgments   ix

Foreword   xi

Introduction   1

1. Praxis, Identity, and the American Writer: *Lives of the Poets* and *World's Fair*   27

2. The Frontier Reconsidered: *Welcome to Hard Times*   47

3. Representing and Facing an "Irretrievable Past:" *The Book of Daniel*   67

4. The American Dream, Insiders and Outsiders: *Ragtime*   89

5. Fathers, Sons, and Class Injury: *Loon Lake* as a Revision of the Proletarian Novel   111

6. Gangsters, the 1980s, and Greed: *Billy Bathgate*   133

7. Postmodernism Reconsidered on an Urban Landscape: *The Waterworks*   151

Afterword   171

Table of Contents

Works Cited   179

Index   191

Preface

E. L. Doctorow's: Skeptical Commitment is divided into seven chapters. Because Doctorow's autobiographical fiction most directly expresses some of the issues of the artist bearing witness to his/her society, I begin with his two autobiographical works, *Lives of the Poets: A Novella and Six Stories* and *Billy Bathgate,* in chapter one. Each of the remaining six chapters is devoted to one of Doctorow's novels, and I discuss the novels in the order in which they were written: *Welcome to Hard Times*, *The Book of Daniel, Ragtime, Loon Lake, Billy Bathgate,* and *The Waterworks*. Doctorow's second novel, *Big as Life*, a science fiction book in which two giants suddenly appear over New York City, is not up to the standards of the rest of Doctorow's work. The plot seems far-fetched and the quality of the writing disappointing. *Big as Life* is the only Doctorow novel that is out of print. For these reasons, I have chosen not to examine it. Also, since I am confining my study to Doctorow's fiction, I do not discuss his only drama, *Drinks Before Dinner* or focus on his numerous essays, though I do relate the views Doctorow expresses in his essays to the themes in his fiction.

Editions Used
Welcome to Hard Times. New York: Random House, 1960
The Book of Daniel. New York: Ballantine Books, 1971.
Ragtime. New York: Random House, 1975.
Loon Lake. New York: Random House, 1980.
Lives of the Poets: A Novella and Six Stories. New York: Random House, 1984.
World's Fair. New York: Random House, 1985.
Billy Bathgate. New York: Random House, 1989.
The Waterworks. New York: Random House, 1994.

Acknowledgments

There are many people who helped bring this manuscript to completion. Goucher College generously awarded me a Nitchie Grant for two summers, enabling me to focus on this book. I was fortunate to find many perceptive readers—Jane Bennett, William Connolly, Penelope Cordish, Cheryl Fish, Sharon Jessee, Mary Marchand, Barbara Roswell, and Paula Uruburu. Heidi Burns was a meticulous editor and sympathetic listener. Robert Welch provided important reassurance when my hard disk crashed in the midst of my editing the manuscript. Some of Goucher's skilled computer personnel—Paulette Comet, Christina Pumphrey, and Leslie Harris—literally helped give shape to this book. Secretaries Madeline Karczeski, Jamie Winter, and Jean McGregor saved me valuable time by retyping chapters lost to format errors. Finally, I thank my husband, Paul Groncki, for his continued support and faith in me.

Foreword

Bruce Robbins

"E. L Doctorow is the epic poet of the disappearance of the American radical past," Fredric Jameson wrote in 1984. Though Doctorow is "one of the few serious and innovative leftist novelists at work in the United States today," Jameson declared, he is also a prisoner of postmodernism, and thus politically handicapped. He exemplifies the postmodern "crisis of historicity" that cuts us off both from the struggles of the past and from the transformative potential lurking unrecognized in the present.[1] "The historical novel can no longer set out to represent the historical past," Jameson concluded; "it can only 'represent' our ideas and stereotypes about that past (which thereby at once becomes 'pop history')." In our "new and original historical situation," we are "condemned to seek History by way of our own pop images and simulacra of that history, which itself remains forever out of reach" (25).

Michelle Tokarczyk does not neglect the upper-case History that always seems to evade the novel's grasp, but she pays more attention to the everyday social grime and mess in which Doctorow delightedly dirties his hands. Asking "what it means to write political fiction in America . . . at this historical moment," Tokarczyk uses the word "political" in its enlarged contemporary sense, a sense instructed by feminism and other recent social movements to remember that strikes and barricades do not exhaust the subject of politics. If "the personal is the political," then most if not all novelists must count as political novelists. But Tokarczyk refuses to take this easy way out. She gives Doctorow full credit for his commitment to politics of a literal or traditional kind—for example, his treatment of Boss Tweed in *The Waterworks*, which she presents as an allegory of Reaganism—and she takes for her real subject what she calls Doctorow's "politics of indirection": the tense zone of subtle and unpredictable interactions that Doctorow sets up between such large, public, historical matters and the "personal" materials of the novel. She wants to know, for example, what Daniel's sexual sadism has to do with the politics of the Rosenberg case in *The Book of Daniel*, what the unashamed and uncriticized upward mobility of Tateh and Houdini has to do with the historical trajectory of *Ragtime,* what Joe's strange identification with the union-busting detective next door has to do with the strike episodes of *Loon Lake*. It is mystifying, piety-resistant puzzles like these that call for skepticism and commitment to pool their resources.

Perhaps because Doctorow's protagonists are so often upwardly mobile, they tend to be evasive about what they are committed to. Uneasily balanced, as Tokarczyk observes, between proletarian consciousness, gangster consciousness, and literary consciousness, they sometimes call the object of their desire "life." Only something as vague as "life" can cover, for example, the amoral jumble of desires that opens Joe of Paterson's narration in *Loon Lake*: "I stole what I needed and went after girls like prey. I went looking for trouble and was keen for it, I was keen for life, I ran down the street to follow the airships sailing by, I climbed firescapes and watched old women struggle into their corsets, I joined a gang and carried a penknife I had sharpened like an Arab, like a Dago, I stuck it in the vegetable peddler's horse, I stuck it in a feeb with a watermelon head, I slit awnings with it . . . I only wanted to be famous!" (2). The cascading rush of clauses won't let you pause to take in the difference between commonplace sadism and aesthetic spectatorship (the airships and firescapes), between the disinterested or perhaps even sympathetic contemplation of the old women struggling into corsets and the appetitive scrutiny of girls as prey, between the budding criminal's need to dominate and the budding writer's need to see for himself. This daredevil indiscriminateness, which flows from but also overflows the standard moral confusions of the picaresque first-person, can lead you to see the writer as criminal, or the criminal as writer, or the aspirant to upward mobility as some combination of the two. In any event, it leaves the object of their commitment anything but clear.

But perhaps that is just Doctorow's point. One of Tokarczyk's strongest arguments for Doctorow's political seriousness rests on the premise that the endpoint of his plots is still more unreliable than the narrative voices that seductively lead us there. Joe's upward mobility story ends, for example, in a dark inversion of Horatio Alger. Like Billy Bathgate, who identifies with and attaches himself to the gangster Dutch Schultz, Joe chooses in the end to become son, heir, and successor to the man we have come to recognize as the ruthless and virtually omnipotent center of an evil social system. Despite the richness of "life" that Joe's voice and adventures ensure, the reader is meant to recognize the costliness of his error, Tokarczyk argues, even if Joe is never punished for it. Deciding that the protagonist is the very opposite of an eligible role model, we are meant to reflect on the politically demobilizing consequences of upward mobility aspirations for the working class: not just the ease with which a keenness for "life" can come to mean aiding and abetting CIA campaigns of liquidation—an item on Joe's curriculum vitae—but also a loss of respect for the parents, who are inescapably seen as failures, and a loss of the sense of cross-generational continuity that radical politics requires.

There is clearly something important here. Yet it can hardly be the whole story. The moral is too neat and familiar to sum up such a strenuous wrestling match with American society. Moreover, the adventurous energy that flows between Doctorow's narrators and the American Dream forms a high-voltage circuit; even at the end of the novel, many and perhaps most readers will have trouble pulling away into respectably buffered alienation. Thus it is perhaps necessary to seek for Doctorow's political commitments in as well as against the narrative force of the American Dream. On the first page of *Loon Lake*, Joe describes Paterson, the nightmarish neighborhood of his parents: "What, after all, was the tragedy in their lives implicit in the profoundly reproachful looks they sent my way? That things hadn't worked out for them? How did that make them different from anyone else on Mechanic Street, even the houses were the same, two by two, the same asphalt palace over and over, streetcars rang the bell on the whole fucking neighborhood. Only the maniacs were alive, the men and women who lived on the street" (1). Reinventing his world metaphor by metaphor, Joe seems to share with the streetpeople all the available "life"; his parents at any rate have none. His case for leaving natural parents behind and fleeing toward a parental surrogate like auto magnate F. W. Bennett seems open-and-shut. Yet the novel does not in fact allow Joe to put his neighborhood behind him. It obliges him to act out his commitments even while submitting to the impulsive violence of unconsidered desire.

He is a homeless person himself, and thus a kind of neighborhood representative in spite of himself, when he arrives at Bennett's mansion on Loon Lake, and it's as if only that arrival can make sense of the violence he has already revealed in himself. Penfield, the poet who self-consciously parallels Joe, dots the i's and crosses the t's: he too arrived at Loon Lake, treed by Bennett's dogs, in order to murder Bennett, and he did so because homelessness like his is the result of Bennett and his corporations. "People I loved died because of the policies of one of his companies" (53). Does that mean the death-in-life of Joe's parents can be traced back to Bennett as well? This is precisely the suggestion when the flight from Loon Lake takes Joe and Clara Lukacs to Jacksontown. Here the plot borrows from the paranoid thrillers of the 1960s and 1970s: running away from Bennett, they find themselves of all places stuck in a Bennett company town, where Joe works on an assembly line in a Bennett autobody factory and his friend and next-door neighbor turns out to be a Bennett company spy. But if the hint of inescapable total system, with police and company working hand-in-glove, prepares for Joe's final offscreen conversion, or anti-conversion, into a CIA director and Bennett's successor, the episode also plunges Joe back into the lifeless life of his factory-worker father that he had tried so hard to avoid, and that he now learns to look at with more respect: "It was enough to make me think of my father. The man was a fucking hero" (188). The novel will give this recognition nowhere to go, politically speaking, but that does not cancel the power of this inadvertent return to the parents' neighborhood.

The world left behind by his mobility also reasserts itself, at the very heart of the mobility story, as the disguised social substance of Joe's passion for Clara Lukacs. As Tokarczyk notes, Clara both echoes and further justifies Joe's own desire for mobility. But she does so by means of Joe's epiphanic quasi-memory (we are not told that Clara herself remembers it) of the "outrage" her face registered when she was forced, as a small child, to urinate before strangers in the street. Returning obsessively to this image, Joe turns mobility itself into an expression of outrage at casual, taken-for-granted indignity. The struggle for possession of Clara is thus something more than what it sometimes seems, a struggle of and between men over an abstract feminine trophy. In a sense, Joe's love for Clara can be taken as an indirect mode of political commitment.

Tokarczyk points out how, like other Doctorow heroes, Joe concentrates his desire on the act of stealing or rescuing (the two acts are difficult to distinguish) a beautiful woman who belongs to an older and more powerful man. Clara belongs to the union-busting gangster Tony Crapo, and perhaps also to Bennett himself; Drew Preston in *Billy Bathgate* belongs first to gangster Bo Weinberg, then after Weinberg's murder to Dutch Schultz. Within *Loon Lake* itself, the same scenario comes back with a minor twist when Joe takes to the road with Red James's recent widow. Joe himself is "not unaware of his attraction to other men's wives, he was not unmindful that his life since leaving Paterson had been a picaresque of other men's money and other men's women, who in hell was he to get righteously independent with anyone?" (272). Yet there is much in this flagrantly Oedipal fantasy structure of which both Joe and Doctorow do indeed seem unaware, including the way it teases the rags-to-riches story of egotistical independence back in a more righteous direction. On the psychological level this motif registers a simple displacement of Oedipal conflict (it is more palatable to imagine stealing a woman from a surrogate father than from a natural father). But on the political level it also registers an undeclared assault on the powerful surrogate father. And this assault can then be interpreted, without pushing too hard, as an indirect defense of the natural or lower-born father—the scenario that Doctorow stages with more direct political implications in *The Book of Daniel*. Instead of simply displaying contempt for the family of origin, then, the upward mobility plot turns out to channel the energies of personal ambition into a devious but erotically charged vector of neighborhood loyalty.

Thus Doctorow can have the cake of mobility and eat it, too. The fact that Joe's story does not end well means that Joe is no positive hero, but it does not erase the intermittent elements of attractive, even compelling moral sensibility with which Doctorow has infused his character. A central scene of the novel, announced early, delayed, and finally repeated in detail, presents Joe stealing a large wad of bills from a woman with whom he has just made love, then tossing the money away into the wind. The money, we learn, comes from the sexual exploitation of a third party. The sex that precedes the theft is itself unmistakably and unforgivably sadistic. On this evidence, Joe is a sadist, a thief—and a disinterested agent of justice, refusing to share in these ill-gotten gains. He does not simply play to win.

A similar scene and a similar moral structure informs *Billy Bathgate*. The novel opens with Dutch Schultz's murder of his trusted lieutenant, the handsome Bo Weinberg, then his confiscation of Weinberg's girlfriend Drew, all of it witnessed by the young Billy. Cut up and surrendered only in reluctant bits, this scene becomes an organizing center of the novel, like the bills in the wind in *Loon Lake*. Indeed, Billy's power over Drew—another woman of absolute if not fully convincing beauty whose possession stands in for all the promises of upward mobility—seems to reside largely in the power of having witnessed and being able to narrate Weinberg's death. Another father figure whose woman our hero will inherit, Weinberg is aligned by his imminent death with the poor natural fathers, not the rich parental surrogates. Billy's narration, neither entirely false nor entirely true, bestows upon him a dignified death—a death singing "Bye Bye Blackbird." And this is how Billy achieves his most novelistically gripping success. As in the short story "The Writer in the Family," which Doctorow sometimes uses in his public readings and which comes closer than the novels to the facts of his own downwardly mobile childhood in the Bronx (see his autobiographical book, *World's Fair*), the young man gives himself a place in the world by lying, imaginatively and responsibly, about the death of a father whose life has been a failure. Here too, the son's upward mobility is secured, in part at least, not by setting his "life" against the father's lifelessness, but by using his lively creative powers to invest the father's death, or failure, with the dignity it deserves.

Tokarczyk brilliantly sums up the family romance theme of natural versus surrogate fathers by suggesting that Doctorow's "search for a father-figure to complement or replace an inadequate one" is "resolved through the representation of writing as the ideal parent." This formulation makes sense of Tateh's trajectory in *Ragtime*, where upward mobility can be legitimately embraced, it seems, if it can be seen as the story of an artist successfully selling his vision. But it does not of course settle the political question with which Tokarczyk begins. Does the term "skeptical" in "skeptical commitment" signify detachment, a merely personal solution to social conflict rather than a genuinely public one? Is literariness a synonym for playful disengagement? Is this what Jameson means when he calls Doctorow postmodern?

The Doctorow who emerges from Tokarczyk's engaged and engaging interpretation is postmodern too, but in a somewhat less judgmental sense. Whatever his commitment to some sort of transformative action, his novels do not pretend that action offers any escape from epistemological and moral uncertainty. Her Doctorow might be described as a juggler who, like Billy Bathgate, tries to keep as many balls as possible in the air. The act of juggling—which first gets Billy noticed by the gang and in this sense begins his story—is also an act in the theatrical sense, an artistic spectacle. Hence it is one of the many parallels to his own vocation that Doctorow democratically invites the reader to detect among his characters. A spectacle of strenuous stasis rather than historical dynamism, juggling is both a personal way up in the world and a defiance of gravity that exerts a universal appeal. At the very least, it encourages us to think that in the social world, too, things are not fixed at their natural and unalterable level.

Notes

1. Fredric Jameson, *Postmodernism, or, The Cultural Logic of Late Capitalism* (Durham: Duke University P, 1991): 21.

Introduction

I

E. L. Doctorow's: Skeptical Commitment argues not only for a political reading of a particular writer's work, but for a reconsideration of what it means to write political fiction in America, especially what it means for a white Jewish male to do so at this historical moment, when the study of political writing is often devoted to women and minority writers. My intensive study of E. L. Doctorow's fiction is in essence a "local" effort at understanding how political views and stances may inform an author's fiction, and how a member of the intelligentsia could be passionately committed to politics, highly skeptical of political action, and write aesthetically fine fiction that oscillates between indeterminacy and commitment. *E. L. Doctorow's: Skeptical Commitment* shows how such an author can use a variety of literary techniques (such as shift in voice or point of view, or ambiguous narration) and genres (such as the romance, the western, the crime story, or the *bildungsroman*) to achieve excellent politically conscious fiction. Of course, I can make no predictions as to Doctorow's future fiction or evolving political attitudes (and suspect he would be uncomfortable with the label "political fiction," finding it reductionist). Nonetheless, this book argues that Doctorow has from *Welcome to Hard Times* through *The Waterworks* continually represented his political vision in challenging, aesthetically fine fictional works. By doing so he has enriched the possibilities for political fiction; works such as Don De Lillo's *Libra*, Robert Stone's *Dog Soldiers*, and Russell Banks's *Cloudsplitter* owe a debt to Doctorow's inroads in historical and political writing. Moreover, especially if, as Doctorow claims and as many of us sense, political discussion in the public sphere has become limited and has failed to engage many crucial issues of justice and equity, his fiction may begin to encourage a genuine political dialogue.

II

The political content of Doctorow's fiction has often been commented upon by reviewers and authors of short articles.[1] Yet there is no book-length scholarly study of how politics informs Doctorow's work.[2] This gap compromises our ability to appreciate Doctorow's fiction, which is best understood by apprehending his political vision in combination with the specific genre choices he makes in each work, with his stylistic experimentation, with his continual revision of American myths.

Presently there is such excitement over some socially conscious fiction, such as Don De Lillo's *Underworld* and Toni Morrison's *Beloved*, that it may be difficult to recall how disparaged political writing has been as recently as the 1980s, when what some have described as more insulated fiction was far more popular.[3] To understand Doctorow's pull toward political fiction, as well as the particular contours of politics in his fiction, it is useful to review his biography. E. L. Doctorow was born in the Bronx (New York City) in 1931 to lower-middle-class Jewish-American parents. His paternal grandfather was an intellectual, a socialist, and an atheist. His family's and to some extent Doctorow's own political and religious views have been characterized by critic John Clayton as radical Jewish humanism, "It is the heritage of Jewish writers to deal with suffering, especially suffering as a result of some essential injustice in the human or divine world, suffering to which they offer a response of compassion and yearning for a life modeled on human kindness" (in Trenner 109). Furthermore, Clayton argues that the politics of Jewish immigrant culture was largely radical—anarchist, socialist, communist, Zionist, or some amalgam of these with faith in the labor movement (110). Religious practice need not play a critical role in defining oneself as a Jew; rather, one's sensibility and ideals might.

As an undergraduate in the 1950s Doctorow attended Kenyon College, majored in philosophy, and studied with John Crowe Ransom, one of the New Criticism's foremost critics at a time when this approach reigned. The New Criticism perceived of a literary work as a "well-wrought urn,"[4] a self-contained artifact that could be understood by examining its formal techniques, not by examining the context in which it was written. The insular approach of this criticism, coupled with the conservative political climate of the 1950s, made many critics wary of political novels, ready to dismiss them as propaganda.[5] In a conversation with me years ago Doctorow acknowledged the tension between his upbringing in a New York progressive Jewish home and his schooling in a college stressing formalism, but emphasized that the tension was ultimately productive, enabling him to avoid the excesses of both formulaic political writing and the academic dandy novel.⁶ He navigates between these extremes through his adaptation of popular and literary genres as well by his insistence on certain themes.

Unlike some contemporary authors who seem to glow in celebrity status, Doctorow is predisposed to privacy. Certainly he has inserted himself into public debates, having written numerous essays that critique government policy or public sensibility in matters such as nuclear weapons.⁷ But unlike some other writers, such as Amiri Baraka, who boldly assert their political views, Doctorow is wary of direct statements. Consider his words in the introduction to his collection of essays *Jack London, Hemingway and the Constitution*, "With one exception the pieces in this book were written because someone asked me to write them. Left to my own devices I will write fiction. I will choose the thrown voice and its tropes" (ix). The image of the novelist as ventriloquist evokes Bakhtin's concept of indirect discourse and prompts me to describe Doctorow's politics as a politics of indirection. It is a politics borne out of a combination of a private personality, a particular upbringing, and coming of age at a particular historical moment.

Certainly Doctorow shies away from direct political involvement in part because he is afraid of taking too much time away from his writing. But more importantly, he adheres to a vision of the artist as detached witness, similar to the filmmaker in *Rent*, who chronicles his friends' lives while remaining at a distance from them. Part of this distance may be attributed to Doctorow's skepticism about the possibility of affecting change, a suspicion that takes many forms. First, it may manifest itself in novels such as *Welcome to Hard Times* by expressing distrust of progress and Enlightenment ideals, a skepticism commonly associated with postmodernism. Alternatively, it may take the form of distrust of political processes, a particular concern of *The Book of Daniel*. In his introduction to *Jack London, Hemingway*, Doctorow reflected on his experience of coming of age during the McCarthy era, a time when many politicians shamelessly jumped on an anti-Red bandwagon and blacklisting destroyed many lives. Dissent was dangerous; conformity was enforced. It was also a time during which news of Stalin's atrocities and other revelations about Russian communism shattered the vision of some leftists that communism was an extension of democratic ideals. Doctorow and other members of the so-called Silent Generation reacted to these two phenomena with detachment and withdrawal from the political process. As Doctorow himself once explained in an interview with Larry McCaffery, "It's the fate of my generation that we've never shared a monumental experience. We think of ourselves as loners" (37).

While he may not identify a collective experience that has shaped his generation, Doctorow constantly seeks to re-envision the familial, social, and historical forces that have shaped his life and inform his fiction. The resultant stance, manifested differently in various works but present throughout Doctorow's fiction, I have termed skeptical commitment. The postmodern vein in Doctorow's fiction and in essays such as "False Documents," widely commented upon,[8] might be seen as a skeptic's position—the belief that true knowledge or knowledge of a particular area is uncertain; hence, one adopts an attitude of doubt or disposition toward incredulity. For Doctorow absolute certainty of one's position or the possibility of definitively answering questions is itself a danger. Yet while he remains suspicious of definite answers and, more importantly, of the possibility of knowing with certainty, he is also suspicious of radical uncertainty and passionately committed to certain idea and causes. In an interview with Richard Trenner, "Politics and the Mode of Fiction," Doctorow refers to being characterized as someone with a primitive sense of justice, of what's fair and what's not (52). There is, I believe, a very keen perception of Doctorow's political vision in this assessment. Throughout his fiction he depicts inequality in what we have come to call the "trinity of oppression"—especially race issues in *Ragtime*; class issues in *Welcome to Hard Times*, *The Book of Daniel*, *Loon Lake*, *Billy Bathgate*, and *The Waterworks*; and gender issues in *Ragtime* and *World's Fair*. Doctorow's fiction is particularly sensitive to class issues, often suggesting sympathies with the underclass while critiquing individual greed and its concomitant lack of community values. This fiction does not, however, address only this "trinity" of inequities. Rather, his vision of the just society is one which would enable people to self-actualize. According to Doctorow, in a truly just society, ". . . everyone [would] be able to live as he or she is endowed to live; that if a person is in his [sic] genes a poet, he be allowed to practice his poetry" (Trenner 55). It is a yearning that is particularly expressed through the artist figures in *Ragtime*, *Loon Lake*, and *Lives of the Poets: A Novella and Six Stories*.

This vision of personal fulfillment has ramifications far beyond an individual's life, for in Doctorow's fiction the personal is indeed political. In part, this equation stems from Doctorow's suspicion of organized politics; in part, it is the logical outgrowth of his aversion to political sloganeering typical of the 1960s and 1970s, and perhaps an awareness of the futility of leaders trying to change countries when they could not change themselves. To quote Doctorow advocating a view he attributes to Wilhelm Reich, "there is no hope for political progress until people can be freed from their neurotic character structures"(Levine "Writer" 64).[9]

Hence, the quest for personal fulfillment, or at least for some personal resolution, is a crucial part of the "commitment," that is, the word "commit" means to oblige or bind, to carry into action deliberately, to assign or pledge to some particular course. Essentially, "commitment," even if it begins on a micropolitical level of work on the self, suggests attachment, and often some form of public action.

American literature has, since the time of the Puritans, featured the jeremiad as a prolonged complaint, a prophet's indictment of his society characteristic of work such as the muckrakers' novels or Allan Ginsberg's "Howl." Doctorow struggles to accommodate this form to his artistry (as successful practitioners of the work have always done). To this end, he has repeatedly adapted genres such as the Western, the romance, and the detective novel, often playing with accepted conventions, and thus avoiding didacticism. Rather than having an omniscient narrator report on situations, Doctorow's novels often feature narrators who agonize about their ability to comprehend and render events, but who nonetheless "bear witness." For many contemporary authors, the idea of the writer bearing witness is indeed important. Consider the poem "It Was My First Nursing Job" in *Dark Blond* by Belle Waring. Here she describes a doctor's indifference to a patient, which results in a stillbirth. Reflecting on how she told a father of his newborn's death, she ponders that today, "I *would say, I am your witness./* No. I have never told the whole truth./ Forgive me" (7–9). Waring's speaker does not tell the truth because, in part, she is a nurse and her loyalties are to the institutions and the doctors with whom she works as well as to the patients. To be effective witnesses, writers must be, according to Doctorow, "independent witnesses . . . not connected to the defense of any institution, whether it be the family or the Pentagon or God" (Levine "Writer" 69). The echoes of Stephen Dedalus here reinforce the notion of the artist's detachment, but for Doctorow the detachment is from official institutions, not from ideals such as justice, equality, and the like. Cynical detachment is one possible response, suggested particularly by Daniel in the earlier parts of *The Book of Daniel*, but ambivalent involvement represented in the figures of Jonathan at the end of the novella *Lives of the Poets* or McIllvaine in *The Waterworks* is another, more desirable one.

III

Each of Doctorow's major novels raises questions about the artist's relation to political and social issues, whether it is possible to progress, and what it means to be committed. None do so as directly, however, as his two autobiographically based works: *Lives of the Poets: A Novella and Six Short Stories* (1985), and *World's Fair* (1986). Hence, it is useful to begin close examination of Doctorow's fiction with these works. *Lives of the Poets: A Novella and Six Short Stories* (1984) contains stories, presumably by the writer of the novella that follows, *Lives of the Poets*. This metafictional element is virtually the only experimental feature of this volume. Critics Carol Harter and James R. Thompson in *E. L. Doctorow* have pointed out a common theme of dereliction in these works (105). "The Leather Man" depicts a person who grotesquely dresses in layers of coats and shawls, topped with a leather outer armor and a pointed leather hat. His bizarre attire is not to be taken as a mark of individual maladjustment; rather, "You remember your Thoreau. There's a definite political component of avoiding all other human beings and taking on the coloration of your surroundings" (69). His detached, alienated stance, and that of so many Doctorow characters, may be partially explained by reference to the theories of political theorist Peter Sloterdijk on cynical detachment.[10] According to Sloterdijk, the cynic is often a cutting-edge figure on the urban landscape. The cynic is distinguished by his/her enlightened false consciousness, Sloterdijk's revision of this Marxist concept. In Marxist theory, citizens in bourgeois cultures often develop a false consciousness that identifies with ruling class interests rather than their own. People might, for example, vote for politicians whose tax policies benefit only the rich. In contrast to this false consciousness that naively embraces reigning ideologies, enlightened false consciousness recognizes a futility in many activities such as voting in elections, trying to become upwardly mobile, and so forth, but nonetheless goes through the motions because doing so is necessary for economic, and to some extent emotional, survival. If, as Sloterdijk claims, enlightened false consciousness characterizes the modern period, there is a certain typicality to The Leather Man's bizarre behavior; his behavior is in fact common to those who are unable to commit to a political or even a personal belief system.

Alternatively and somewhat paradoxically, "The Leather Man" may be seen as a grotesque. The term "grotesque" here is one Doctorow has adapted from Sherwood Anderson's *Winesburg, Ohio*. In Anderson's work, an elderly writer (a frequent Doctorow narrator) observed hundreds of truths that were all beautiful, but "the moment one of the people took one of the truths to himself, called it the truth, and tried to live his life by it, he became a grotesque and the truth became a lie" (4—5).[11] (Notice here the suggestion that the nature of truth is constantly shifting.) "The Leather Man" may be seen as a grotesque of an often revered American type, the rugged individual. Indeed, *The Political Fiction* argues that extreme individualism at the expense of community values is often depicted as grotesque in Doctorow's fiction.

A sense of disconnection inherent in "The Leather Man" also runs through other stories such as "The Water Works" in which the body of a young boy who has drowned in a water tower is found. Here and throughout the stories in this volume Doctorow questions whether there is a possibility of community. In "The Writer in the Family" Doctorow more directly represents some of the choices writers must make as they bear witness to their subjects. The narrator is a boy whose father has recently died and who has fine writing skills. Unwilling to break the news of the man's death to a frail grandmother, the boy's family goads him into pretending to be his father and writing letters to the elderly woman. In the course of narrating his subject the boy comes to understand his father, a failure by many standards. Realizing that his father's dream was to go to sea, the boy finally writes a letter stating he [the father] is dying and wishes to have his ashes scattered in the ocean. In the act of writing the boy recreates his father's life and memory, effectively bearing witness to the man's dreams and giving him an appropriate death.

The theme of the writer's isolation and responsibilities is more extensively developed in the novella *Lives of the Poets*. The main character, Jonathan, a middle-aged New York City writer, is suffering various minor physical ailments and a general sense of dissatisfaction with his life. His cohorts are other successful writers whose lives might be described as typical Updike lives: living in comfortable ennui, married for the second or third time. Jonathan is still married to his first wife, but the two of them live apart; she in their suburban home, he in New York City. Although a recognized writer with a seemingly comfortable life, he is obviously estranged—from other people, his wife, and himself. In stating that each book he writes took him further away from himself, he is suggesting the alienation that a writer's isolation can bring, as well as the separation that accompanies success, suggested in his friends' having uniformly stopped taking public transportation in favor of taxis. Many of the male behaviors and attitudes in this novella might be understood by considering theories by feminists such as Carol Gilligan and Nancy Chodorow; the men privilege individuation and autonomy at the expense of connection. As a result, they often feel alienated and detached. In his restless, dissatisfied state Jonathan perhaps needs only the impetus to connect with others, an impetus provided by a woman who asks him to shelter illegal aliens. The image of his teaching the alien boy to type is one of father-son nurturance strikingly different from the strained father-son relationships that permeate much of Doctorow's work. It is an image of activism that only half succeeds because it is only half-believable that Jonathan would involve himself in such a risky project. Still, the novella is one of the earlier works that suggests Doctorow is striving to develop an appropriate praxis. As represented in this novel, the praxis is local and specific to the writer; the writer will nurture someone who will perhaps bear witness to his own experience with oppression. The commitment is qualified (Jonathan teaches one boy to type) yet definite.

World's Fair (1985) is a *künstlerroman* about a New York Jewish boy developing into a writer in the 1930s, a pivotal decade for many Americans on the left and one that is the frequent setting of Doctorow novels. In keeping with the themes of connection expressed in *Lives of the Poets*, *World's Fair* includes the voices and perceptions of narrators other than the boy Edgar—his mother, brother, and grandmother. For example, his mother Rose says, "Phil admired your father very much. We had wonderful friends. Only now do I see that our lives could have gone in an entirely different direction" (29). *World's Fair* thus continues the experimentation Doctorow began in his first novel, *Welcome to Hard Times*, and reflects his interest in language's oral quality.

Edgar has much in common with typical *künstlerroman* protagonists, notably Stephen Dedalus from *A Portrait of the Artist as a Young Man*: while Stephen has poor eyesight, Edgar is asthmatic; both boys' families experience downward mobility; Stephen is bullied by classmates, Edgar threatened by anti-Semites. Yet as the latter example suggests, *World's Fair*, far more than most *bildungsromane*, suggests Edgar coming of age in his society by finding his place in it—not rejecting it as Dedalus did. In addition to resolving his feelings about his somewhat dreamy father and detached, critical mother, Edgar must come to terms with consumer culture represented by the World's Fair. This fair ironically holds out the promise of progress at a time when Hitler is gaining control in Europe, and America is struggling for economic recovery; as in so much of Doctorow's fiction the definition and possibility of progress itself is questioned.

But most importantly, Edgar's prize-winning (albeit second prize) essay on "The Typical American Boy" suggests the necessity of a writer's stating his/her Jewish identity in a public document. Written in the aftermath of the confrontation with anti-Semitic thugs whom Edgar escapes only by telling he is not Jewish, the essay states that the typical American boy should hate Hitler. Furthermore, "if he is Jewish he should say so. If he is anything he should say what it is when challenged" (244). This is the impetus, the voice that will inform the young boy's fiction.

Unlike many novelists, Doctorow did not publish autobiographical pieces early in his career. Indeed, his first novel *Welcome to Hard Times* (1960) is a western, and Doctorow had not yet been west of Ohio. As critics have noted, *Welcome to Hard Times* is an inverted Western, a genre that dates back to Stephen Crane's "The Blue Hotel." These revisions of popular westerns emphasize the region's dark side and complicate notions of good and evil. *Welcome to Hard Times* also bears the mark of the very recent memory of the Holocaust and the existentialist philosophy that so influenced Doctorow and other intellectuals in the 1950s. In this first novel Doctorow establishes the political themes that would in various ways be expressed throughout his work—the responsibility of the artist as historian and witness, the destructiveness of greed in a community, the problematic notions of history and progress.

Significantly, the Bad Man who destroys the town is named Clay Turner; Frederick Jackson Turner's *The Frontier in American History* forms a background for many of the ideas and actions in this novel. In a sense, the Bad Man, who indeed appears larger than life, is a grotesque of Turner's rugged individual. According to Turner, frontier society created a primitive organization based somewhat on the family, but fundamentally antisocial. The survivors of the Bad Man's carnage—Blue, the prostitute Molly, and the orphan Jimmy Fee—form a loose family that unfortunately mirrors its society. Both Blue's family and the town of Hard Times evolve out of self-interest and greed rather than a sense of community.

After surviving a harsh winter, Blue, Molly, and Jimmy Fee become what is the first of many blended families in Doctorow novels. On a personal level, the blended family represents issues of dealing with the past, for their coming together suggests a hope in the future despite their having been traumatized by past wounds. Blue is optimistic when new settlers arrive and economic activity flourishes. Significantly, he resumes the record-keeping he maintained before the conflagration, but with an important change. Rather than simply logging deaths and births, he writes down events. The latter record is much more problematic, for Blue constantly questions the accuracy of his memory as well as the possibility of recording what occurred. *Welcome to Hard Times* indeed articulates many of the concerns that have preoccupied historians, historiographers, and literary critics—the relationship between history and interpretation, between history and memory, and the role of contingencies in history. The uncertainty about history and interpretation is a key component of the "skepticism" that marks Doctorow's skeptical commitment.

Within *Welcome to Hard Times* the "commitment" is best suggested in the fable-like tale of a town that cannot recover from its past. While Blue glories in the town's prosperity, Molly grows increasingly anxious that the Bad Man will return. Ironically, Blue tells her that the town is ready to stand up to the Bad Man, failing to recognize that Hard Times is a typical gold rush town whose only institutions are brothels and saloons: the antithesis of a community. Because the town fails to balance individual gain with community welfare, it is indeed vulnerable to scoundrels. When the boom dies, the people who have overextended themselves are ruined and become vicious. In a multiplication of evil, two Bad Men ride into town. The cycle is fully repeated when the town is not only burned to the ground, but when Jimmy Fee, trying to defend Molly, kills her and the Bad Man, and he himself becomes an outlaw. Jimmy Fee is the first of many Doctorow children whom society fails to nurture. Witnessing such destruction, the dying Blue hopes only that the wood remains may be useful to someone. Blue could not fight against the Bad Man, but perhaps his works and remnants could. Barbara Foley, discussing proletarian fiction and praxis, would say, suggest a "way out," an end to impasse for future generations.[12]

Doctorow has described his next novel, *Big as Life* (1966), a science fiction book, as his *Mardi*, a book that, despite years of effort, did not work. The plot is far-fetched, and the style not up to Doctorow's usual quality. In speculating as to why this second novel failed, Doctorow suggested that it is not dark enough and he did not take enough risks in writing it. If this is so, perhaps what he learned from the shortcomings in *Big as Life* facilitated his writing his brilliant third novel, *The Book of Daniel* (1971). As Doctorow would say, this novel was "occasioned" by, or we might say inspired by, the Rosenberg Case. In "False Documents" Doctorow articulates how a controversial case such as the Rosenberg could be an inspiration to him: "Facts are buried, exhumed, deposed, contradicted, recanted. There is a decision by the jury and, when the historical and prejudicial context of the decision is examined, a subsequent judgment by history. And the trial shimmers forever with just the perplexing ambiguity characteristic of a true novel" (in Trenner 23). In *The Book of Daniel* Doctorow finds a way to further explore and complicate questions concerning the possibility of actually recording and knowing history. Far more than any other Doctorow novel, *The Book of Daniel* engages the central tenets of postmodernism. The novel's style is boldly experimental, frequently shifting chronology and point of view, seemingly combining genres as diverse as the dissertation, history text, travelogue, and memoir. It is also metafictional, suggesting the difficulty of writing and interpretation themselves. The continuing controversy surrounding the Rosenberg case upon which the Isaacson Case is closely modeled suggests important questions about the relationship between indeterminacy and commitment. *The Book of Daniel* walks a line between representing that, as Daniel says after meeting the long-sought Selig Mindish, "the truth is irretrievable" and demonstrating that certain events, such as infringements on individual liberty during the McCarthy era, are true, verifiable, and must be acknowledged. For example, during her trial Rochelle Isaacson logically assesses factors affecting the trial—the nature of the jury and the prosecution, the news coverage, the Korean War—and soundly concludes that they will be judged guilty. In a novel in which there is so much indeterminacy, the fact that some things are apparent and can be objectively assessed is striking. Because it walks the line between indeterminacy and verification so well, *The Book of Daniel* can be seen as an example of what critic Alan Wilde calls "midfiction"—fiction that uses postmodern techniques and accepts the primacy of surface, but nonetheless tries to be referential and establish truths.[13]

Daniel's difficulty in understanding political oppression as well as his parents' and other communists' complicity in it are graphically represented in the novel's structure. Three of its sections are named for holidays, and the fourth is titled "Starfish." The obviously disjunctive section refers to the starfish's points, all converging at the center, and indeed this section takes us to "the heart of the matter" in the book—the actual trial, Susan's catatonic state, the March on the Pentagon. Such material can never be completely integrated into the book.

In this novel Doctorow further develops the connection between the personal and the political suggested in *Welcome to Hard Times*. He has moved back to the urban setting that repeatedly energizes his work as well as heightens the apparent alienation of characters. In *The Book of Daniel* the protagonist Daniel's depiction as a cynical, bitter, and often sadistic man undercuts sentimental caricatures of survivors, particularly orphan children. As a detached urban figure going through motions of getting a degree, marrying, and having a child, Daniel fits Sloterdijk's profile of a modern cynic. Daniel is so thoroughly disillusioned and cynical in part because there are no heroes in the Isaacson case—Jews, communists, the left, and the Isaacson themselves are shown to be complicit. Daniel perpetuates the resultant political wounds on a personal level, being a cruel spouse and parent. He cannot embrace any social institution because his own participation in the society that killed his parents not only rankles him, but also raises questions as to his own complicity in his society's wrongdoing. In many respects, *The Book of Daniel* is an effective political novel because it not only portrays complicit characters, but, in accordance with Barbara J. Eckstein's theory of the characteristics of good political fiction, it makes readers feel complicit in the wrongs about which they read and thus prompts them to reevaluate their relationship to power structures in their society.[14]

The Book of Daniel is the most obviously political Doctorow novel because it represents an espionage trial. It also depicts a time of post-war hysteria when outgroups—Jews and communists—were frequently persecuted. The Peekskill incident, in which buses of leftists returning from a Paul Robeson concert are ambushed and attacked by rabid "patriots," is a microcosm of what happens in the Isaacson case. Groups of people are endangered until the "patriots" find a specific target on which to focus their hatred.

Furthermore, *The Book of Daniel* is about two generations of radicals, the Old Left of the 1930s and the New Left of the 1960s. Artie Sternlicht represents the ahistorical, opportunistic segment of the New Left that tries to take advantage of the media, but ironically gives no evidence of being more effective against the government than were Old Leftists. Two other examples of ahistoricism are Linda Mindish, who denies her past and remakes herself in California and Disneyland, appropriately descried as a Baudrillard-like simulacrum substituting for the real. The challenges for Daniel and for readers is to acknowledge the burden of history without becoming immobilized by it.

In the hopes of rescuing his mentally ill sister and silencing the demons in his own head, Daniel begins a detective-like search to discover the truth about his parents' guilt or innocence. But as the novel progresses, Daniel moves from searching for the truth to searching for an appropriate ritual or way to mourn, first suggested in his participation in the March on the Pentagon and finally in the three endings. He realizes he will never uncover the truth about his parents' case, but he is nonetheless able to mourn them and to love his new immediate family even as he accepts, in Barbara Eckstein's terms, his own and his society's complicity, "a network of personal, social, political, even aesthetic conditions which perpetuate the stereotypes and in turn rationalize the suffering" (32–33).

While *The Book of Daniel* is a densely written, challenging novel that would suit a highly intellectual audience, *Ragtime* (1975), a novel focusing on the years 1902 to 1919, also often characterized as postmodern, is marked by a sense of play and easy accessibility. Its style has been described as mock historical, imitating the simple facts and characterizations of history books. Consider, for example, these lines from the beginning of the book: "Everyone wore white in the summer. Tennis racquets were hefty and the racquet faces elliptical. There was a lot of sexual fainting. There were no Negroes. There were no immigrants"(3–4).

These lines parody the dry, supposedly objective prose of conventional history texts, what Bakhtin might call monolingual discourse (60–61). They do so playfully by including information that would not be in history books, such as descriptions of tennis racquets. However, the playful prose also underscores important points, for in just a few paragraphs the narrator reports that there apparently were Negroes and immigrants—and indeed the novel as a whole bears this out. In some ways *Ragtime* is then a revisionist history text including those who had been omitted from official accounts. It is also a novel that toys with the preponderance of illusions in human lives—Houdini's magic, the advent of filmmaking. Both illusion and official history should be reconsidered. A key to the novel's political insight might be summed up by the epigraph at the beginning of the novel, "Do not play this piece fast. It is never right to play Ragtime fast." Indeed, this apparently light, entertaining novel is filled with as much social criticism as Doctorow's more jeremiad-like works, especially criticism of race and class inequities.

There are two governing clusters of images that structure *Ragtime*: those of repetition suggested in Ford's assembly line, the Boy's fascination with baseball; and the image of metamorphosis suggested in the Boy's fascination with stories from Ovid's *Metamorphoses*. Playfully, *Ragtime* teases out the relationship between these two images, questioning how the repetitious historical patterns of injustice and discrimination affect the myth that in the United States people can transform themselves.

As critics have noted, *Ragtime* is a romance. While an earlier generation of American Studies scholars saw the romance as evading direct engagement with sociopolitical issues, new Americanists find the romance an essentially political document. According to Michael Wilding, "The confrontation of the hopes of romance with the actualities of realism runs throughout political fiction . . . The formal polarities arise from the situation, the politics, the character choices" (8).[15] Romance dreams are suggested in figures such as Tateh; realism is suggested in characters such as Emma Goldman, Mameh, and Coalhouse Walker, Jr.

Although there are numerous historical figures such as J. P. Morgan, Sigmund Freud, and Emma Goldman in the text, *Ragtime's* plot centers on three families—a WASP one whose members are simply named Mother, Father, Younger Brother, Grandfather, and the Boy (whom many believe to be the clairvoyant narrator); Jewish-immigrant Mameh, Tateh, and the girl; and African-American Coalhouse Walker, his girlfriend Sarah, and their baby. In the spirit of much proletarian fiction, the characters seem to be types representing their ethnic and socioeconomic groups rather than individuals. The novel depicts a period of rapid change in American society—new inventions, changes in gender roles, the transition from a rural to an urban society, the advent of the automobile and mass production. Readers are given a quick, somewhat distanced panoramic view of the era. Characters' potential to thrive in this society is marked first by their ability to adapt to change and second, perhaps more importantly, by their being allowed to change. Father, who cannot adapt to change, conveniently sinks on the *Luisitania*, leaving the novel's landscape. In contrast, Tateh and Mother evolve into happier human beings, achieving what Mother might call a "life of genius," perhaps an ultimate form of justice for Doctorow. Other, more controversial characters such as Evelyn Nesbit, Emma Goldman, and Younger Brother vanish from the novel: They either die or their lives are no longer followed. Emma Goldman and Younger Brother do not strive for conventional success, but others do. The difference between who is allowed to succeed and who is not is graphically illustrated in the contrasting fates of Tateh and Coalhouse Walker. When Tateh stops being an artist and a socialist activist, he hides his former life and his Jewish identity, blends into the American mainstream, and prospers. Coalhouse Walker, a proud, self-made man wants to achieve the American Dream, but is thwarted by racism. He cannot hide being an African-American. Unable to secure justice when his car is vandalized, he becomes a terrorist, ironically reinforcing materialist American values by conflating his identity with his car. Like Michael Kohlhaas, the character in Kleist's short story on whom this subplot is based, Coalhouse Walker's only choice is to die with dignity. That Harry K. Thaw, Stanford White's murderer, marches in the Armistice Day Parade long after Coalhouse Walker has been shot down underscores the injustice in this society.

Doctorow played more freely with history in *Ragtime* than in any other novel, and yet the fact that Coalhouse Walker is not a historical character while Evelyn Nesbit is does not make the fates of the two any less real. Each story is true to the "facts" of American history as we understand race, class, and gender dynamics in the early 1900s. *Ragtime* is, like *The Book of Daniel*, an effective piece of midfiction because it does not merely accept the primacy of surface, but rather engages it to bear witness. Like the history texts it mimics, the prose initially seems to be a surface accounting of events. But this prose actually prompts readers to recognize the social problems and continuing injustice that mark an era when, on the surface, technological progress is rapid and the quality of life seems to be improving.

While his abandonment of his art and socialist goals is somewhat problematic, Tateh's upward mobility is essentially benign; he does not destroy others in his attempt to succeed. In *Loon Lake* (1980), often described as a Depression-era inverted Horatio Alger story, the main character moves from poverty to great wealth through his ruthlessness, cunning, and luck. Doctorow's interest in the Depression, his skepticism of the possibility of progress, and his interest in father-son relationships as mirrors of political issues coalesce in this highly innovative adaptation of the proletarian novel. As a 1970s adaptation of this genre, *Loon Lake* examines parallel lives of working-class characters, focuses on union activity, and reconfigures a *bourgeois* plot. The novel might disappoint some dogmatic radicals, however, for it depicts assimilation rather than radicalization and deals with issues such as complicity and betrayal.

While the 1930s proletarian novel often eschewed experimentation, *Loon Lake* is highly innovative and challenging. Initially, it is difficult to determine whether Joe or Penfield is narrating. Furthermore, the plot line is interrupted with poems, computer printouts, and short biographies, suggesting several interpretations of events. While in *World's Fair* the presence of other voices enriched and complicated Edgar's narrative, in *Loon Lake* the official biographies reduce the complexities of characters' lives and again remind readers of the drawbacks of official "factual" history. The dryness and lifelessness of such documents are implicitly contrasted with the passion of Joe's love for Clara, a passion which cannot endure in a world that Bennett seemingly controls.

Loon Lake is a successful adaptation of the proletarian novel in part because it is not formulaic; it includes many contingencies, one of the most apparent ones being the parallels between Joe's and Penfield's life, and to a lesser extent the parallels of Bennett with both men. All men share the same birthdate. Joe and Penfield were both poor boys alienated from their families; they both survived the dogs' attack, they both fell in love with Clara, a working-class gun moll who nonetheless becomes a Daisy-esque figure to these men. Such parallels undercut bourgeois notions of individuality and stress how common environments mold people.

In conversation Doctorow said that in part *Loon Lake* is about a man who chooses the wrong father, and essentially, suffers the loss of his soul.

Penfield does indeed see in Joe a surrogate son; he goes so far as to tell the younger man "You are what I would want my son to be." Yet Joe sees Penfield, a failed poet-in-residence kept at the lake as a curiosity, as no more desirable than his own parents.

Essentially, Penfield as a poet suffers from a lack of community and a lack of subject matter. Having rejected his father's admonition to write about the workers' lives, he can find nothing inspirational at Bennett's lake. The image of his body straining in the meditative poses of Zen Buddhism suggests his emotional and intellectual desire to understand and represent suffering, as well as a typically Buddhist desire to escape repetitive cycles through death and rebirth into Nirvana. It is fitting that someone who had always wanted to transcend suffering—one proletarian artistic response—would die in an airplane with a woman who wished she were without a body and would, like her, die without an heir.

Warren Penfield, like Joe, disliked his own parents. Their common disdain can be understood in part by reference to Richard Sennett and Jonathan Cobb's *The Hidden Injuries of Class* in which the authors argue that in a society where everyone supposedly can be middle class, working-class youths often come to see their parents as failures whom at all costs they should avoid imitating. The need to reject one's parents contributes to the ruthlessness and anger that characterize Joe and actually mold him to fit into the oppressor class.

Yet Joe tries to build a working-class life, and graphically describes the rigors of factory work. His bold attempt to live with Clara as an auto worker in a company town Bennett indeed controls might have succeeded had the budding union not been infiltrated by Bennett's spies. The effectiveness of Crapo Industrial Services represents how difficult it is for solidarity to develop among workers. Ironically, the shrewd Joe is duped by a seeming hillbilly. This act is but one of the inversions in *Loon Lake*, one that again reflects Doctorow's interest in the lines between appearances and reality. The carnival (evoking Bakhtin's concept of the carnivalesque), in addition to representing an escapist form of entertainment popular in the 1930s, is a mirror society of Bennett's lake. People are commodified, disposed of when no longer useful. Power is exerted by inflicting physical and sexual pain, most graphically illustrative in Joe's vengeful sex with Magda Hearn.[16]

Because Joe is ruthless and cunning, he is Bennett's rightful heir, and hence rather than kill him, Joe, in what Harter and Thompson have interpreted as a baptismal gesture, jumps into the lake and emerges a Bennett. Presumably taken from something like a *Who's Who*, the biography of Joe at the novel's end tells readers that he has repeatedly unsuccessfully married, indeed replicating his surrogate father's emotionally empty life. In informing readers that Joe's last name is Korzeniowski, the biography also complicates the *doppelgänger* theme and, like the inclusion of Tateh in *Ragtime*, suggests the assimilation of immigrants into the American Dream rather than their critique of it.

Despite the information it contains, this biography is a mock biography as *Ragtime* is a mock history. It lists Joe's hobbies as *petit* larceny, humorously legitimizing his crimes, embracing him as one of the nation's wealthy industrialists who earned their fortunes at the expense of others. *Loon Lake* thus does not suggest a "way out" of what seems to be *bourgeois* determinism, but its experimental techniques coupled with its proletarian themes suggest what Barbara Eckstein calls complicities, not only among the characters, but likely among any readers who wished to sever their roots for upward mobility. Doctorow does not embrace the easy hope of radical change still present in some leftists of the 1970s, but in *Loon Lake* vividly represents the values that sustain the current regime and undermine the possibility of such change.

While *Loon Lake* depicts a callous young man achieving wealth through a chance inheritance, Doctorow's eighth novel, *Billy Bathgate* (1989) represents a teen coming of age as a gangster. As in *Loon Lake*, Doctorow in this novel uses inversions of the Horatio Alger story and the proletarian *bildungsroman*. The book is set in the 1930s, but it actually suggests the danger of 1980s social and monetary policies, policies that Doctorow frequently criticized.[17] In an interview Doctorow stated that he, like many Americans, was fascinated not by the actual gangsters, but by their mythic appeal. His adaptation of an American myth in *Billy Bathgate* harkens back to *Welcome to Hard Times*, *The Book of Daniel*, and *Ragtime* particularly. We might reflect on Barthes's notion that the world gives myth a historical reality, and in turn gets back a natural image of it. The public then is not in love with the actual, violent gangsters, but with their naturalized renegade image. *Billy Bathgate* effectively engages readers at both levels: the actual in representing violent acts, the mythic through Billy's adulation of Dutch Schultz.

Again, Doctorow adapts a popular genre, the crime novel, with a tradition that has implications for *Billy Bathgate*. Unlike the detective novel—which will soon be discussed—the crime novel does not manifest an implicit faith in law and justice. Rather, it reflects a more cynical society, and some theorists and practitioners might even argue a more criminal society. As an urban figure living on the fringes of society, and one who has personally experienced the failure of social institutions, Billy has some affinities with Sloterdijk's criteria for a modern-day cynic. Yet Billy does believe in the possibility and satisfaction of upward mobility, a dream that distinguishes him from the cynic and somewhat ironically marks him as an average American.

In *Billy Bathgate* a high-school aged boy, whose father has deserted the family and whose apparently mentally-ill mother barely holds their lives together,[18] dreams of a life beyond the poverty of his tough Bronx neighborhood. Ultimately, he achieves this life through crime. It has often been observed that in the United States historically there have been two possible quick escapes from the ghetto: sports and crime. Young Billy shows no athletic prowess and states that many of the neighborhood figures were mobsters. Hence, Billy, an aspiring criminal, manages to attract the attention of one of the crime bosses, Dutch Schultz (who was an actual crime boss during this period) and begin a sort of apprenticeship to the mob.

As a novel focusing on a boy trying to escape from the ghetto, *Billy Bathgate* is a highly class-conscious novel. First, class is suggested in the sheer number of times Billy says the word in references to "class act" or "real class." It is reinforced in Billy's simultaneous attraction and intimidation in the presence of the upper-crust Drew, this novel's equivalent of *Loon Lake*'s Clara. Finally, the dream of class mobility is represented in the image of Bathgate Avenue with its abundant fruits evoking Schultz's references to wanting the fruits of his labor. Although many may dream of upward mobility, Billy has specific traits which will enable him to achieve it—primarily his tolerance for violence and his ability to juggle. In this novel, even more than in *Ragtime*, America itself is a "big juggling act" which requires citizens to effortlessly balance many diverse roles without showing signs of strain. Juggling also signifies performance, acting itself, which, if we look at *Billy Bathgate* as an allegory of the 1980s, brings to mind the character of Ronald Reagan. Reagan's acting, like Billy's, other characters' in this novel, and indeed many Doctorow characters in general, is tied to his mutability. Billy has the ability to blend in with the gang, even in the small town, Onandoga. His mentor, Dutch Schultz, however, exemplifies mutability, moving from urban crime boss to small-town good citizen, converting from Judaism to Catholicism. When Schultz loses his chameleon-like traits—when he loses his temper, impetuously killing—is when his survival is threatened.

To Billy, Dutch Schultz is the father he never had. In this novel the personal/political family dynamics that are crucial in much of Doctorow's fiction are played out in the boy's identification with Schultz. Some of the sentiments Schultz expresses about the need to oppose a government that stood against him reflect not only a criminal consciousness, but also an anti-government bias prevalent among many on the extreme right. Dutch Schultz's being based upon, indeed named after, a real character suggests that Doctorow is again playing with the boundaries between fact and fiction.

In his death-bed monologue, Dutch Schultz significantly calls for this mother. Billy's relationship with his mother is likewise crucial. Terry Caesar argues that in many contemporary novels mothers are disruptive voices, and that in a patriarchal society a mother's job is to police her son: having a criminal son merely literalizes her work. Caesar's otherwise provocative analysis ignores the class dimensions of this father-son relationship. In many ghetto homes fathers are missing and mothers are dependent on the agility and cunning of youth for support, even if this support involves criminality.

Ultimately, Billy's mother (who is given no name) becomes functional because of Billy's actions. Through his cunning and luck, Billy uncovers the gang's fortune after Dutch Schultz is murdered. As heir to Dutch Schultz, Billy is in many ways like Joe of *Loon Lake*: an inverted Horatio Alger protagonist. Moreover, he is an inversion of the protagonist of the proletarian *bildungsroman*. The end of the novel indicates that Billy has achieved respect by, in a typically cynical fashion, going through the motions of getting an education. Yet it is doubtful that Billy has escaped the gang life, even though as a youth he may have thought he could do so. As Dutch Schultz told him, once in the rackets, always in the rackets.

In *Billy Bathgate* Doctorow destroys or unpacks the myth that gangsters are outsiders and constructs an image of them as grotesques. Again, for Doctorow, as for Sherwood Anderson, a person becomes a grotesque when he/she embraces a particular truth (such as economic opportunity) too tightly or at the expense of all other truths. Hence, in different ways "The Leather Man" and the Bad Man from Bodie are grotesques of American individualism and unchecked greed. Similarly, Donald Pease asserts, in a review of this novel, that gangsters were "firm believers in the spirit of capitalism." In their world, "a different ordering of the relationship between needs and wants prevailed, transforming the need for thrift into the wish to get rich quick at the numbers" (458). This is the spirit that fueled Reaganomics, some of the Wall Street scandals, and the Savings and Loans debacles. Considering Eckstein's theory that good political fiction makes readers recognize complicity, we might ponder the extent to which this novel holds up an imperfect mirror to those who lived through the 1980s. Partially that mirror would reflect a failure to nurture.

It would further represent a lure of wealth so great that an essentially good boy is drawn to ruthless crime figures.[19] The text's ending suggests the frightful possibility that crime might indeed pay. *Billy Bathgate* does not, however, depict any possible way the course of events might have been altered.

Doctorow's 1994 novel, *The Waterworks,* can be read as a provisional resolution of many questions raised in *Billy Bathgate,* and indeed in all his previous novels. Here Doctorow suggests that praxis is possible and potentially effective against evil people and corrupt institutions. In *The Waterworks* evil is represented as a collusion between science, wealth, and government. The depiction of a diabolical scientist, Sartorius, whose hubris prompts him to violate what many would consider human laws, has its roots in nineteenth-century American writers such as Nathaniel Hawthorne and Edgar Allan Poe. As in *Ragtime* the romance genre is adapted, and it is again worthwhile to consider new Americanist assessments of the romance. Polarities are represented in Sartorius's destruction coupled with Martin's imperfect recovery, for example.

The Waterworks also could be considered a detective novel, for it, like *The Book of Daniel,* involves a search for the truth. As was previously mentioned, the detective novel (a popular genre) typically manifests a faith in reason, law, and justice; *The Waterworks* certainly exhibits these themes. Hence, this novel is perhaps Doctorow's most effective piece of midfiction, but one that slants in the direction of determinacy. Its themes share much with a reconsideration of postmodernism examined in *Telling the Truth about History* by Appleby et al. in which the authors uphold, "the human capacity to discriminate between false and faithful representations of past reality and beyond that to articulate standards which helped both practitioners and readers to make such discriminations" (261).[20] As did *The Book of Daniel, The Waterworks* insists that although "truth" might be slippery, there are some "truths" that are indeed verifiable and evident.

In addition to grappling with questions of praxis and verity, *The Waterworks* insists upon the importance of community. This is first suggested in the nineteenth-century newspaper's layout, somewhat similar to the contemporary *New York Times*: "In those days we ran stories straight down, side by side, a head, subheads, and story. If you had a major story you ran it to the bottom of column one and took as much of the next column as you needed" (114). In essence, the layout visually represents interdependence. Furthermore, *The Waterworks* actually represents community action by depicting McIlvaine, Donne, Grimshaw, and Emily working together to find Martin Pemberton, and ultimately bring Sartorius to justice. Simultaneously, the newspaper suggests the failure of community, for McIlvaine iterates that there is no need for papers in village societies in which residents spread news among themselves, and keep track of all residents. Hence, there would be no undernourished paperboys or street urchins that populate this novel and indeed populated nineteenth-century urban centers.

While the theme and plot of this novel are relatively determinate, and indeed may harken back to more realistic fiction, the style is decidedly postmodern and experimental. As he did in *World's Fair*, Doctorow strives for an oral quality in *The Waterworks*. As did Conrad in *Heart of Darkness*, Doctorow imagines a narration, one between the elder McIlvaine and a stenographer taking down his remembered tale. The same questions of reliability that marked *Welcome to Hard Times* are implicit in *The Waterworks*, but philosophical speculations on the reliability of his account do not trouble McIlvaine as they do Blue. Rather, narrative gaps are visually suggested in the numerous ellipses, left for readers to consider.

McIlvaine is a lifelong, albeit ambivalent, urbanite who remained in New York City rather than follow what was purportedly the great story of the 1800s, the settlement of the West. In fact, the growth of urban cities was the other, less commented upon, great story of the era. The booming decade after the Civil War was the beginning of the Gilded Age (the later part of which was depicted in *Ragtime*) when the gap between the haves and the have nots widened.[21] In cities, which swelled as a result of immigration, the divisions among a supposedly classless society were especially apparent, for the rich and poor lived in relatively close proximity to one another, and exploitation could be easily observed.

The Waterworks suggests that determined and rational effort can prevail against evil (if not against all the manifestations of social injustice). The novel is, however, very skeptical about the possibility of scientific achievement. As was previously discussed, Doctorow came of age in the 1950s, in the aftermath of the Second World War, and hence in many ways shares outlooks on science described by Appleby et al. According to these authors, this post–World War II generation had seen science produce and then been unable to control the nuclear bomb; hence, it was far less optimistic than its predecessors about science's potential to improve human life (172). As important, Doctorow in conversations about possible influences on this novel referred to the Nazi experiments, an awareness of which would undoubtedly make one wary of scientific experiments on vulnerable population groups and prompted him to reconsider the role and limits of science, to examine the lines between genius and hubris, a line Sartorius clearly crosses.

Like many Doctorow characters, Sartorius might be seen as a grotesque: a mad scientist or rabid individualist, especially in view of the fact that the has no professional affiliations. He is a symbol of the excess that Doctorow, in the name of community values and social justice, has repeatedly cautioned against through his fiction. Also, his invention of his own name suggests a common American practice of trying to better one's status by changing one's name. That he was able to turn normally cynical men into "acolytes" illustrates the persistent power of the con man who plays upon rubes' vulnerabilities, in this case a desire for immortality.

It is ironic that Augustus Pemberton trusts Sartorius, for he has so few ties with others. In fact, he is estranged from Martin who risks his life to find his father. In *The Waterworks* the theme of failed nurturance is manifested not only or even primarily in Martin's strained relationship, but most graphically in the orphan children whom Sartorius exploits. Martin Pemberton is similar to Joe in *Loon Lake* in that he is given two surrogate father figures—Sartorius and McIlvaine—to choose between. Unlike Joe, Martin ultimately transfers his affections to the poorer, struggling man rather than the richer, corrupt one. This choice not only signals Martin's redemption, but harkens back to *Loon Lake*, suggesting, in Eva Goldbeck's terms, a "way out" of the impasse in that novel: Joe's life might indeed have been different had he chosen another father figure.

Although Martin is saved from Sartorius and restored sufficiently to marry his fiancée, he is, like Marlow in *Heart of Darkness*, profoundly altered by his experience, which is in keeping with Doctorow's view of history's lasting power. In *The Waterworks* pernicious patterns of scientific hubris and political corruption are broken, but they nonetheless leave their mark. The narrator, McIlvaine, who struggles to recreate historical events and their meaning, does not doubt the hold this history has upon him and his contemporaries.

McIlvaine's desire to understand and communicate history is best exemplified in his desire to write something that would transcend mere reporting, something along the lines of a novel or a memoir. By accomplishing his desired task, McIlvaine would be breathing life into history in a manner that historiographers have long argued historians must do. That he decides not to publish what was undoubtedly the greatest story of his career possibly reflects his anxiety about accurately rendering this story, as well as a communal concern that if "the horror" of Sartorius were to become widely known people would be overwhelmed by the magnitude of his evil.

Ultimately then, the romance ending, with its dual wedding and depiction of the peaceful winter city, apparently frozen in time, stands in juxtaposition to McIlvaine's ruminations of the past. These elements combined help to make *The Waterworks* a highly effective piece of midfiction, a novel that combines postmodern indeterminacy and stylistic experimentation with an implicit claim that there are some definite truths one should try to discover and that there is possibility for praxis and positive change. In accordance with postmodern thinkers such as Foucault, Doctorow practices a version of "micropolitics." Action is local, situated in the community, in individual deeds and work on the self rather than in mass movements of which Doctorow has persistently remained skeptical. And yet action is possible

Notes

1. See in particular Clayton "Radical Jewish Humanism," Estrin, "Surviving McCarthyism" for sympathetic assessments of the politics in Doctorow's fiction. Alter, "The American Political Novel" finds *The Book of Daniel* polemical; Pearl K. Bell comes to similar conclusions about *Loon Lake* in "Singing the Same Old Song."

2. Of the five books that have been published about Doctorow's work, four are intended as general overviews and the fifth is a deconstructive study. See Levine *E. L. Doctorow*, Harter and Thompson, *E. L. Doctorow,* Parks, *E. L. Doctorow,* Fowler, *Understanding E. L. Doctorow* for general introductions to Doctorow's work. Morris, *Models of Misrepresentation: On the Fiction of E. L. Doctorow* gives a deconstructionist reading of Doctorow's novels through *Billy Bathgate,* as well as of some of his interviews and of a series of short prose pieces titled "The Songs of Billy Bathgate."

3. One might think of the fiction of John Updike or Ann Beattie as typical examples.

4. The reference is, of course, to Brooks's landmark book, *The Well-Wrought Urn*. Other influential books espousing the New Criticism are Ransom, *The New Criticism*; Empson, *Seven Types of Ambiguity*; and Wellek and Warren, *Theory of Literature*. Ransom coined the term "New Criticism."

5. Although the New Criticism has been widely attacked in the past two decades, there are defenders who claim, in part, that this criticism was not as monolithic and apolitical as it is now represented. See in particular Hartman, "The Philosophical Bases of Literary Criticism."

6. From 1984 through 1993 I had two or three informal conversations with Doctorow.

7. Recently Doctorow has taken a more public role by participating in discussions of the musical *Ragtime*, although he has lamented that doing so has taken time away from his writing.

8. See in particular Hutcheon, *The Politics of Postmodernism,* Bevilacqua, "Narration and History in E. L. Doctorow," Harpham, "E. L. Doctorow and the Technology of Narrative," and Morris, *Models of Misrepresentation*.

9. Paul Levine, "The Writer as Independent Witness" in Trenner 64. Wilhelm Reich (1897–1957) was an Austrian-born psychologist who became a U.S. citizen. Largely known for his work advocating sexual freedom, he also studied mass psychology and Marxist theory. See in particular *The Mass Psychology of Fascism*.

10 *Critique of Cynical Reason.* The title is a play on and rebuke of Immanuel Kant's *Critique of Pure Reason* (1781). As Huyssen explains in the "Foreword," Sloterdijk argues that cynicism is "the dominant operating mode in contemporary culture, both on the personal and institutional levels . . ." (xi). Sloterdijk, a German intellectual, in his exhaustive study examines the manifestations of cynicism in areas as diverse as technology, religion, the military, and social interaction.

11 In "A Gangsterdom of the Spirit" Doctorow applies Anderson's concept of the grotesque to modern values. The genre of the grotesque has been widely studied, particularly in German fiction, but in American literature as well. See especially Uruburu, *The Gruesome Doorway* and Meindl, *American Fiction and the Metaphysics of the Grotesque.*

12 I am indebted to Foley for her thorough study of the various kinds of proletarian novels as well as for her analysis that often proletarian fiction failed because it was not radical enough.

13 Wilde creates the category of midfiction to account for a substantial body of contemporary fiction that could not be classified as either reflexive or realistic, in essence fiction that occupies a middle territory between these poles. See "Strange Displacements of the Ordinary" and *Horizons of Assent.*

14 The concept of complicity is crucial to Eckstein's theory of good political fiction and will be discussed in later chapters.

15 For information on the new Americanists and their approach to literature see Crews, "The New Americanists," Pease, *"National Identities and Post-Americanists' Narratives,"* Dekker, "Once More," and Budick *Fiction and the Forms of Historical Consciousness.*

16 For a discussion of escapist entertainment in the 1930s see Dickstein, "Depression Culture." For a particularly insightful discussion of commodification and the evil of money in Doctorow's fiction see Gross, "Tales of Obscene Power."

17 For Doctorow's critique of the Reagan Administration, see "A Gangsterdom of the Spirit." Although this essay was published during the Bush Administration, it addresses values associated with Reaganomics. See also "For the Artist's Sake," and "The Character of Presidents."

18 Much of Doctorow's fiction—"The Leather Man," *The Book of Daniel, World's Fair,* and *Billy Bathgate*—includes mentally-ill characters. In many cases the genesis of mental illness can be traced to social pressures and injustice. Billy's mother deteriorates after the father leaves; Susan and the grandmother in *The Book of Daniel* become ill after losing several family members and seeing life-long dreams destroyed. The theme of mental illness might thus be tied to the themes of injustice.

19 In my interview with him Doctorow said, "Billy Bathgate is everything that you would want a boy to be; he's bright; he's enterprising; he's observant, a quick learner." "The City," 34. That we never see Billy Bathgate commit acts of vio-

lence and behave ruthlessly, as Joe in *Loon Lake* does, indicates he is basically decent.

20. The authors give an overview of western attitudes toward history and progress and attempt to resolve a postmodern skepticism of historical objectivity and veracity, understandably and in some sense rightfully born out of a post World War II distrust of science in the aftermath of nuclear weapons, as well as part of the postmodern critique of modernity. In many respects their project has affinities with my own project of resolving the skeptical and committed aspects of Doctorow's political outlooks manifested in his fiction.

21. O'Connell focuses on New York City's representation in and inspiration for literature, but he also offers a concise account of major developments in the city's history.

Chapter 1

Praxis, Identity, and the American Writer: *Lives of the Poets* and *World's Fair*

In many of his essays, Doctorow addresses the situation of contemporary American writers, but he most clearly articulates his view of contemporary fiction and its reception in "The Beliefs of Writers." Here he laments what he sees as a lack of passion in contemporary writing and a related inability of writers to represent politics. In contrasting American writers with Europeans he finds his cohorts, "With certain exceptions . . . less fervent about the social value of art and therefore less vulnerable to crises of conscience" (*Jack London* 106). He further argues that withdrawal from and distrust of society has been prominent in American fiction since Hemingway's *For Whom the Bell Tolls*, and that fiction suffers from a "reduced authority" because it neglects the issues that are critical to contemporary life. Moreover, critics have not developed a way of writing about social and political fiction: "There is no poetics yet devised by American critics that would treat engagement as anything more than an understandable but nevertheless deplorable breakdown of form" (112).[1] Doctorow ends this essay with a charge to writers themselves to write books about, "the way power works in our society, who has it, and how it is making history" (116).

Each of Doctorow's novels, I believe, attempts to address this imperative, but in fleshing out the conflicts contemporary writers face and the difficulties of formulating an acceptable aesthetic and praxis, it is instructive to begin by examining his two autobiographical works, *Lives of the Poets: A Novella and Six Stories* and *World's Fair*.[2] In his interview with Larry McCaffery, Doctorow stated that his first attempted novel was autobiographical, but that he quickly realized this type of writing was not his strength ("Spirit" 34). As a middle-aged man, however, he was perhaps better able to return to the subject of his life not as an example of isolated, atomistic experiences, but rather as a "case study" (to use a social science term admittedly too impersonal for Doctorow's fiction) of the writer's place in American society. In both *Lives of the Poets: A Novella and Six Stories* and *World's Fair*, Doctorow grapples with the boundaries between art and practice, between individual and community, that will inform all of his fiction. Nowhere is the artist's position to his society, the artist's role as witness, more clearly articulated.[3]

Like Doctorow's other fiction, *Lives of the Poets* and *World's Fair* are in many ways specific to time, class, and region. Both works are set in New York City, where Doctorow has spent the majority of his life and with which he strongly identifies. Class mobility is prominent in each work, although in *Lives of the Poets* the protagonist has moved up while in *World's Fair* the family is downwardly mobile. Furthermore, as in much of his fiction, the search for a father-figure to complement or replace an inadequate one is an important theme which is, in each work, resolved through the representation of writing as the ideal parent.

Lives of the Poets is composed of six short stories and a novella that is supposedly about the author of these stories. Hence, while the prose in this book is not generally experimental, especially when compared with *Ragtime* or *Loon Lake*, the book's composition is distinctly self-reflexive, reflecting the postmodernist bent in Doctorow's writing.[4] The stories' subjects are very different, but all feature characters who are outsiders, misunderstood and often thwarted; appropriately Harter and Thompson see dereliction as a motif in this work, for many characters face actual or emotional abandonment (105).[5] Significantly, the collection begins with "The Writer in the Family," which is about a boy whose father has died and whose family is afraid to break this news to the ailing grandmother. Because of his letter-writing skills, young Jonathan is enlisted to write "fictional" letters from his deceased father. The boy makes up adventures for his less-than-successful father of whom the narrator tells us, "In his generation the great journey was from the working class to the professional class. He hadn't managed that either" (4). Eventually, Jonathan learns his father had been in the navy and realizes the man's dreams were to be at sea. Angry at himself for not recognizing his father's dreams earlier, the boy drafts a letter from the father stating he has a fatal disease, should never have traveled to Arizona, and wishes his ashes to be scattered at sea. As a writer, the boy, like many Doctorow characters, bears witness to the emotional rather than the literal truth.

In its focus on a boy estranged from his father, "The Writer in the Family" is typical of Doctorow's work. Ellen G. Friedman has argued that a preoccupation with the father is characteristic of much male fiction that features a missing father and often represents Oedipal conflicts, "The missing father is the link to the past that, for the protagonists, determines identity" (241). While Friedman's formulation cannot be applied to *Ragtime*, in which Father often appears as an outdated buffoon, it is useful in considering most of Doctorow's fiction, including "The Writer in the Family." In this story, as in some of Doctorow's other work, the father's strained "linkage" is related to his role as breadwinner. The father's financial irresponsibility puts a barrier between himself and his son that, the boy discovers, writing helps dissolve. As Doctorow says in discussing this story, writing leads Jonathan to the truth about his father's desires and causes for his failures (Morris "Fiction" 448). Presumably, this story is an autobiographical piece by the writer Jonathan in *Lives of the Poets* and might shed some light on him.

"Willi" also focuses on childhood experiences, but they are recalled by an old man years later (a technique repeatedly employed by Doctorow). The eastern European narrator remembers his mother's repeated infidelities for which his father beat and finally murdered her. There is a tension in the text between the child's romantic vision, "I imagined the earth's soul lifting to the warmth of the sun and mingling me in some divine embrace" (27) and the harsh realities of his life, a tension reminiscent of the polarities associated with American romance but present in other fictional forms as well. Furthermore, there is an irony in the story being set in the early twentieth century, for at the end the narrator points out, "This was in Galicia in the year 1910. All of it was to be destroyed anyway, even without me" (35). Like so much of Doctorow's work, "Willi" suggests the impossibility of isolating private tragedy from political turmoil.

While most of Doctorow's fiction is about males and often about male themes (such as searching for a father figure), as Harter and Thompson point out "The Hunter" is unusual in that it is written from a woman's point of view (107). The female voice and experience of becoming interested in a man who sees her only as a sex object are gender specific, but her loneliness and alienation are common to many of the male characters in this book.

This alienation reaches a peak in "The Leather Man," a tale about someone who grotesquely dresses in leather. Trying to understand this character, the narrator ponders, "What is the essential act of the Leather

Man? He makes the world foreign.... He is estranged. Our perceptions are sharpest when estranged" (74). Furthermore, the narrator views this character with a mixture of revulsion and admiration, "You remember Thoreau. There's a definite political component to avoiding all other human beings and taking on the coloration of your surroundings, invisible as the toad on the log" (69). The Leather Man's identification with Thoreau, an admirable if impassioned figure determined to live simply, brings to mind Doctorow's specific interpretation of the grotesque as exemplified in Sherwood Anderson's stories, "that all about us there are many truths to live by, and they are all beautiful.... But as people ... snatch up a truth and try to make it their own predominating truth, to the exclusion of all others ... what happens, says Anderson, is that the moment a person does this, clutch one truth too tightly, the truth so embraced become a lie and the person turns into a grotesque" ("Commencement" in *Jack London* 84–85). In *Lives of the Poets* the truths of writerly detachment and self-reliance are embraced to an extreme degree so that the narrator and his peers become grotesques of themselves.

This final description of The Leather Man's state in many ways fits Jonathan in the novella *Lives of the Poets*. The main character is a successful fifty-year-old writer who lives in New York City's Greenwich Village. In an apparent mid-life crisis, he contemplates his own life as well as the lives of his fellow writers. Like characters in Updike novels, Jonathan's cohorts are estranged from their spouses and/or contemplating second or third divorces. Jonathan himself is still married to his wife of twenty years, though she lives apart from him in Connecticut and he is involved with a much younger woman.

It is easy to see the outlines of Doctorow's life in Jonathan's New York-suburban lifestyle,[6] in his age and profession, and in the writers described who resemble some of Doctorow's colleagues, such as Norman Mailer. However, it is also easy to see why Doctorow would disavow claims that the narrator is actually based on himself, for the lives described here represent some of the problems contemporary writers face as well as Jonathan's shortcomings (McInerney 152–55). In a sense *Lives of the Poets* is not Doctorow's or even Jonathan's life; rather it is the collective life of contemporary successful male authors. Samuel Johnson's *Lives of the Poets*, in contrast, focused on individual lives. Interestingly, scholars have pointed out that the critical judgments in Johnson's biographies obviously bear the stamp of his neoclassical time (Hardy vii–xv). Hence, the allusion to Johnson's work suggests that the writer is constructed by his time and his literary cohorts.

Lives of the Poets might be read as a model, or perhaps a parody, of the diminished fiction against which Doctorow has cautioned. Private angst certainly dominates Jonathan's life. As the novella begins he complains of minor physical ailments that characterize middle age. Additionally, he focuses on his own and his colleagues' marital difficulties and his need for isolation. At the core of many problems is a conflict between a need for autonomy and a need for solidarity with other people—not just for companionship but for a sense of shared human purpose. Marital problems become symbolic of the conflict between the need for bonding with another person and the need for freedom and isolation; Jonathan describes the many marriages between couples not divorced but not entirely together (such as himself and his wife) as wavering between two "archetypes," touching on both but committing to neither. These problems also represent Jonathan's doubts about his self-worth as a man, doubts that might stem from his relationship with and opinion of his father. When his wife Angel goes into a tirade against male perfidy, Jonathan reinforces her views. His willingness to condemn males partially reflects an insecurity rooted in his relationship with his own father. Again, it is useful to consider "The Writer in the Family" as a story reflecting the childhood experiences of its fictitious writer with his own father as well as hose of Doctorow himself. (For one, the father in "Writer," reportedly loved the city—a trait Jonathan in *Lives* and Doctorow share.) As the Jonathan of the novella remembers his father, he recalls, "How I loved him. The man who disappointed millions. Make promises, fail to keep them" (114). Clearly, Jonathan tries to distance himself from his father, for he reflects on both his success and his financial responsibility.[7] Moreover, he points out that he is a "true Capricorn," an earth sign implying a stable character as opposed to the father who loved the sea in "The Writer in the Family." In a sense, Jonathan has achieved the American Dream constructed as a child economically surpassing his parents. Yet achieving or even striving for this dream can have many dark sides. In their study *The Hidden Injuries of Class* sociologists Richard Sennett and Jonathan Cobb analyze the often-hidden costs of the assumption that in the United States everyone who works hard can be at least middle class.[8] One of the more detrimental effects of this ideology upon working-class families is parents' tendency to in effect tell their children not be like them and for working-class children to see their parents as failures. Hence, the child may be encouraged to "desert [his/her past] . . . leave it and the parents who have sacrificed for it behind" (131). But those who alienate themselves from their parents and their pasts are likely to feel guilty. So it is not surprising that Jonathan sees his financial responsibility as atonement for success. Most likely, other actions are also penances.

For one, Jonathan's isolation is self-inflicted. New York City functions as a metaphor for this isolation and as an ironic preserver of it. According to some social critics and historians, a common theme among writers and historians from the nineteenth century until today has been the sense of estrangement urban inhabitants feel—estrangement from their surroundings, themselves, and from people of other classes (Vidler 11).[9] The urban landscape itself and the particularly dense population of New York City can foster a sense of anonymity and isolation. For this reason among others, cities have in postmodern novels often been represented as labyrinths where memory is cut off from experience (Lehan 240–45).[10] While Jonathan is perhaps better at connecting memory and experience than are the characters in *White Noise* or *The Crying of Lot 49*, he is no more able to learn from experience. In addition, he is unable to connect with other people in any meaningful way. Throughout the novella there are images of the body as fort; while riding the subway he sees his skin as a border. He condemns people who talk too much, thereby violating their own privacy. These images suggest that the city functions both to isolate and to insulate. Jonathan's neighborhood, Greenwich Village, is a former bohemian haunt. Yet in the 1980s much of the housing is affordable only to the affluent. Hence, Jonathan, like most New Yorkers, lives in close proximity to the poor, but otherwise removed from their lives. In stating that most of his acquaintances eventually switched from riding the subways to taking taxis, he is referring to the class mobility among his peers and to their growing reluctance to mingle with other classes.

While there are economic and psychological roots of Jonathan's isolation, there are also important ones in his being a writer. Writers require isolation; to write novels they must, in most cases, work alone for several hours a day. Moreover, the writer is often working on something of dubious value; in interviews with me and with Christopher Morris, Doctorow talked of how the author is often filled with doubts about the value of his work, of how difficult it is to determine the worth of literary labor as compared with other kinds of labor (Tokarczyk 36–37; Morris 455). Such anxieties are likely related to the increasing commodification in American society—especially in the 1980s when some artists in all fields became stars and visual artists in particular sometimes had six-figure annual incomes. It is perhaps these concerns taken together that prompt Jonathan to refer to writing as "like a sentence—it's a prison image. It's an exclusionary image as far as I'm concerned" (96). The exclusion here refers both to non-writers being excluded and to the author being excluded from everyday society. As Fred Pfeil stated, the writer's engagement with others seems "indirect, incomplete, filtered through this premeditated skein of words, a process by which what I do now, writing the words, loses the name of action" (25). Like *Ragtime*'s Houdini, the author here laments not being to create, a "real world act"; fiction, despite the substantial power Doctorow assigns it, does not have the immediacy of many forms of communication. Moreover, in the act of writing fiction the sources of the fiction are lost or mutated; hence, in a desperate tone Jonathan tells a friend "each book has taken me further and further out so that the occasion itself is extenuated, no more than a weak signal from the home station, and even that may be fading" (142). Jonathan is not only isolated and alienated from others, but to an extent from his own work, which may explain his inconsolable nature.

But Jonathan's problems are the problems of contemporary American writers and to some extent other intellectuals; as was discussed earlier, the book is titled for "poets," all writers, not Jonathan as an individual. As such, the book questions not only how writers should respond to their own dilemmas, but also how they should address the social and political realities in society. John Williams argues that often Doctorow's characters are escapees from a social power structure who try to assert writing as resistance to life-denying forces in culture (11–12). This is certainly the role into which the Jonathan of "The Writer in the Family" falls, and, as we will see, one which Edgar of *World's Fair* discovers. But it is not one into which Jonathan has found entrée. He has not yet been able to finish his work *Lives of the Poets*, perhaps because he has not found the kind of fiction he wants to write, a fiction similar to that endorsed by Doctorow in "The Beliefs of Writers."

Because he has not found a way to address his own problems or those of his society, he adapts a stance similar to that of a modern cynic as conceptualized by Peter Sloterdijk. According to Sloterdijk, contemporary culture is marked by a universal, pervasive cynicism. "Modern cynicism presents itself as that state of consciousness that follows after naïve ideologies and their enlightenment" (3). In other words, cynicism results from the exhaustion of seemingly failed ideologies and social institutions. This pervasive modern figure has its roots in ancient culture in which the cynic, typified in Diogenes, is "a lone owl" and "an urban figure who maintains his cutting edge in the goings on of the ancient metropolises" (4). In the modern world the city becomes a fertile breeding ground for cynics, for in this anonymous setting cynics can perform their daily duties, apparently effectively blending into society, while having little faith in this society. This performance aspect is crucial, for Sloterdijk sees cynics as having enlightened false consciousness. In traditional Marxist ideology, false consciousness described the state of the proletariat identifying with the ruling class and actually believing that it shares in the upper class's benefits. The cynic, in contrast, knows that many social policies and institutions are meaningless, but nonetheless goes through the motions of accepting them. What might appear to be false consciousness is then "a constitution of consciousness afflicted with enlightenment that, having learned from historical experience, refuses cheap optimism" (6). Indeed, according to Sloterdijk one of the hallmarks of cynics is their ability to work and be successful, even though they are often borderline melancholics. The distinction between cynicism and skepticism, I would argue, is the degree to which one accepts enlightened false consciousness.

In many respects Jonathan fits Sloterdijk's profile. He is an urban figure on the periphery of society; he might also be seen as a melancholic nonetheless able to control symptoms and work, if with reduced efficiency. Jonathan withdraws from his society in what Sloterdijk describes as "mournful detachment." His sense of existential absurdity is to him something to be ashamed of, so it is repressed and internalized and consequently useless for taking preemptive action. Possibly he perceives himself as being more marginal to society than he actually is. Having shown some fascinations with derelicts—those without home or work who live on the edge, he reflects "between the artist and simple dereliction there is a very fine line" (101). Furthermore, he believes that dereliction is a state of mind common to middle-aged men, but not women. We might speculate that to the extent this perception rings true it does because, as theorists such as Carol Gilligan, Nancy Chodorow, and Mary Belenkey have in various ways shown, women tend to value connection over individuation, while men have contrary priorities. Hence, intimacy and connectedness are often threatening to men; they may avoid these states and thus become isolated.

Although Jonathan is relatively isolated in his society, he is far from apathetic. In particular he laments the plight of refugees and the actions of the U.S. government that made the refugees' lands unlivable. Furthermore, he refers to the U.S. president embracing sociopathic murderers, and at this point contemplates whether he has become "estranged" from his calling. Such estrangement is presumably what prompts him to offer his home as sanctuary to illegal aliens, an act a local minister calls "bearing witness"—a term Doctorow might use to describe the writer's art.[11]

Despite his fears of commitment, he decides to take the leap of becoming a political activist and returning to live with his wife. In typing with the alien boy, relying on the child to reach his quota of pages, he is resolving his father-son issues by realizing that his battle with his own father is over and it is time for him to be a father figure. Rather than wish for a son to surpass him economically, he will "adopt" an "orphan" and try to give that boy a new life.

In discussing American literature, Katherine Newman argues that its governing theme is not the American Dream, but rather the selection of a cultural model that will satisfy spiritual and emotional needs. Novels are often about choices of assimilation, accommodation, and successful rebellion. Despite concern about the legal ramifications of his actions, Jonathan, who had the guise of an assimilationist, chooses to rebel against his society, and despite his ideals of writerly detachment, Jonathan gets involved; he changes from cynic to activist.

In theorizing Jonathan's action, it is useful to consider Frank Lentricchia's *Criticism and Society* in which the author argues that society is unreasonable, most critics recognize this is so, and it is the intellectual's task to go about transforming society. To do so, one must keep in mind a fact that might seem like a commonplace, but nonetheless has powerful implications: that the ruling culture does not define all culture; it excludes marginalized voices that the oppositional critic must work to amplify. In teaching the young boy to write, Jonathan is enabling him to someday voice his own concerns. In his essay "Foucault's Legacy," Lentricchia speculates that the central if unacknowledged desire for historicism is to find a space of freedom in which people are not forced to become what they do not wish to become. Drawing on Raymond Williams's notion that determinism is a complex and interrelated process of limits and pressures in the social process, we might see the pressures for commitment conflicting with those for isolation, the fact that Jonathan, for his weaknesses, is not emotionally crippled, and understand his willingness to commit on various levels (87–104). We might also utilize Barbara Eckstein's concept of complicity. She explains that in the *OED* complicity is related both to "complicate" and "accomplice," and that its roots ("com" and "plic") mean to "fold together." In contemporary definitions "complicity" means both "being an accomplice" and " [the] state of being complex and involved." Hence, "If evil befalls the other, the self is not simply guilty, to blame, but rather complicit in a network of personal, social, political, even aesthetic conditions which perpetuate the stereotypes and which, in turn, rationalize the suffering. The self is an accomplice in this complexity. But in the web of complicity the self also suffers" (32–33). It might be argued that Jonathan becomes acutely aware of his inevitable complicity, and then decides to undermine immoral policies of the country to which he nonetheless owes allegiance and supports with his taxes.

While the previous analyses are appealing, some critics have found the ending of *Lives of the Poets* unconvincing.[12] It is indeed difficult to believe that Jonathan could so quickly commit to his wife and become an activist who takes legal risks. That the ending is strained most likely reflects Doctorow's continued ambivalence concerning the writer and political activism, an ambivalence attributable both to a solitary nature and to a New Critical schooling. The move to activism in this novel is perhaps best seen as an ideal that the writer is still struggling to envision a way to achieve.

While *Lives of the Poets: A Novella and Six Stories* probes the conflicts of a mature writer, *World's Fair* is a *küntslerroman*. It includes key features of the genre—a sensitive boy misunderstood by his peers struggling to come to terms with religion, family, and politics, and discovering himself as a writer.[13] In specific ways, *World's Fair* imitates James Joyce's *A Portrait of the Artist as a Young Man*: most notably, it begins with a bed-wetting scene. While Stephen Dedalus has to cope with poor eyesight, Edgar is an asthmatic child with numerous allergies. Like the Dedalus family, Edgar's family includes a financially irresponsible father whose business fails, and as a result the family has to move to more modest quarters. Although Edgar is not teased by his peers as Stephen is, he is a loner who says he prefers his own company to any "miserable wretch of a child" (19). His solitary nature, however, is not the most significant marker of his difference. Instead, his position as a Jew in the 1930s, even in the Bronx where there were many Jews, is the most problematic part of his identity. *World's Fair* is an American *bildungsroman* in part about situating ethnic *and* American identity, as some would say riding the hyphen, balancing Jewish and American identity.[14] With this in mind we may conclude Edgar's father is correct in the explanation he offers his son in consolation for attaining honorable mention rather than first place in the essay contest on the typical American boy: Edgar simply is not a typical American boy. Edgar's project is to claim the typicality he wants—the aspects of American life he desires—while formulating a positive Jewish identity under siege.

The most pervasive influence in Edgar's life is, not surprisingly, his family. Again, in a manner typical of *künstlerromane* such as *A Portrait of the Artist as a Young Man* and D. H. Lawrence's *Sons and Lovers*,

World's Fair represents a tumultuous family in which the boy often feels torn. Of his parents' relationship he writes, "The conflict between [them] was probably the major chronic circumstance of my life . . . irreducibly opposed natures" (15). The tension is most apparent in the mother's complaints about and disparagement of the father. Edgar himself views his father with a sense of wonder and concern; he contrasts the relatively carefree father with his hardworking brother Donald; while Donald earns his rewards, the father seems to attain them by "magic." His childlike use of the word may, in context, suggest Edgar will, like *Ragtime*'s Houdini, want to work his own magic—to exercise control over the world or at least make it appear that he does.

In contrast to the adults, the brother Donald is an ally to Edgar, someone to be admired and trusted, making Edgar a less isolated figure than many *künstlerroman* protagonists. After Donald tells Edgar their pet dog has been taken to the pound—not given to a family, as his parents said, Edgar reports "Implicit in what my brother said was the truth, I knew, that adults could be loved but never trusted; only Donald could be trusted" (83). When Donald fails out of college, he becomes, for Edgar, another adult to be watched and worried about, but given the nature of gender roles in this book, it might be more accurate to state Donald becomes another adult male to be watched and worried about.[15]

Edgar depicts his mother as a far stronger figure than her husband.[16] She is presented as a vigorous "buxom" woman who endures the breech birth of the "accidental" Edgar and goes on to manage the family's lives. At one point Edgar reflects, "here she was in the Depression, with her sick mother, her improvident brother, her two children, a yapping dog, and maintaining an entire family while in economic dependency to her unpredictable husband" (68). Her life in actuality is similar to that captured metaphorically by Nora's mother at the World's Fair, swimming in a pool with Oscar the octopus, trying to avoid being snared. Edgar's concern for his mother and sense of inadequacy about his father shape his own sense of identity and vision of what it will mean to be an adult.

Although Edgar's voice and perceptions expectedly dominate the novel they are not, as are the protagonist's in some *künstlerromane*, the only perceptions. Rather, short oral narratives by the mother and Donald are included, offering other perspectives on the family situation and thus avoiding the solipsistic feeling that some *bildungsromane* have.[17] Hence, although this novel's prose style is not experimental, its inclusion of different voices expands the possibilities of the traditional *bildungsroman* and thus continues Doctorow's efforts to experiment with the novel's possibilities.

The novel begins with Rose's narrative telling Edgar about her own life and how she met his father Dave, thus explaining her feelings and leaving us to speculate on the effect of her narrative on the boy. Similarly, a crucial point in one of her later narratives is when she tells of losing her two older sisters in the 1918 flu epidemic, reflecting on the grief of her own mother and the "black space" in her own life. When Edgar becomes dangerously ill, readers can speculate on the way memory intensified her own fears. But the most persistent theme in Rose's narration is that their lives could have taken another direction, that she needn't have married Dave or moved away from her beloved Rockaway. For the mother as for other characters in *World's Fair* and the collection *Lives of the Poets*, the sea is associated with freedom, depicted as a source of life that continually nourishes it.

This source is so important because, paradoxically, a fear of death permeates the book. Initially, when Edgar finds his grandmother dead he is struck by "the overall stillness of her, a declared inanimateness, the monumental event of death recorded for me as another kind of life, a superseding condition with more visible torment than I could have imagined was possible" (96). Significant here is the word "recorded," for it suggests the event's imprint on his mind. Since Edgar found his grandmother he is now privileged, having a firsthand knowledge of death and his grandmother's passage out of their lives. His privilege extends to the magic he attempts to exert over death, becoming almost obsessed with it, thinking of and imagining death in order to avoid it. Such an attempt at magical control over his world, while typical of childlike thinking, also prefigures the control an artist has over his universe, the need for which might become more acute given the circumstances of Edgar's specific confrontations with death—his appendicitis, the explosion of the Hindenburg, and Hitler's victories in Europe.

When asked about the importance of death in his fiction, Doctorow responded that there would be no need for a moral understanding of death if one didn't need to understand its injustice: why one is struck down and another is not. Once a person asks this question, he/she is no longer talking about death, but about injustice (Morris "Fiction" 44). The specter of death in *World's Fair* then raises questions about the nature of injustice and people's complicity in it. Specifically, some of the questions it raises are not why Edgar was spared, but why any child should die, why any Jew should be killed by Nazis.

Although this novel focuses on the daily family life of a boy, there are many hints of political struggles that affect the lives of private families.

Despite the father's noted lack of aptitude for business and his financial irresponsibility, his business failed partially because of the Great Depression. When the family income declines, Edgar's family behaves as did many in this era and moves to a cheaper rental. (Some families moved constantly to get a free month's rent.) In this respect *World's Fair* is similar to *Welcome to Hard Times*, *The Book of Daniel*, and *Loon Lake*; as John Clayton points out, the three latter works examine a collective experience of their century ("Radical" 113). Additionally, *World's Fair* clearly conveys the experience of American Jews during the 1930s. Initially, Edgar fears being beaten by anti-Semites in his neighborhood and analyzes his fear, "A little boy who went to Hebrew school would live in endlessly concentric circles of danger, beginning with my part, and rippling over the globe" (101). He first experiences these "circles of danger" when he sees swastikas scrawled in a neighborhood yard and is warned by his mother to avoid young anti-Semites. Like the meaning of the stories told by Marlow in *Heart of Darkness*—meaning which is not inside the "kernel" tale, but in the context around it—the significance of Edgar's brushes with anti-Semitism is not so much in their immediate threat to him but rather in what they suggest about danger in the world at large.

Edgar responds as a child would, at times imitating Hitler in the mirror trying to appropriate his power and drain the danger from himself. The Hindenburg's crash, from which many people fell from the sky in flames, becomes a metaphor for the Holocaust. In a kind of adaptation, Edgar sees himself as falling all the time but living in close proximity to the pavement, again perhaps reassuring himself that he can work magic and thus will not be hurt. But by far his most serious adjustment is after he is attacked by the anti-Semitic boys and denies being Jewish, when he "struggle[s] to understand Christianity as something that would shove a knife into my belly" (238).

Edgar is able to deny his Jewishness and thus escape his attackers. His situation represents that of American Jews who, in varying degrees, have been able to blend into the American population. Indeed, at one point American Nazis go into Edgar's father's store and try to sell him a subscription to their publication, presumably not realizing he is Jewish. Edgar is able to perceive what is necessary to survive, but his survival compromises his integrity. One of his goals, expressed in his prize-winning essay, becomes to tell the truth, to claim his Jewish identity.

In portraying Edgar as a sensitive boy coming of age in the troubled 1930s, Doctorow has positioned him to develop as a writer. Harter and

Thompson depict Edgar, as Daniel from *The Book of Daniel* describes himself, as a "criminal of perception" (109): one whose insightful nature enables him to penetrate the secrets of others. His perceptions enable him to realize the shortcomings of his parents' marriage and to recognize the difficulties of adult lives. As he reports he gradually gains an awareness of his private life, one that will enable him to separate himself from his family and envision a different kind of future for himself. Such an awareness is a necessary balance to a perceptive nature, for it enables him to perceive himself in relation to others.

Through the perceptions of this young narrator, Doctorow suggests the concerns with cycles of history and illusions that mark so much of his fiction. Edgar is fascinated with repetition. One of his first readings is of nursery rhymes, and he is struck by recurrences, "Whatever happened to them kept happening to them over and over, good or bad, and I perceived a true moral in this repetition of fate, this recurring inevitable conclusion to the flaws in their beings" (93). Juxtaposed with Edgar's fascination with the World's Fair that glorifies progress, this sentiment represents a dilemma: how does one remain aware of recurring patterns in history while retaining faith in the future? To the extent that the novel resolves this question, it does so through the figure of Edgar as budding artist with a sensitivity to his time, as represented in his making the time capsule, and a faith in the future. In a highly optimistic appraisal, Shaun O'Connell argues that New York City, despite the gloom of the Depression, prepared its youth to emerge triumphant (227). Edgar seems to embody this claim.

Edgar first becomes aware of the power of art while at the circus marveling at illusion. In the clown's acts, Edgar perceives a way to capture a audience, and reveal "the truth" slowly in the actor's/writer's own time. His first attempt to do so is in his essay on the theme of the Typical American Boy, worth quoting in its entirety because its simple prose so effectively conveys the issues with which Edgar grapples:

> The typical American Boy is not fearful of Dangers. He should be able to go out into the country and drink raw milk. Likewise, he should traverse the hills and valleys of the city. If he is Jewish, he should say so. If he is anything, he should say what it is when challenged. He roots for his home team in football and baseball but also plays sports himself. He reads all the time. It's all right for him to like comic books so long as he knows they are junk. Also, radio programs and movies may be enjoyed but not at the expense of important things. For example, he should always hate Hitler. In music he appreciates both swing and symphony. In women he appreciates them all. He does not waste time daydreaming when he is

doing his homework. He is kind. He cooperates with his parents. He knows the value of a dollar. He looks death in the face. (244)

One is initially struck by the number of commonplaces here—root for the home team, cooperate with parents, and so forth. What marks this essay as unique is its insistence on proclaiming Jewish identity and the intrusion of Hitler into the prose itself; stylistically, "For example, he should always hate Hitler" does not clarify the previous sentence. The sentence's intrusion is important in illustrating the intrusion of anti-Semitism on Edgar's imagination. Although horrible and terrifying, the experience of bigotry is a key component to Edgar's genesis as a writer.[18]

Edgar's essay touches upon less crucial issues as well. As critics have pointed out, one of the themes in *World's Fair* is the rise of consumer and popular culture, a concern that is to some degree also present in *The Book of Daniel, Ragtime,* and *Loon Lake.* Christopher Morris sees *World's Fair* as recreating American 1930s culture as one defined by consumer products that market meaning (*Models* 166). Morris does not, however, address the degree to which the modern writer must negotiate with popular media such as television, radio, and publications designed for fast reading. Weaker writers may find themselves consumed by the culture around them; extremely "high brow" writers may be unable to attract an audience. Some successful writers, such as Doctorow himself, are able to use the material of popular culture to express themes of importance to them. Edgar's essay marks him as potentially such a writer.

Newman argues that liberation is a continual theme in minority literature (8). References to traversing the hills and drinking raw milk certainly suggest a yearning for freedom and adventure. Edgar desires liberation as both as a member of an ethnic group and as a member of a family that has often seen its dreams destroyed. In seeming contrast to his parents, Edgar is able to envision a dream and act to achieve it. Perceiving that the family had not gone to the World's Fair because they could not afford the admission, he resolves to win tickets for them. Again, there is a contrast between Edgar's hopefulness matched by the optimistic vision of the 1939 World's Fair, and the reality of American people's lives. The fair itself is identified with health and well-being, so much so that when Edgar is recovering from his appendicitis Donald promises that they'll go to the fair when he is well. Collectively the World's Fair seems to promote an escape from the past into the future; hence, the "World of Tomorrow" is its theme. For all its attractiveness, it is a hard world to grasp, as Edgar suggests when he comments upon the problems of perspective, "Everywhere at the World's Fair the world was reduced to tiny size by the cunning and ingenuity of builders and engineers. And then things loomed up that were larger than they ought to have been" (254). The modern age technocrats—builders, engineers, and industry captains—have an ability to create illusion that perhaps once belonged exclusively to artists.

The future represented in Futurama might indeed seem an ideal one in which everything is effectively planned, human needs are articulated and met. Yet the fair presents a vision of world harmony that contrasts sharply with world events.[19] The fair's idealization, as well as its exclusion of Jews and other immigrant groups in its representations, is noted by Edgar's father. (Although there is a Palestine Pavilion that Rose applauds for demonstrating Jews can be like everyone else.) Again, there is a tension among the parental voices, readers' perceptions, and Edgar's naive enjoyment of the fair. His childlike pleasure is, of course, typical of many attendees, and it is undoubtedly a response for which organizers and displayers hoped. Like many forms of 1930s popular entertainment the fair provides escapism. According to Morris Dickstein, there was a split in the era's collective psyche between an effort to grapple with unprecedented economic woes and an effort to escape these woes through popular entertainment that was largely escapist in nature. Furthermore, the fair is an attempt to manage a worried populace. As John Williams notes, the perisphere in *World's Fair* indicates how corporate "toys" on display are actually ideological contrivances masking more unpleasant realities, such as economic inequity and bigotry (188). The acclimation of the frugal, 1930s generation to the post–World War II consumer economy is concisely represented in Rose's agreeing that spending tax dollars to build highways satisfies General Motors' interests, but stating that nonetheless she would like to own a car.

The pervasiveness of consumer culture is perhaps again suggested in the time capsule Edgar assembles and buries in imitation of that at the fair. While Edgar includes an essay on President Franklin Roosevelt's life, the focus is on material artifacts to represent a culture rather than the written word at which Edgar has excelled. Edgar's capsule does allow future generations to interpret artifacts, but what he possibly (and only possibly) gains in objectivity he loses in authority. For this reason, Christopher Morris sees Edgar not so much as a dedalus or maker but as a byproduct of texts that generate him along with new signs (*Models* 161). Edgar has more passion and budding creativity than Morris grants; the young boy's essay is a promising beginning. However, the shift to material culture focuses attention on Edgar as consumer rather than maker. The meaning of this time capsule is further complicated by Edgar's last-minute decision not to bury the book on ventriloquism, but to attempt again to learn this skill. A budding writer, Edgar will focus not on finding his own voice, as we might say, but to throw his voice, to find the proper medium and illusion for his art, as Doctorow characterizes his own choice to write fiction rather than essays, to "choose the thrown voice and all its tropes" (*Jack London* ix). The time capsule might then represent the thrown voice, the indirect approach Doctorow favors; future generations are given materials to interpret rather than a text that necessarily reveals its author's interpretations. Nonetheless, Edgar leaves us with material artifacts while Stephen Dedalus leaves us with an aesthetic theory. Even given that Dedalus is at least a decade older than Edgar, it seems the written word has been shortchanged in *World's Fair*.

If the ending of *World's Fair* is somewhat confused, it is because the book only partially succeeds in depicting the genesis of a political writer; readers get only a glimpse of Edgar's talent and interest in writing.[20] The novel is most effective in giving a sense of New York life in the era, a strength that much of his fiction has. Doctorow's autobiographical underpinnings are apparent not so much as surface similarities between his and the protagonist's lives, but in the often sentimental rendering of episodes, most notably at the end when Edgar walks away from the time capsule with tears in his eyes. *Lives of the Poets: A Novella and Six Stories* is more successful in rendering the contemporary writer's psyche and conflicts, but stops short of envisioning praxis. Yet both these autobiographically based works effectively represent writers' imperative to bear witness to their society and its history, to come to terms with their "complicity" in it while maintaining fierce allegiance only to their art. They both depict the author's struggle to balance skepticism and commitment through the act of writing. In various ways, the imperative to do so shapes Doctorow's more "impersonal" historical fiction. This historical fiction, which forms the bulk of Doctorow's work, further probes questions only touched upon in *World's Fair*: the seemingly cyclical nature of historical events and its implications for the possibility of progress, as well as the constructed nature of truth and narrators' related difficulty in perceiving and rendering what actually happened.[21]

Notes

1. Doctorow's assessment of the apolitical nature of American criticism is undoubtedly less true today than when "The Beliefs of Writers" was first published as "The Passion of Our Calling." One might think of the work of critics such as Barbara Foley, Frank Lentricchia, and Paul Lauter, to name a few.

2. Doctorow has quibbled with the distinction between autobiographical and other fiction, stating the two books discussed in this chapter draw upon his life no more than other works. While it is likely that Doctorow did draw upon his experiences to create the characters in all his fiction, the resemblance between features of Doctorow's life and those of characters in *Lives of the Poets* (the novella) and *World's Fair* is far more obvious than in other works.

3. For a thorough discussion of the role of the artist in Doctorow's earlier, more impersonal work—*Welcome to Hard Times*, *Ragtime*, and *The Book of Daniel*—see Cooper "The Artist as Historian."

4. "The Leather Man" with its discontinuous narrative, is the most experimental piece.

5. "The Water Works" is interesting in that this dark tale of a child found drowned in a water tower is the inspiration for Doctorow's novel of the same title.

6. Jonathan, like Doctorow, has a second home outside the city.

7. According to Fowler (2) Doctorow's own father was charming, but financially unstable.

8. The authors of this pioneer conducted 150 in-depth interviews with working-class people over a four-year period in order to determine the effects of the ideology of class difference and upward mobility upon them. Their concept of class injury, especially as it affects family relationships, informs much of my reading of Doctorow's work.

9. While Vidler focuses on nineteenth-century responses of social critics and romantic writers to rapidly growing metropolises, the representation of cities as places of alienation and estrangement appears in the work of many twentieth-century writers.

10. Lehan traces the evolution of cities from commercial to industrial to multinational centers and their resultant representation in European and American literature.

11. Doctorow has referred to writers as witnesses in Levine "The Writer as Independent Witness."

12. See in particular Bruce Bawer, "The Human Dimension." It is not surprising this conservative critic disliked the book and Doctorow's work on the whole. While I

believe Bawer's criticisms of the collective nature of Doctorow's fiction are unfounded, Bawer nonetheless has a point in questioning the believability of Jonathan's conversion to activism.

13 The prevalence of children, particularly alienated and orphan children, in Doctorow's fiction has been commented upon. See especially Morris, "Fiction."

14 I use *bildungsroman* rather than *künstlerroman* here because I want to emphasize the importance of "the education of a young ethnic (wo)man," not necessarily an artist. Edgar is of course educated both as an ordinary man and as an artist.

15 For a discussion of women's roles in Doctorow's fiction see Gentry, "Ventriloquists' Conversations."

16 The grandmother, however, is rapidly becoming senile and worries all her family. Hence, we cannot conclude women are always represented as stronger than men in this novel.

17 Valerie Miner in particular has written *bildungsromane* that include other voices and thus are less centered around a particular individual. Visions of a new *bildungsroman* are attributable in part to a left-wing focus on community and to postmodern skepticism about individual fixed identity.

18 Of course, after World War II there was a flowering of Jewish-American literature by writers such as Saul Bellow, Phillip Roth, and Bernard Malamud, in part because of a deepening sense of the Jewish experience.

19 See Morris, *Models* for a discussion on this point.

20 Reviews tended to praise the novel as a Jewish *bildungsroman* and as an effective period piece with a documentary feel. The novel was faulted for a lack of plot, and sometimes perceived to be more like a memoir. The prose was often described as lyrical, but overwritten at times. Many found the book sentimental. For generally positive reviews, see Bluestein, "Time Capsule"; White, "Pyrography"; Shelton in *National Forum* (Shelton sees *World's Fair* as Doctorow's best book to date). For negative reviews see Koenig, *New York* 18; Sheppard, "The Artist as Very Young Critic" *Time* 126; and especially Iannone "E. L. Doctorow's 'Jewish' Radicalism." Iannone's review essay might be seen as an answer to Clayton's article on radical Jewish humanism. She argues that Doctorow's writing is influenced not by Judaism, but by ideology and that this ideology undermines all his fiction to date. My own reading of the novel is most closely aligned with critics who find the period evocative and the depiction of childhood emotions effective, but the ending sentimental.

21 Christopher Morris in *Models* argues that there is a contradiction in Doctorow's work and vision of fiction between the imperative to represent the truth and the perception that truth is constructed. While Morris sees this contradiction as pointing to meaning's indeterminacy, I see a tension, not a contradiction, and argue that the tension enriches and complicates Doctorow's political vision.

Chapter 2

The Frontier Reconsidered: *Welcome to Hard Times*

While Doctorow's historical fiction deals less explicitly with the problem of the artist representing his or her community and developing a suitable kind of praxis, it foregrounds the problems of actually bearing witness, of perceiving and rendering history. Moreover, this history often challenges American "myths," or governing ideas by which we live. In his essay on the genesis and quality of modern myths, Roland Barthes discusses the relationship between myth and history: "What the world supplies to myth is a historical reality, defined, even if this goes back quite a while, by the way in which men have used and produced it, and what myth gives us back in return is a *natural* image of this reality (142).[1] In *Welcome to Hard Times* Doctorow debunks or denaturalizes one of the most powerful American myths that had particular resonance when the novel was published—the conquest of the American frontier.[2] By debunking this myth Doctorow reveals his skeptical nature, and through the character of Blue suggests how difficult it can be to interpret events. Moreover, this first novel is most clearly influenced by existential philosophy, and thus has a fatalistic, even deterministic, vision of history and human nature.

The novel tells of a town that is burned to the ground by an outlaw, rebuilt largely through the efforts of its mayor and "historian," has a Gold Rush and the social problems that accompany it, and is finally burned again by outlaws. Critics such as David S. Gross have placed *Welcome to Hard Times* in a tradition of counter-westerns dating back to Stephen Crane's "The Blue Hotel," and "The Bride Comes to Yellow Sky," stories that present, "a pessimistic 'realism' [that] constantly reveals new ways in which the traditional version rests on values, assumptions, views of reality which are unreal, false, insubstantial."[3] This first novel is perhaps Doctorow's most accessible and certainly his least experimental: *Wel-*

come to Hard Times, in keeping with Doctorow's penchant for indirection, can be read as a fable with a hint of prophecy in it. On one level *Welcome to Hard Times* is the story of the town being twice burned to the ground by the Bad Man. On another level, it is about the toll of self-interested economic ventures that undercut any possibility of community cohesiveness. The struggle to find community is echoed in the novella *Lives of the Poets*, and much of Doctorow's fiction is juxtaposed with greedy self-interested behavior of individuals. Christopher Morris states that *Welcome to Hard Times* has been critiqued around two themes: one as a critique of American civilization, especially capitalism, and second as modernist, focusing on, through Blue's narration, "the debility of writing in the modern world." "The obvious problem," according to Morris, "is that these themes contradict each other. If the novel espouses a political critique, then the modernist view of Blue—that the narrative questions the validity of truth—becomes less plausible" (*Models* 26). Again, rather than a contradiction between political critique and modern questioning of the written word, I see an effort to make a political critique without claiming the certainty that some political critiques have, to acknowledge both an political ideology and a authorial skepticism.

In explaining how he came to write this book, Doctorow recalls that while working as a reader of screenplays, he read innumerable westerns. As someone who had never been west of Ohio, he'd had neither an interest in nor an affinity for them. "But from reading all these screenplays and being forced to think about the use of Western myth, I developed a kind of contrapuntal idea of what the West must really have been like. Finally, one day I thought 'I can lie better than these people.'" The result was a short story that was eventually, on the advice of an editor, turned into a novel (McCaffery 34).

Aside from Doctorow's notion that stories of the West are lies—a notion that is related to Doctorow's views on history and fiction that will be discussed later—the most interesting description of his idea of the West is "contrapuntal," a word defined both as "the combination of two or more independent melodies in a single harmonic texture" and "a complementing or contrasting item."[4] Taken together these definitions suggest the novel is offering a new perspective on the West; Doctorow's "lie" represents an alternative view of the frontier, especially in 1960 when skepticism of the frontier mythology was less widespread than it is today. In one sense the novel itself, as an inverted Western in which the "good guys" die and the bad ones triumph, suggests a contrapuntal view. Yet there is another sense in which Doctorow's understanding of the West is itself contrapuntal, and this explains why he produced such a revisionist western.

The novel's very title evokes an intertextual reference to Dickens's *Hard Times* and the economic exploitation that novel depicts, thus suggesting affinities between urban problems and the frontier. As a born and bred New Yorker who has lived outside the city's environs for only short periods of time, and who has a deep affinity with the city, Doctorow was shaped by the experience of living in a place described by Shaun O'Connell as both separate from the rest of the nation and as an intensified version of it (2).[5] That New York is often seen as separate from the United States as a whole is evident in the remarks by politicians such as Gerald Ford, Dan Quayle, and Newt Gingrich, who at various times have castigated the city as a center of waste and failed social policies. What such politicians are reacting to is New York's liberal reputation and policies that in part grew out of immigrant culture, what Doctorow has variously described as socialist Jewish culture and the trade union spirit.[6] Some of the more familiar components of this progressive politics are a vision of human interaction as essentially communal and a de-emphasis of isolated private gain. These progressive ideals coexist with the often brutal realities of urban life—great economic disparity and ruthless exploitation of the vulnerable. These are the concerns that inform *Welcome to Hard Times*, that affect Doctorow's composition of a landscape very different from New York City, but also harsh and extreme.

The seminal piece depicting mainstream America's vision of the frontier is, of course, Frederick Jackson Turner's *The Frontier in American History*.[7] It is thus useful to examine some of the key concepts of this document in relation to *Welcome to Hard Times* to illuminate specifically how this novel revises traditional concepts of the West.

According to Turner's thesis, a new "man" emerged through a process of "Americanization" that took place in America's wilderness. So important was this development that, Turner asserts, "The true point of view in the history of this nation is not the Atlantic Coast, it is the Great West" (3).[8] In particular, Turner credits the frontier with promoting individualism, and he defines individualism in opposition to group identity: "The tendency [of the frontier] is antisocial. It produces antipathy to control, and particularly to any direct control" (30). While Turner does acknowledge the possibility, indeed necessity, of group solidarity and cooperation, particularly in uniting against Native American tribes, the thrust of his piece is on the frontier's shaping self-reliance and a belief in human agency. Furthermore, implicit in Turner's thesis is an optimism that the "new man" is in essence beginning anew, almost *tabula rasa*, free of any past mistakes or undesirable influences.

Critics of *Welcome to Hard Times* have commented on the significance of the Bad Man from Bodie's actual name: Clay Turner. Frank R. Shelton in particular has viewed it as an ironic reference to Frederick Jackson Turner.[9] The first name has been interpreted as a reference to the land itself, suggesting a relationship between the Western land and its mythology. Certainly the Bad Man is represented as larger than life, indicative in Florence's perception that she had never seen a man so big (3), as well as in his generic name equating him with evil itself. The suggestions of larger than life, even mythic status, indicate he may represent the epitome of Frederick Jackson Turner's antisocial individual, a grotesque of the West. According to Doctorow's adaptation of Sherwood Anderson's ideas, when an individual holds a particular truth too tightly, or exaggerates it to an extreme, excluding all other truths, the individual becomes a grotesque and the truth he/she holds becomes a lie. Hence, the outlaw is an exaggeration or a grotesque of the American ideal of the rugged individual who not only shuns community but actively destroys it.

The town's values are best represented by its first settlers, Zar and his prostitutes. Zar explains his decision to go West by stating that when he had heard there was gold in the region he knew there would be many men working alone who would have a need for women. The use of "need" here brings to mind the Marxist concept that capitalism creates false needs. Men do not need sexual intercourse in order to survive, though they may want it badly. Perhaps more crucial, the collection of individuals convening for economic gain is not a good basis for a community. As Blue says, "People naturally come together, but is that enough? Just as naturally we think of ourselves alone" (192).

While Frederick Jackson Turner's work and Westerns in general have often been viewed as narratives of establishing civilization in the wilderness (a more contemporary version of the founding of Rome), the settlers of Hard Times show no concern for those institutions (schools, churches, community organizations, etc.) commonly associated with civil society. Rather, their lives are focused around saloons, brothels, and stores; essentially they survive economically by servicing base desires. Hard Times is certainly not unique in its origins; most towns or cities grow up because there is an economic impetus and decline when it is gone. What is disturbing and ultimately fatal is the town's sole focus on individual economic opportunity and exploitation.

From the early days of the American republic there has been speculation that the nature of opportunity (or perceived opportunity) in this nation has shaped the way people conceptualize themselves and their communities. According to de Tocqueville, Americans labor because they are accustomed to seeing prosperity as the fruits of their exertions (VI, 243). In *Welcome to Hard Times*, the new settlers might appear to labor for this reason, but some scrutiny of the text points out the flaws in this reading. The prostitutes who work for Zar do not advance; they, like typical proletarians, work for their boss's profit. Similarly, a number of people come to town hoping to work on a railroad that is never built, expending money and time on vacuous dreams. Blue, sensing the danger of empty promises, cautions Zar about profiting from settlers who have yet to make money, "You can't just take out, you have to put back in too, you're a businessman, you know that" (177). As the settlers' behavior points out the dangers in an American tendency to glorify individual opportunity, it also validates de Tocqueville's assessment of American character and values. According to him, Americans see public order and public prosperity as proceeding side by side. In fact, when Hard Times's prosperity declines, chaos breaks out, and the Bad Men (Turner and a cohort) re-emerge. As Blue had warned Jimmy, "They [Bad Men] don't need much to grow, just a few folks together will breed 'em, a little noise and they'll spring out of empty hell" (165). There is a vast difference between "a few folks together" and a community; the frontier town Hard Times cannot evolve into the latter.

"It is difficult to draw a man out of his own circle to interest him in the state because he does not clearly understand what influence the destiny of the state can have upon his own lot" (104). These observations might be applied to Jonathan and his peers in *Lives of the Poets*, for these isolated individuals cannot recognize their complicity in social and political problems; in *Welcome to Hard Times* detached individualism has far more serious consequences. De Tocqueville's words underscore the difficulty of building a community when individual achievement is privileged and seems attainable. When economic conditions are *apparently* improving and when the class structure is less obvious than it might be in some older European societies,[10] the number of economically self-sufficient people increases. Because such people believe they are indebted to no one else for their good fortunes, they are in the habit of considering themselves first, of indeed taking their destinies in their own hands. So Americans, de Tocqueville notes, have a propensity for explaining—and, by implication, justifying—actions by motives of self-interest. This self-interest is not necessarily destructive because, de Tocqueville believes, each American knows when to sacrifice some of his/her own interest to save the rest, when to give up individual gain for the larger good.

The only character in *Welcome to Hard Times* who understands the importance of balancing individual interest with community welfare is Blue. As is typical of Doctorow's narrators, he is initially detached and doubtful his actions can yield results, for he refuses to fight the Bad Man. But as the novel progresses he becomes increasingly committed to the town's welfare and vigorous in its promotion. In an effort to stabilize the thriving town, he urges Ezra Maple (brother of the missing Ira Maple), Zar and his prostitutes, and other newcomers to remain. Genuinely believing in the "good signs" he sees, Blue trusts that the resurrected Hard Times will last, that Turner or another Bad Man cannot threaten a community. He cannot, however, truly envision a way to build a healthy town, for his visions, revealed in his word to Molly, are filled with self-deception, "But you see this time we'll be too good for him . . . I don't mean I'll stand up to his gun, I mean I won't have to . . . You fight them, you just look at them and they have you . . . I've seen them ride into a town, a bunch of them, feeling out the place, prodding for the right welcome . . . But a settled town drives them away. When business is good and life is working they can't do a thing, they're destroyed"(149–50).This passage reveals several important features of Blue's construction of community and its relationship to the Bad Man, some of which are contradictory. In stating that if people fight then the Bad Men "have" them, Blue evokes the idea that violence recreates violence. His words are suggestive of Molly's fate, for she creates in Jimmy the Bad Man—what she fears and what indeed kills her. Then, in stating that a settled town "drives away" Bad Men, Blue suggests that outlaws prey on those who are vulnerable by virtue of being unsettled and isolated. In a sense, an outlaw is an extreme, a grotesque of the rugged individual as the Leather Man was.[11] Finally, Blue reveals his own naïveté of, some might even say complicity in, the fate of Hard Times.[12] In the manner described as typically American by de Tocqueville he collapses business thriving and life working, overemphasizing economic boom. His confusion of the two perhaps causes him to misinterpret the atmosphere of Hard Times; if he had perceived more accurately, he would have realized the town was becoming the kind of place that would welcome the Bad Man. Inhabitants reside in alleys; men urinate in the streets; Zar and the other merchants charge exorbitant prices.

Blue's effort to commit to building a community and his tragic inability to do so are most graphically and poignantly illustrated in the failure of his "blended family"—himself, Molly, and young Jimmy Fee. In recent years the family, its health and construction, have become a rallying point in American politics, perhaps because it represents the desire for community and nurturance of future generations.[13] For Blue, the newly-formed family is obviously a source of hope: he feels some love for Molly, who very briefly returns his affections, and tries to be a stepfather to the boy. Yet because Blue cannot satisfy Molly's thirst for revenge on the Bad Man, she trains her adopted son Jimmy (who is strongly attached to her) not only to protect her but also to hate and fight the man she hates.

This family's fate is crucial in that it represents both key elements in the conception of the West and dynamics that are typical of other groups. As John E. Williams notes, John R. Milton posits that the typical western hero finds rootedness not in society itself but in some tradition, sense of brotherhood, or in the biological family. Frederick Jackson Turner makes a similar point in explaining his conception of the frontier's shaping of American individualism, "Complex society is precipitated by the wilderness into a kind of primitive organization based on the family" (30). While Turner sees the family as the crucial Western organization, his analysis implies that the individualism inherent in the Western spirit, antithetical to control, is necessarily hostile to the control of the family itself. In *Welcome to Hard Times* this thesis is proven true in Jimmy's behavior; the boy, like characters in later Doctorow novels, has been groomed by Molly and by his life circumstances to resist all control, including Blue's. Since the father cannot control the son, the son loses respect for him, and the father becomes an ineffectual, scorned figure. Blue thus becomes the first in a series of male figures in Doctorow novels who is a potential father figure rejected because of his perceived flaws. For the rejecting son, renouncing this father means renouncing an honest and meaningful life.

The ineffectiveness of families in this novel is further underscored by the scant attention given to them. Aside from Blue and his blended family, the only familial relationships mentioned are Ezra Maple wearily seeking out his brother and the Swede and his wife Helga, who settle at great psychic cost to the woman.[14] Although Blue states he records the town's births and deaths, readers are not told of one birth, and no children besides Jimmy are mentioned. The one wedding between Bert Albany and the Chinese prostitute with whom he has fallen in love is noteworthy because it is so unusual. The other prostitutes are perplexed by Bert's feelings, unable to comprehend love. Blue himself reacts with wonder rather than expectation that as a town grows people in it will love and marry, "For me it was a revelation that such a thing was happening here . . . I wanted to nurture something like that, keep it going" (127).

Some of the specific difficulties of Blue's family, however, are characteristic of blended families—new families made up of two former families that suffered death or divorce—which in this novel signify the hope to build something new out of loss (Vischer & Vischer). Frequently blended family members experience bitterness, anger, or fear of intimacy because of their pasts. Certainly this is true of Blue's family. Molly has been severely mutilated by the Bad Man; Blue lost his wife years earlier, and Jimmy has been orphaned by the Bad Man's carnage. Characteristically, in blended families bonding is hampered because some of the members, most often the children, have not chosen to join the new family. In Blue's family the situation is aggravated: no one has chosen to live with the others; the members just happened to have been placed in the same horrible situation by the Bad Man and they stay together because they have few options. They are thus like the town itself, people who "naturally" came together and just as naturally destroy one another in the end. In many respects, human relationships in this novel resemble contingencies such as the harsh winter with which the settlers must cope.

On a personal level, the dynamics and fate of Blue's family indicate the error of American exceptionalism, one of the significant characteristics of Frederick Jackson Turner's interpretation of the frontier. In the view of exceptionalists, America is a radically new and different place that will not be plagued by the evils that affected older European cultures. Trauma gives the lie to exceptionalist thinking, for traumatized individuals such as Molly and, to a lesser extent, Blue carry the burden of the past and thus are not free to begin life anew. Hence, they suggest the futility of trying to effect change.

The past's power is most graphically represented in Molly's burns covering her back, giving her a perpetually stiff walk, a permanently grim facial expression. It is this embodiment of suffering that Blue loves, for he explains to readers that he introduces her as his wife to Zar and the prostitutes because he felt he and she had been wedded by the Bad Man. Any love Blue and Molly share is rooted in, and ultimately warped by, the initial destruction of Hard Times and Molly's torture at the Bad Man's hands. With a smirk on her face, she tells Blue of her desire to murder Turner. At this point Blue senses the futility of trying to build a town and a family anew, "An awful sense of hopelessness came over me . . . What was the use? The woman in John Bear's shack was no longer Molly, what had happened in Avery's saloon could never be undone. The only hope we have is that we can pay off our failures, and Molly's grin had burned the hope right out of me" (36).

Molly's desire for vengeance distorts not only her own character and relationship with Blue, but also her relationship with Jimmy. The orphan boy sees her as a mother, and in ways she indeed behaves like one, nursing him through a dangerous illness, and tenderly singing him to sleep. Yet she also teaches him to kill. One night she even stages a "rehearsal" in which she calls Blue to her bed, and then summons Jimmy as though she were being attacked. The only strong emotions Molly can consistently sustain are for Clay Turner, with whom she ultimately does struggle again as if "in embrace," and the only response possible for Jimmy is to shoot the two of them. Trained for nothing but killing, Jimmy leaves the destroyed town a bad man.

In grooming Jimmy as a warrior, Molly is taking on what is usually a male role. As do women in many Doctorow novels Molly represents a hard-edged, realistic alternative to men who are idealistic or dreamy. While in the later fiction women often suggest promising alternatives to prevailing male behavior and values, in *Welcome to Hard Times* Molly represents the failure of a warrior code. Frederick Jackson Turner emphasizes the frontier's importance as a military training school that keeps alive men's power to fight aggression and to develop necessary rugged qualities (15). Jimmy's actions and ultimate fate revise Turner's thesis, illustrating the danger in societies' glorifying aggression and battle. Years later, Doctorow explicitly rejects the warrior code in "An Open Letter to the President" written to President Bush on the eve of the Gulf War, "A modern nation's honor is not the honor of a warrior; it is the honor of a father providing for his children, it is the honor of a mother providing for *her* children" (6). For Doctorow, training children in violence and crime is failed nurturance, using them for one's own gain rather than attending to their needs. Such behavior guarantees that past mistakes will be repeated and that cycles of violence will indeed recur.

Suggesting failed or warped nurturance is but one of the ways *Welcome to Hard Times* indicates people may have limited agency to correct past errors and ensure a better future. Christopher Morris believes that the novel's vision mocks Constitutional and Enlightenment ideals (*Models*). Other critics have similarly commented on the novel's bleak vision of the possibility of progress. Most notably Marilyn Arnold argues that the town's settling, destruction, rebuilding, and final destruction are metaphors for the historical process. Certainly, as David Gross discusses in his insightful article, and as I have further argued, individual greed causes many of the town's problems. Yet Doctorow's coming of age at a time when existential philosophy was prominent and when the memory of the Holocaust was especially raw influences him, I believe, to avoid generalizing that greed is the sole cause of suffering. Clay Turner's rampages were not economically motivated. The Holocaust likewise has causes far more complex than economic ones (though there were some economic causes). Ultimately, *Welcome to Hard Times* depicts people's relationship and response to evil, responses which in this novel are impotent.

The problem of evil is personified in the land itself, from which the Bad Men seem to spring and thrive. The survivors—Molly, Blue, John Bear, and Jimmy—too, are associated with the earth, having dug into it, built a winter shelter barely high enough to stand under, and "resurrected" in the summer. The term "mother earth" seems oxymoronic, for the land's winters are bitterly cold; its summers are devoid of breeze, and water is always scarce. In such a harsh environment, Jimmy's evolution as a Bad Man, though heart-wrenching, cannot be completely unexpected to Blue, for he recognizes the boy as being "fitted to the land, using all his senses to live with what it gave him" (89). Here the suggestion that the boy is appropriate for his natural environment reinforces the idea that his behavior—lawlessness, radical individuality—is a grotesque of an idea associated with the Western landscape, and ultimately associated with what has been conceptualized as the American character.

The issue of evil's intransigence—dealt with in all of Doctorow's fiction—in *Welcome to Hard Times* confounds human optimism and visions of progress, and forms one component of Doctorow's skepticism. In this novel Blue often represents the good, rational man who cannot comprehend evil. His naïveté is perhaps revealed in the decision to remain in Hard Times, even though Molly urges him to leave. He continues to hope for happiness in the face of a history of suffering. In explaining how his own outlook had been colored by life on the prairie, he reflects on his many expectations upon first coming to the West, "But in time my expectations wore away with the weather . . . I learned it was enough to stay alive. Bad Men from Bodie weren't ordinary scoundrels, they came from the land, and you could no more cope with them than you could cope with dust or hailstones" (7). Again, in equating evil with the landscape itself he suggests evil cannot be overcome. It is furthermore impossible to outrun evil. At some point, Blue migrated to the West, and perhaps had spent most of his life moving, searching for a stable, orderly life. Now, with his having exhausted possibilities, there is a sense that Hard Times is his fate; he must "fix" himself to the land, face whatever there is to face there, be it a Bad Man or a harsh winter.

However, Blue does not stand completely apart from evil, despite his valiant efforts to build community. In so dubiously framing Blue's refusal to fight the Bad Man (was it principle or cowardice?), Doctorow has suggested Blue is complicit with the town's demise and with the Bad Man himself. Furthermore, in portraying Molly's destructive urge for vengeance as the result of her brutal rape and horrible scarification, the novel evokes reader sympathy and perhaps complicity. *Welcome to Hard Times* might thus be read as a kind of political fiction which, according to Barbara S. Eckstein, is effective because it represents and enables readers to feel complicity. As she says, when evil falls on another, "the self is not simply guilty, to blame, but is rather complicit in a network . . ." (32–33). In this vision, the town of Hard Times is a web of individuals, forces, and behaviors that all contribute to its demise. Complicity is thus different from guilt, for there is no sense of blame in the recognition of complicity, only a realization that no human actions fall outside the "web." Blue's record-keeping, Molly's anger, the town's economic activity, are all factors in its sad fate. In the act of reading, readers too, become enmeshed in the web, perhaps consciously recognizing the role they play as participant-observers in their own society as well as in readers of the town's demise.

If evil is intrinsic to all people, then one possible response to suffering is to endure in an existential sense.[15] The contrast between such existential endurance and the exceptionalism intrinsic in Frederick Jackson Turner's thesis is especially striking because Hard Times's development fits Turner's model for the settlement of the West. In his narrative of progress, Turner discusses the stages of Western settlements and the resultant political transformations they produced. The first settlers were pioneers and homesteaders, followed by farmers who purchased land, and finally by "men of capital and enterprise" (19–20). Hard Times moves rapidly from desperate settlers (Blue, Molly, Jimmy, and John Bear) to the entrepreneur Zar, to the speculators, and finally to the directors who come from the East.

The evolving disillusionment of all settlers is borne out in the words of Mr. Gillis, who has come to survey the area, "Nothing fixes in this damned country, people blow around at the whiff of the wind. You can't bring the law to a bunch of rocks, you can't settle the coyotes, you can't make a society out of sand" (140). This perpetual instability might be described as the downside of what Turner saw as perennial rebirth, fluidity in continual westward expansion. Such a geography complicates the possibility of committing to a community in a land that seems to shift with every seasonal shift of the wind, a land that resists settlement and interpretation.

Critic Marilyn Arnold sees Doctorow in this novel as "[looking] at the historical process through the consciousness of an observer-recorder and [suggesting] that such processes tend to create the future in the image of the past, producing an inevitable cycling of history" (207). As if trying to deny this recycling of history, Blue rejoices in any sign of new beginnings, such as the Swede and his wife settling: "I can't deny how I felt seeing this farmer settle in the town. Molly was right. I would welcome an outlaw if he rode in. I felt anyone new helped bury the past" (123). Uncertain of his relationship to the past, Blue is both afraid of the Bad Man and hopeful the town he helped to rebuild will repel men like Turner. At some level, he does realize the past cannot be undone, for he tells his imagined audience, "You could step out the door and the scar of the old town was blocked from your sight, but the scar was still there" (149). Often, however, Blue seems to underestimate the magnitude of the past's scar, instead hopefully focusing on the future. In his dissertation on Doctorow's fiction, John E. Williams refers to John R. Milton's discussion of the importance of the expansive landscape in westerns. Partially in response to this landscape, Milton argues, characters often take "the long view" that often blinds them to the present situation (48). Blue, Williams argues, mistakenly does so (although Blue is one of the first to perceive the town is in trouble).

Rather than conclude that Blue focuses on the future at the expense of learning from the past, I believe that his relationship to the past and future are somewhat more complex: he tries to reconcile hope for the future with an acute awareness of the past's very harsh lessons. Again, I do not think we can underestimate Doctorow's Jewish identity in examining the world view informing *Welcome to Hard Times*. John G. Parks has likened *Welcome to Hard Times* to Holocaust literature in that the novel is a narrative of a dying man who finds hope in not having been forgotten (99). It is also the narrative of a man who wants to say "never again," but who has seen that the most recent carnage is a recreation, on a more horrible level, of earlier ones. Blue's status as mayor of Hard Times particularly suggests the impotence of authority figures against both human greed and evil that defies understanding.

Although Blue cannot alter the course of events, his recording them is in itself significant: he is the first of Doctorow's several narrator-historians whom many critics have seen as representing the writer himself.[16] Blue is motivated not by a desire to see himself or the town remembered, but rather initially he sees his log as a means of imposing order and organization on the chaotic West. For him as for historians, recording and making sense of events is a crucial human activity (not, as it was in *World's Fair*, preserving artifacts themselves). The record's importance is clearly indicated in the extent that Blue agonizes over it, fearing that he has misrepresented events or written down his flawed recollections rather than what actually occurred. His misgivings themselves result from the record's evolution. At one point while writing the narrative he scorns the bookkeeping he had done earlier and the mistaken (if somewhat unconscious) notion that his notations could control things (185). He further recognizes the inadequacy of the historical narrative written over the log on another plane, "I have the cold feeling everything I've written doesn't tell me how it was, no matter how careful I've been to get it all down it still escapes me: like what happened is far below my understanding, beyond my sight. In my limits . . . have I shown the sand shifting under our feet, the terrible arrangement of our lives?"(199).

With these words Blue underscores one of the basic problems in historical understanding. Christopher Morris sees lines such as these as indications that Doctorow's fictions are in fact models of inevitable misrepresentation; in the very attempt to represent, one is cut off from the world which one is representing. Brook Thomas addresses a similar problem in commenting upon the tension in new historical criticism between the new historicist idea that knowledge of the past matters for the present and the poststructuralist idea that all history is constructed. The dilemma is expressed in somewhat different terms by philosophers of history such as Collingwood, who claim that in order to capture the past effectively historians must breathe life into empirical data and observations by interpreting it and emphasizing with the agents they study. In attempting to resolve such issues, other theorists have compared the historian's role to an individual's memory in recalling and interpreting the past. Dominick La Capra in his *Rethinking Intellectual History* makes use of Freud's transference theory to explicate the situation of a historian entering into an exchange with the past. Use of this model, La Capra argues, would facilitate an understanding of history (intellectual history) as a dialogue with the past rather than a reconstruction of it. The patient undergoing transference is in a dialogue with the therapist, and is thus trying to create a new understanding of his/her relationship to past life events, not simply recreate life events.[17] Similarly, the historian—in this case Blue—in writing his account of Hard Times's history is striving not to recreate crucial events, but to develop an understanding of them.

La Capra's model provides a way around the problem exemplified by Blue's realization that data without interpretation, represented by his log, is useless; yet the historian who interprets facts necessarily alters them. For the misgivings Blue expresses—that his memory may not capture change as quickly as it occurs, that any interpretation is in some respects a distortion—signal the problems with viewing history as a human creation. These problems cannot be corrected, but rather can only be acknowledged through the historian's active transference of his feelings on to the past and explicit goal of enhancing understanding of it.

Still, the problem of accurately interpreting the past itself further reflects Doctorow's own struggle to balance a skepticism about empirical observation and tendency to see meaning as indeterminate with a desire to bear witness to some truth that is at least relatively determinate and verifiable. La Capra's distinction between documentary and worklike aspects of texts might be useful in resolving this problem as it is exemplified in Blue's attitude toward his recordkeeping. The documentary aspects are texts' factual or literal dimensions, involving reference to empirical reality and conveying information about it. Worklike aspects supplement empirical reality, add and subtract from it. In the documentary model of historical understanding, understanding is limited to filling in gaps in the record, "getting the facts straight." If historians are to contribute to historical understanding, they must define what meaningful historical understanding is. Filling in gaps in past records is not likely to affect attitudes toward the present and future (though of course it is necessary to try to ensure that records are as complete and accurate as possible). Again, as a Jew writing in the post–World War II era, Doctorow is especially sensitized to people's need to know what happened in the past and know how to interpret the past so it can yield some lessons. In a shift from emphasizing documentary to worklike aspects, Blue records the narrative of the town's history over the log of births and deaths, giving prominence to the narrative but nonetheless relying on the foundation of the factual, verifiable elements.

Despite the uncertainty surrounding interpretation of the causes and results of Hard Times's destruction, the fact that the town did exist and was destroyed is not contested—an important point when considering views that all reality is constructed. My own interpretations, similarly, have relied upon empirical evidence available or omitted, such as the lack of recorded births. Blue may scorn facts without interpretation, but he has not scorned facts entirely; *Welcome to Hard Times* is cautious about an overreliance on facts, but it does not completely discard them. Here as in his other fiction Doctorow depicts skepticism toward an overreliance on data—and at times he has perhaps overstated such skepticism.[18] But a careful reading of *Welcome to Hard Times* suggests a need to weigh both documentary and worklike elements in order to understand historical texts. Such a reading further suggests Doctorow's struggle to develop a fictional form that accommodates worklike and documentary elements, as well as reconciles realistic and postmodern fictional elements.

As he reflects on his record, Blue increasingly feels the town's demise was preordained: "I told Molly we'd be ready for the Bad Man, but we can never be ready. Nothing is ever buried, the earth rolls in its tracks . . . it never changes . . ." (211). Here we find suggestions that there is something intrinsic in human nature, as there is something intrinsic in the landscape, that cannot be altered. Similarly, at one point earlier in the novel, Blue addresses readers, apparently chiding presumed exceptionalist beliefs, "Do you think, mister, with all that settlement around you that you're freer than me to make your fate? . . . Your father's doing is in you, like his father's was in him, and we can never start new, we take on all the burden, the only thing that grows is trouble, the disasters get bigger, that's all" (184).

In addition to human frailty and the burden of history, there are many variables that contribute to the final destruction of Hard Times—the harsh winter, the original rumor that there was gold in the area, the arrival of the Bad Man in the beginning and in the end—that can be viewed as contingencies, chance occurrences that are not usually viewed as prime causes of historical events but without which the course of history would have been different. The power of contingencies again illustrates the flaws in the Enlightenment belief in the power of reason to control events and the error of American exceptionalism that holds America is immune from many of Europe's plights. Contingencies also point out the constructed nature of historical accounts, for many contingencies are difficult to incorporate, but if they are left out the accounts will not be accurate. To some extent, most of Doctorow's later fiction recognizes the role of contingencies in human life and in various ways weaves their role into the text.

One of the novel's most thorny problems for political interpretation is how to balance the implicit determinism with a hope of agency, if only in learning from the past. In his *Marxism and Determinism*, Raymond Williams defines determinism as never only the setting of limits, but as always also the exertion of pressures. Hence, determinism in the novel is reflected in the town's isolation, the severe weather, the difficult interpersonal relationships—several forces act together to determine the course of events. There was no single cause for the town's demise, so many factors together contributed to it. Recognizing the concept of overdetermination might be a catalyst for change, for this concept implies not that events are preordained, but that many factors together make them almost inevitable. If one or two of these factors were changed, the course of history might be altered, or perhaps mitigated, even given intangibles, such as the problem of evil. There is thus a chance that Hard Times could have been saved, but only a slight chance; a possibility, not a likelihood. (Indeed, Doctorow's later fiction, like Horatio Alger stories, will often illustrate how contingencies can drastically improve lives.)

While there is a tinge of hope in Blue's final decision not to burn the wood because someone may want it for building, his enduring record is the greatest source of hope that, ironically, gives some credence to Frederick Jackson Turner's thesis that, though the wilderness might initially prove too strong for settlers, eventually they would break and civilize it. Although in Hard Times civilization has been destroyed, the record itself is an earmark of civilization. In commenting on Gloria Anzaldua's and other revisions of the frontier, Annette Kolodny defines *la frontera* as a liminal landscape of changing meanings on which distinct human cultures first encounter one another's "otherness," and appropriately, accommodate or domesticate it through language ("Letting Go"). *Welcome to Hard Times* is in part about Blue's efforts to domesticate the land—and to some extent assimilate its people (John Bear and presumably other Native Americans)—through language. Language proves inadequate to the task partially because Blue's account can only reflect upon what happened; it cannot alter the course of events. Indeed, even when Doctorow's novels suggest that some form of praxis is possible, it is not achieved through writing.

In his first novel Doctorow established the earmarks of his fiction—a revision of popular genres, a focus on the importance of narration with a concomitant skepticism of the possibility of accurately perceiving and rendering the truth, a concern with the inability of Americans to develop community but rather to glorify extreme "grotesque" versions of individualism. The intangible, persistent quality of evil also marks *Welcome to Hard Times* and will likewise inform most of Doctorow's later works. The past is recreated not only in the reappearance of the Bad Man, but also in the formation of a new Bad Man in Jimmy, the first of many children in Doctorow's novels who represent failed nurturance. In this novel Blue's skepticism about his ability to render the truth through his narrative is suggested in his fears about the accuracy of his memory and interpretation. *Welcome to Hard Times*, as critics have noted, suggests a relentless pessimism about human ability to alter the course of events while in the figure of Blue representing the artist/historian's intense desire to bear witness to events. These themes will, with variation, be grappled with in Doctorow's later work. There is one important difference in the fiction that follows, however. In *Welcome to Hard Times* the language itself is, to use a postmodern term, transparent. The prose is plain and accessible; it is easy to decipher the meaning of sentences. In much of Doctorow's later work the limits of language are represented through postmodern literary techniques that problematize the difficulty inherent in traditional linear narration.

Notes

1. I am indebted to Winifred Farrant Bevilacqua, "Narration and History" for the application of Barthes's theories to Doctorow's early fiction.

2. In 1960 when this novel was published, John Fitzgerald Kennedy was elected president of the United States, and his vision for the nation's future was referred to as the New Frontier.

3. Some other notable authors writing in the counter-western tradition are Frank Norris, Willa Cather, John Steinbeck, and Walter Van Tilburg Clark.

4. Doctorow would use the concept of independent melodies working together as a governing metaphor in *Ragtime*.

5. One critic, in fact, argues that *Welcome to Hard Times* reflects an urbanite's failure to understand and appreciate the western landscape. See Tanner, "Rage and Order." Most assessments of the novel, however, have been positive; for example, see Gore, "Read 'Em Cowboy" and Starr rev. *New Republic* 173.

6. See Tokarczyk "The City" and Trenner "Politics."

7. Although the myth of the frontier has a strong place in the American imagination, Turner's thesis has always had its critics. For critiques contemporary with Doctorow's novel see Smith *Virgin Land* and to a lesser extent Lewis *The American Adam*. In recent years frontier myths have been challenged most vigorously by feminist, Chicana, and Native American scholars.

8. In *The Waterworks* the urban newspaper reporter states that he neglected the great story of the westward push to write about New York City. His words suggest the importance settlement of the West was given, but the novel underscores the importance of urban life.

9. For other critical comment on the significance of the Bad Man's name see Saltzman "Stylistic Energy" and Arnold "History as Fate." Morris in *Models* also briefly comments on this point, seeing in the name Turner a mocking of the Enlightenment thinking and American exceptionalism intrinsic in Turner's work.

10. In *Welcome to Hard Times* there is a class structure; Blue is the manager; Zar is also a manager, and his women are workers; John Bear is an outsider.

11. I use male pronouns here because the prevailing imagery of outlaws and other Western figures is male.

12. Morris sees Blue as complicit particularly in his delay in handling the letter to the mine boss informing him of the decision to close the mine.

13. There is a long tradition to the equation of family health and national welfare. In his essay, "The Frontier Gone at Last" Stephen Crane says, "Consider the very beginning of patriotism. At the very first, the seed of the future nation was the

regard of family; the ties of birth held common men together, and the first feeling of patriotism was the love of family" (*Responsibilities* 79).

14   Note that each of these families is also a failed and/or unhappy family.

15   As a philosophy major at Kenyon College in the early 1950s, Doctorow was quite influenced by existential philosophy.

16   See in particular Morris *Models* and Cooper "The Artist as Historian."

17   See Morris *Models,* Lentricchia "Foucault's Legacy," Thomas "New Historicism," Collingwood *Essays in the Philosophy of History,* Van Den Haag "History as Factualized Fiction," and La Capra *Rethinking Intellectual History.* For further discussion of history as interpretation and similarities between history and literature see White *Metahistory* and *Tropics of Discourse.*

18   It is possible to read Doctorow's "False Documents" as Morris does: the document may be seen as a radical postmodern manifesto. This reading, however, clashes with grounding in empirical reality that is present in all Doctorow's fiction and that especially marks his later work.

Chapter 3

Representing and Facing an "Irretrievable Past": *The Book of Daniel*

After the publication of the generally well-received *Welcome to Hard Times*, Doctorow turned his attention to a science fiction book, *Big as Life*. In this novel Doctorow moves to the urban landscape of New York City that will be the locale for so much of his work. A pair of giants suddenly appears over the metropolis, seemingly threatening to annihilate it. The book focuses on three people's responses to this possible threat: Red, a jazz musician; his girlfriend, Sugarbush; and Wallace Creighton, a historian working for a government agency that is investigating the giants. Ultimately, the giants' presence proves benign and the city learns to coexist with them.

The plot is somewhat far-fetched and the writing itself is not up to Doctorow's usual quality. In an interview with Christopher Morris, Doctorow speculates that the problem in *Big as Life* is that he never found his nerve in the writing; the book is not dark enough, and perhaps does not contain enough evil ("Fiction" 446–47).[1] *Big as Life* received scant attention and is the only Doctorow novel not in print.

Big as Life is noteworthy, however, in that, like *Welcome to Hard Times*, it grapples with a continuing threat of annihilation and with communities in crisis. Given that *Big as Life* was published during the Cold War years, it is easy to see the giants as a metaphor for nuclear weapons, and to read the populace's response to the giants as a study in group hysteria. In several essays and interviews, Doctorow asserted that post–World War II America had become a "bomb culture," that the fear of nuclear weapons America itself had used had come to taint many facets of daily life.[2] These themes are more fully and successfully addressed in

Doctorow's third novel that established him as a major contemporary writer, *The Book of Daniel*. In this book Doctorow certainly found his nerve. In interviews he has told of having written about 150 pages of this book and, in a fit of despair, realized the writing was awful. He began again, in an urgent, angry voice that turned out to be Daniel's, and as Douglas Fowler notes, for the first time in Doctorow's fiction, a Jewish voice, dealing with Jewish-American issues as the protagonist Edgar in *World's Fair* did.[3]

Paul Levine is correct in assessing that nothing in Doctorow's earlier work quite prepares us for *The Book of Daniel* (*Doctorow* 35).[4] In this book "occasioned" (in Doctorow's words) by the Rosenberg case, the earmarks of Doctorow's finest fiction are evident: a compelling narrative line; sophisticated experimental technique; and speculation on political, historical, and philosophical matters. The novel's most outstanding achievement is its vivid and complex representation of the lasting effects of political oppression on both a personal and national level, while it simultaneously insists that history is a product of interpretations. It is, of course, impossible to pinpoint the roots of an author's genius, but some clues as to why the Rosenberg case proved such an inspiration for Doctorow may be found in his essay "False Documents." Here he expressed fascination with the indeterminacy of controversial trials in which facts surface, are challenged, reviewed, "and then the trial shimmers forever with just that perplexing ambiguity characteristic of a true novel" (Trenner 23). *The Book of Daniel*'s inspiration thus may partially be attributed to the value on ambiguity Doctorow acquired from his undergraduate studies, which were heavily influenced by the New Criticism. As his essay "False Documents," with its references to Barthes and Nietzsche indicates, Doctorow, like many other intellectuals in the 1960s and 1970s, became increasingly suspicious that a record of any human endeavor could exist independent of interpretation. *The Book of Daniel* reflects this suspicion, prompting literary critics such as Linda Hutcheon to classify Doctorow as a postmodernist. Indeed, this novel grapples with some of the central tenets of postmodernism: the idea that history is a construct and that meaning is indeterminate. Ultimately, the novel points to a middle way between indeterminacy and positivism. This middle way is Doctorow's first step toward finding a way for the artist to embrace praxis.

While postmodernism eludes easy definition, certain characteristics have been noted by several theorists—a suspicion of objective truth, resistance to closure, suspicion of grand narratives, and a breakdown of the division between high and low culture. Some postmodernist writers, such as John Barth and Donald Barthelmae, have embraced the notion of fiction as play; others, perhaps less often noted, have a different approach to postmodernism.[5] According to Alan Wilde, there is a school of postmodern fiction in addition to the metafictionists and Surfictionists that often come to mind. This third school, called "midfiction," including writers such as Stanley Elkin, shares with other postmodernist work an acceptance of the primacy of surface, but nonetheless seeks to be referential and establish some truths. Wilde argues "realism and reflexivity mark out the extremes of contemporary literature, leaving between them . . . yet another class of works whose mood is one of interrogation: a questioning of, among other things, the validity of certainties." This other class of "midfiction" "manages to combine the problematic and the assertive—though assent in this case is to be understood as strictly limited, qualified, and local: a gesture of affirmation against a background that remains, if not negative, at least refractory and contingent ("Displacements" 182). Doctorow's postmodernist fiction has much in common with the midfiction described here. I would not say that Doctorow accepts the primacy of surface, because in several essays he has articulated his belief that fiction should bear witness to the writer's world.[6] Moreover, he has disavowed deconstruction, a theoretical movement often linked to postmodernism, for what he sees as its radical indeterminacy (Harter and Thompson 32). Yet Doctorow is suspicious of ideologies that are too confident of themselves as truth, and hence drawn to the relative uncertainty of postmodernism, while holding to the conviction that there are indeed some truths and it is possible for fiction to shed light upon these truths. In the midfiction version of postmodernism Doctorow thus finds a vehicle for expressing his own skeptical commitment.

As a book about an infamous spy trial, *The Book of Daniel* is Doctorow's most overtly political novel. In his reflections on the political nature of Kafka's fiction, Milan Kundera offers some thoughts on the nature of political novels. He asserts that the totalitarian society Kafka represents blurs the distinction between private and public. Intimacy and familial secrets are then not only forbidden but also made impossible. Moreover, it is in the nature of the state to surprise its citizens: in Kundera's words, "The starting point of totalitarianism resembles the beginning of *The Trial*; you'll be taken unawares in your bed" (110–11). As a contemporary political novel, *The Book of Daniel* effectively blends the personal and the political, mingling questions of family relations with ruminations on history and politics and thereby suggesting that nothing is outside the influence of the state.

In *The Book of Daniel*, as in *Welcome to Hard Times*, the historian's role is critical, and La Capra's distinction between documentary and worklike features of historical texts is helpful in understanding Daniel's undertaking. As was discussed, Blue attempts to record what happens to Hard Times and worries about the accuracy of his perceptions. By comparison, Daniel wades through a number of historical accounts of his parents' case and attempts to determine which one is true, in essence sifting between documentary and worklike features in an effort to ascertain the most reliable worklike ones. The job of the historian has thus become more complicated in the postmodernist world *The Book of Daniel* represents. Yet while Daniel cannot uncover "the truth" about his parents' case, he does uncover historically based "truths" about the nature and prevalence of government oppression that should not be dismissed with extreme postmodern relativism. In considering Daniel as a historian, it is significant that while Daniel searches for the truth about his parents' case he is anything but a detached scholar; he is searching for answers that will rescue his ailing sister and heal his own emotional wounds. Daniel's investment, while more personal than most historians', is not altogether different. Historians, too, always begin with some set of special interests, some predilections for a topic that provides the impetus to pursue a history. And historians bring to their subjects their own history; they spend years researching and building a reputation on their work, and thus will be reluctant to admit possible "truths" that would jeopardize their interpretations.[7] The Rosenberg case in particular stirred people's passions on both the left and the right. Even today the government handling of the case, and to a lesser extent the couple's guilt, is still hotly debated. In part, then, *The Book of Daniel* is a novel about the nature of investment in historical interpretations.

The possibly invested nature of Daniel's thinking is graphically suggested in the many manifestations of his emotional wounds—his cruel treatment of his wife and child, his seeming inability to complete his doctoral dissertation, his relative isolation from others. Ultimately, the question of what impact knowledge and understanding of the past have on the present and future are examined through the character of Daniel. Implicitly, the political vision in the novel suggests that there must be personal resolution before political change is possible, particularly when individuals have endured great suffering. As readers chart Daniel's progress, they perhaps reevaluate their own responses to contemporary political upheavals in the United States. To understand *The Book of Daniel* as a political novel that suggests political change starts with personal change, it is again useful to consider Barbara Eckstein's work on politics and fiction in which she argues that good political fiction makes readers first feel complicit and then question the nature of complicity. By doing so, it encourages praxis, for "complicity acts to undo what it has done" (181). If one cannot choose to be outside the web of social and political forces, one can, as a complicit individual, at least consciously try to minimize the harmful acts of one's participation. *The Book of Daniel* suggests the complicity of many groups, including the readers themselves, in the Isaacsons' deaths, which prompts readers to question their complicity in unjust acts.

Nowhere is readers' complicity more graphically and problematically represented than in the scene in which Daniel tortures his wife. Irritated by a remark Phyllis makes, Daniel, driving in the pouring rain, turns off the windshield wipers and accelerates to a dangerously high speed. He will not drive sensibly until Phyllis pulls down her pants and kneels beside him. Then: "Daniel leaned forward and pressed the cigarette lighter. His hand remained poised. Do you believe it? Shall I continue? Do you want to know the effect of three concentric circles of heating element glowing orange in a black night of rain on the tender white girlflesh of my wife's ass? Who are you anyway? Who told you you could read this? Is nothing sacred?" (74). Daniel's address raises questions on several levels. On the political level, it suggests readers' dilemmas in responding to atrocities such as those committed in Vietnam. (The novel is set in 1967.) If readers do not want to learn of such acts, they are closing their eyes to deeds in which they, if they are United States citizens, are implicated. Several times Daniel suggests that Americans have too long ignored the evil of which they are part; for example, he says that most American citizens do not realize Chileans hate them because of their government's policies. Furthermore, the fact that only radical and impoverished people seem to be aware that Lower East Side apartments are often bitterly cold in the winter reflects the ignorance and perhaps denial of the majority of the New York City's population. On the other hand, while Eckstein theorizes action will result from an understanding of complicity, this possibility is complicated by the fact that people often do not know how to act effectively. In part, *The Book of Daniel* is about the failure of radical political action. And if people learn of atrocities and will not or cannot combat them, they become mere voyeurs of suffering. This possibility resonates on a personal as well as a political level. Daniel's wife abuse brings to mind countless instances of familial abuse in which readers/viewers are perhaps tempted to intervene, but fear it is inappropriate to do so. Political and private oppression are linked not only in the ways that people are victimized, but also in the ways that communities are made complicit.

The difficulty of understanding political oppression through a straightforward analysis is reflected in the novel's structure. The book is divided into four chapters, three of which—Memorial Day, Halloween, and Christmas—are named for holidays; and the fourth, Starfish, is named for a defunct zodiac sign. Obviously, the title "Starfish" is disjunctive, suggesting a disruptive component in the book. The chapter headings are but the first in a number of experimental, postmodern techniques. Chronologically, the novel shifts between the 1930s, the 1950s, and the 1960s. In his narration Daniel shifts between first and third person, as well as shifts point of view, as he does in narrating his reactions to his sister's suicide attempt and his strained relationship with her: "To be just, he had started something in the restaurant so as to get to Susan's car. He had needed to see the car. The feeling that crept upon me was of being summoned. They're still fucking us" (35–36). Finally, the document Daniel is writing is a curious hybrid—part autobiography, part political theory, and part history. The range of tone and substance in the prose is suggested in the following two passages:

> Many historians have noted an interesting phenomenon in American life in the years immediately after a war. In the councils of government fierce partisanship replaces the necessary political coalitions of wartime. In the greater arena of social relations—business labor and the community—violence rises, fear and recrimination dominate public discussion, passion prevails over reason (28).

> I have no more of them than the present of their [the Lewins'] lives. Of course, it was more complicated, but the image that returns to me is of a young couple reading about it [the atom spy execution] in the newspapers and rushing down to the subways . . . It is too late for me now to find out who they are or where they came from (93–94).

The various voices and genres that compose Daniel's account reflect his effort to define himself not only as an Isaacson and as an American, but as a writer as well. He has been marginalized in each of these areas, and as a result his tone is one of rage and cynicism.

In many ways Daniel embodies Sloterdijk's modern cynic. Again, according to Sloterdijk, "Cynicism is *enlightened false consciousness* [italics mine]. It is that modernized, unhappy consciousness" (5). Enlightened false consciousness manifests itself, according to Sloterdijk, in people's going through the motions of, for example, working at jobs they find meaningless, voting in elections for candidates whom they do not want to see in office, etc. Daniel goes through the motions of enrolling in graduate school and starting a family, even though these activities seemingly mean little to him: in fact, he treats his education and his family with scorn. His cynicism is so bitter because he perceives few alternatives: he could rebel as Susan does, but he is too politically astute to believe there is a possibility for revolution in America.

Cynicism permeates every aspect of Daniel's life. In addition to the tone of his heated argument with Susan ("This blood money has bought you an education, skiing lessons, and records" [100]) we see his cynicism in his suspicion of the possibility of upward mobility. He contemplates his parents' move from the Lower East Side of Manhattan to the Bronx, "In 1900 you beat the Lower East Side by moving to the Bronx. Only remorselessly does history catch up. And all your secret dreams are open to the light. It is History, that pig, biting into the heart's secrets" (115). While Blue believes it is possible to rebuild Hard Times from the ashes of the past, Daniel sees the past as a burden impossible to escape, and thus, in contrast to Susan's impassioned radicalism, he adapts a cynical stance as the best possibility for coping. His use of the word "pig" to describe history is telling, for in the slang of the 1960s a pig was a policeman or similar enforcer of the "establishment," the status quo. Certain events, such as religious persecution and class inequity, reinscribe themselves from one generation to the next with relentless constancy. In Terry Eagleton's words, "For socialist thought there has indeed been a grand narrative, and more's the pity" (*Illusions* 51). Daniel himself might reinscribe the trend in the "grand narrative." After the Isaacsons' execution, Daniel and his sister are adopted by liberal, upper-middle-class Jews, Daniel, like many other male Doctorow characters, is given two fathers between whom to choose. Characteristic of his cynical response, he neither accepts nor rejects Paul Isaacson or Robert Lewin. Yet the fact that he will not disavow his birth parents signals he is different from the prototypical upwardly mobile son who may see his birth father as a failure.

In historicizing the evolution of modern cynicism, Sloterdijk acknowledges that we might expect the twentieth-century heirs of the Enlightenment to feel some "status cynicism," that is cynicism about socioeconomic status. However: "The retrospective position alone . . . does not explain the particular tone of modern cynicism. The characteristic odor of modern cynicism is of a more fundamental nature—a constitution of consciousness afflicted with enlightenment that, having learned from historical experience, refuses cheap optimism" (6). It is apparent why Daniel has developed a cynical response; his life has been a constellation of events that could strip someone of the "cheap optimism" Blue manifested. Initially, *The Book of Daniel*, set in New York City, paints a picture of a contemporary urban landscape with characteristic class inequities: the janitor is African-American, the working-class Paul Isaacson relies on his dentist friend to drive his family to the beach. The Isaacsons' move from the Lower East Side to the Bronx does not allow them to escape political and/or religious persecution, or the progress of history, as Daniel says.[8] By the time Daniel writes his account, the Bronx has become an impoverished area from which the middle class flees. In addition to the class references, the novel provides many other indications of how "that pig" history has affected the Isaacson family. In her "Bintel Brief" the grandmother refers to relatives dying in pogroms, a sister lost in the Triangle Shirtwaist Factory Fire, and laments, "for thousands of years my people stumbling through the world in their suffering looking for paradise on earth" (80). According to Rochelle, the old woman who immigrated to the United States in search of a better life had nothing to show for her labors when she died.

While *The Book of Daniel* critiques American dreams of upward mobility and certainly criticizes the reality of American justice under the law, it also faults groups associated with the Left: the American Communist Party that abandoned the Isaacsons, the Jews who were so anxious to assimilate into American culture that they did not recognize anti-Semitism in the case, and the Isaacsons themselves (particularly Paul) as naïve pawns.[9] When Paul Isaacson is arrested, the couple's names are taken off the Communist Party rolls, and with the exception of Ben Cohen (whom Daniel always admired) no friends visit the family. If only the United States government had betrayed the Isaacsons, Daniel and Susan might have suffered less emotional damage. But the betrayal of the party in which their parents' believed is a devastating blow that leaves Daniel embittered.

In addition to being disillusioned by the political apparatus of the United States government and the Communist Party, Daniel is severely disillusioned in his interpersonal relationships. Even before their arrests there are signs that the parents, who deliberately walk naked before their children and give lectures on baseball as American propaganda, are so enraptured with their ideals that their ability to relate to their children is compromised. With their arrests, the dissolution of the family is inevitable.

Daniel's disillusionment with family life is best revealed in his adult relationships with his sister and his immediate family. In *The Book of Daniel*, as in most of Doctorow's fiction, the family is a site where social conflicts are acted out; it cannot be separated from its society. In their attitudes toward politics, Daniel and Susan represent different reactions to political repression and betrayal: Daniel, intellectual detachment; Susan, activism. Indeed, the siblings have such different stances toward political activity that they cannot even discuss over a family dinner what to do with their inheritance. In retaliation for what she sees as insults, Susan disowns Daniel, telling him he no longer exists. Essentially, as his birth parents were, he is being told he cannot dissent and be allowed to exist. While trying to carry on her parents' legacy, Susan has unwittingly carried out the behavior of the government that destroyed them. Daniel's own relationship with his wife and baby (who, on a casual outing, Daniel tosses higher and higher into the air, catching ever closer to the ground) mirrors most accurately and painfully the destructiveness he has experienced. He, like the Biblical Daniel who emerged apparently unscathed from the lions' den, is a survivor. Yet unlike popular depictions of unscathed survivors, he has been radically changed by what he has endured; he has metaphorically gone through the fire and, as he says of Linda Mindish, has been "forged," perhaps into something beyond recognition.[10] The characters of Susan and Daniel graphically represent how the oppressed often take on the qualities of their oppressors.

In concluding the Isaacsons were oppressed, I am drawing upon material in *The Book of Daniel* that has a historical basis. Daniel contemplates the polarization that occurred between the Soviet Union and the United States during the Cold War, and the hysteria that pervaded the nation after World War II. While some people believe the Rosenbergs were guilty, very few believe that the death sentence was warranted or would have been given in a less politically intolerant environment. Alan Dershowitz reconsidering the case in an editorial is perhaps typical in concluding that the couple were likely both guilty and framed (Zins). In *The Book of Daniel*, there are references to repressive laws (such as the Mundt-Nixon Bill, which would have, in effect, outlawed the Communist Party) proposed during the McCarthy era. The fact that there were such injustices undercuts a component of American exceptionalism, the belief that the United States is a country where justice is available for all.[11] In the background of Daniel's analyses are references to rights secured in the Constitution (a document reflecting the Enlightenment). Repeatedly Daniel questions the usefulness of a document that purportedly protects people's legal rights if these rights will be protected only if the current political culture allows.

In addition to the many references to the McCarthy era, the novel gives a specific example of political oppression. The Peekskill incident is both a microcosm of persecution in the United States and a precursor of what will happen in the Isaacson case. In this episode based upon an actual event (but not one in which the Rosenbergs were involved) the Isaacsons and other American Communist Party members rent a bus to attend a concert given by the African-American Communist Paul Robeson. A permit authorizing and protecting the concert has been secured. After the concert the Communists' bus is rerouted to an isolated section and attacked by American Legion members who hurl stones while shouting epitaphs such as "kike," "Commie," and "nigger-lover." The attackers are determined to "teach a lesson" to the left-wing intellectuals in the bus, thus showing that intellect can be powerless against brute force. As Daniel crouches in the bus, he (and everyone else there) fears that the attackers will kill them all. Then his father steps toward the bus door, calmly removes his glasses, and goes outside, allowing the "patriots" to "zero in" on their target" (63). Paul Isaacson suffers a broken arm, but the bus is saved because the attackers are provided with a scapegoat.[12] During the McCarthy era many Communists were blacklisted and arrested. Given the hysteria of the time, there seemed to be no way for intelligent people to outwit the repressive forces. Public fear that American Communists were endangering their country threatened to explode, but the focus on one couple who allegedly had betrayed the United States diverted some anger from other leftists.

The attack is also a warning to American Jews, often perceived as being left-wing and "pink." Indeed, a CIA memo relating to the Rosenberg case dated January 22, 1953 (approximately six months before the couple's execution) states that if the Rosenbergs would agree to "appeal to Jews in all countries to get out of the Communist movement and seek to destroy it" their sentences might be commuted (Cook 25). Furthermore, as the Nazi years vividly demonstrated, anti-Semitism was fierce and worldwide; *The Book of Daniel* claims that America's Henry Ford was an anti-Semite. That the fear of those in the bus relates to the very recent Holocaust is further suggested in Rochelle's murmured insults, "Fascist scum. Nazi pigs. Murderers" (62). In the context of this attack, the words of the spiritual Robeson sang "Didn't my lord deliver Daniel . . . Then why not every man" suggest the situation of the American Jews who were by the luck of geography saved from the Holocaust, but who could find that the history they have tried to escape has caught up with them.

Given his background and experiences, as well as his own fear with which he tries to cope by detaching himself from his emotions, it is easy to see how Daniel could become a cynical intellectual. Yet his cynicism is not nearly as caustic as that of the 1960s radical Artie Sternlicht,

Doctorow's representation of New Left attitudes. Sternlicht's stance toward history is typical of the New Left, for compared to the Old Left, its vision was less historically based—even ahistorical, as is suggested by the saying on the collage of enemies Sternlicht keeps in his Avenue B apartment, "EVERYTHING THAT COMES BEFORE IS THE SAME." In essence, this is the attitude described by Daniel Bell in *The End of Ideology: On the Exhaustion of Political Ideas in the Fifties*: "For among the 'New Left' there is an alarming readiness to create a tabula rasa, to accept the word 'revolution' as an absolution for outrages . . . in short to erase the lessons of the last forty years with an emotional alacrity that is astounding" (405). Doctorow, I believe, would share Bell's alarm at the New Left's dismissal of history; as *Welcome to Hard Times* indicated Doctorow may question the nature of historical interpretation, but he does not doubt history's importance. According to Paul Levine, *The Book of Daniel* is "an imaginative revisioning of the radical movement in America that attempts to bridge the generation gap, to reconnect the new radicalism to its history" ("Writer" 67). Yet the possibility of any connection between the New and Old left in itself would be an anathema to Sternlicht.[13]

Aside from his disdain for history, the most notable quality of Sternlicht's revolutionary philosophy is its focus on spectacle. At one point Daniel mockingly describes his parents' arrest, "The Isaacsons are arrested for conspiring to sell the secret of television to the Soviet Union . . ." (143). As a man who owned and ran an appliance store, Paul Isaacson is, in fact, a harbinger of the future.[14] Daniel and Artie Sternlicht's generation is the first to grow up with television. A postmodernist revolutionary,[15] Sternlicht sees potential in exploiting the television's power: "In less than a minute a commercial can carry you through a lifetime . . . Commercials are learning units . . . We'll be on television. We're going to overthrow the United States with images" (172). He complains that the Isaacsons and other Communists were politically naïve, and, in essence, dull: "They were into the system. They wore ties. They held down jobs. They put people up for President" (185).

Sternlicht's idea of how he would behave if he were in the Isaacsons' position is, however, vague, not easily captured by an image as we might expect. He simply insists that revolutionaries should be prepared to die and that *when he is* arrested he will not play the authorities' game; rather, he will act as their accuser and their judge. Perhaps most important, his trial will be a spectacle, "I will turn that courtroom on, and what I say and do in that courtroom will go out on the wire, and the teletype, and kids all over the world will be at the trial and say 'Man, who is that dude, dig the way he's got his shit together'" (186). Indeed, the press conference

Sternlicht is giving to *Cosmopolitan* indicates his willingness to exploit the media, regardless of their political orientation, for publicity. In his critique of both the American government and radical groups other than his own, Sternlicht is utterly contemptuous. The only factor mitigating his cynicism is his belief that a grassroots, spontaneous revolution—not one rooted in theory as the old style Communists or the intellectuals envisioned—will indeed emerge from the people. Although we know little about Sternlicht's background, he is obviously scarred by the injustices he has seen and ruthless in his response to power. Like Susan, Sternlicht is an example of the oppressed taking on the qualities of their oppressor, one who will have to experience personal change if he is to be an effective revolutionary. The examples of Sternlicht, Susan, and the Isaacsons together point out the difficulty of taking political action; they all fuel Daniel's cynicism and reflect Doctorow's skepticism of direct political action.

While Sternlicht is certainly attuned to the powers of television, it is not clear that he understands the difficulty he might have in utilizing it. He talks as if those in control of the media are objective reporters who will recount his actions, not people driven implicitly or explicitly by ideology to decide what is important news, to perhaps even cut and distort Sternlicht's spectacles. Thus I believe Fowler errs in asserting that any political optimism in the novel is "centered on Sternlicht's insights" (54). His insights are illusory; he is no less naïve than the Old Left he rails against, and no more equipped to wage an effective revolution. As Gerald Graff asserts in his "Co-Optation" one of the powerful themes in the new historicism is that societies exert control over their subjects not only by imposing constraints on them but also by predetermining ways that they [subjects] attempt to rebel against constraints by coopting strategies of dissent (169). Fredric Jameson notes that urban squalor itself is often pleasing to the eyes if it is expressed in commodification (*Postmodernism* 33). It is highly likely that the article in *Cosmopolitan* will make radical activity appear chic and harmless.

But Sternlicht's brutal if theatrical plans, since they are not acted upon, reveal little about American justice. The actual Isaacson trial is the arena where questions of justice in the United States are played out. Significantly, the trial is in the "Starfish" section of the novel, which examines core issues in various areas of Daniel's life. Upon seeing Susan in the hospital in her catatonic-like state with arms and legs extended, Daniel compares her to a starfish and ponders the nature of the animal: while it often appears that the starfish's five points lead away from the center, in reality they all lead toward it. Similarly, in *The Book of Daniel* the novel's

Representing and Facing an "Irretrievable Past"   79

diverse threads—from ruminations on atrocities around the world, to family problems, to Daniel's search for the truth about the Isaacson Case—all lead to the actual trial. Moreover, the shape has specific relevance to the Atom Spy Trial. Sketches of the atom bomb's mechanism placed in evidence at the Rosenberg trial resemble a starfish's shape (see illustration). Hence, the starfish is a rich, overdetermined symbol bringing together the

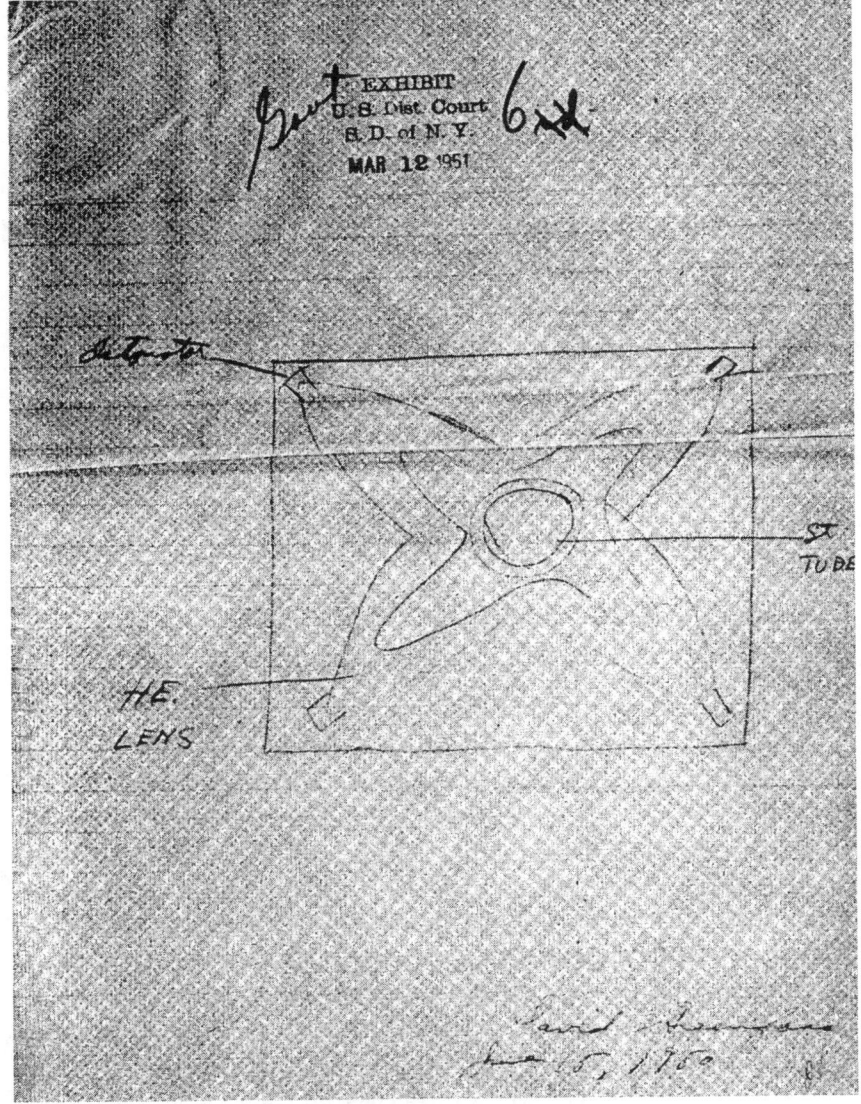

Prosecution Exhibit 6 at the Rosenberg Trial

trial, Susan's demise, the disintegration of Daniel's birth family, and the nature of radicalism itself.

The account of the trial begins with Paul Isaacson's perceptions of the courtroom, the judge, and jury. Immediately, he senses his isolation: after months in prison Paul is ill-at-ease among people in a room without bars and acutely aware of his difference from comfortable mainstream Americans. Here Doctorow stresses the conformity demanded in 1950s America, recognized by many historians and sociologists but nonetheless at odds with the rugged individualism America supposedly venerates in documents such as Frederick Jackson Turner's exposition of the frontier. While Paul's isolation is in part an inevitable result of his imprisonment, it is heightened by breaches of the spirit of justice. The supposed jury of peers includes no communists or Jews.[16] The Jewish Prosecutor Feuerman (modeled on Judge Kauffman in the actual Rosenberg trial) is an "arch-assimilationist" who graduated from St. John's University, married an Irish woman, and had seven children. His career is described as "meteoric"; the highly-publicized Isaacson case will no doubt further speed his ascent.

While Paul Isaacson quiets his misgivings about the trial with a naïve confidence that justice will prevail, Rochelle coolly and objectively analyzes the situation: "Implications of treason are fed like cubes of sugar to the twelve-headed animal which is Justice" (245). The stress on treason is crucial, for as Rochelle realizes, although the charge against them is conspiracy to commit espionage, they will actually be sentenced for treason. The analysis she employs to reach the conclusion that they are doomed is not radical thought, but what Daniel describes as "bookkeeping." She rationally assesses the factors for and against them, and comes to the resounding deduction that she and her spouse cannot win.

The presence of objective tallying is striking in a novel in which the possibilities of various interpretations are so important. That such objective tallying is possible qualifies the postmodernist themes critics have so often commented upon in this novel and reflects Doctorow's midfiction postmodernism. In brief, the postmodern thread is that Daniel, in trying to determine the truth about his parents' case, interviews many people. Finally, after locating the senile Selig Mindish who betrayed the Isaacsons, he realizes that the truth is "irretrievable." At best Daniel can gather and consider the various truths about the Isaacson case and tentatively embrace one. Rochelle's insightful and correct analysis, however, has other implications: It indicates that there are objective classes and conditions whose effects are predictable. As Terry Eagleton says, "There are propotions which are true of all times and places, yet which are not simply vacuous or trivial" (112). If a Jewish communist couple is tried for selling atomic secrets during the McCarthy era, and if this couple has a hostile, ambitious prosecuting attorney, a judge who favors the prosecution, a jury of "middle Americans," and a well-meaning but simple defense lawyer, the couple on trial will be found guilty. Rochelle's analysis might usefully be applied to the debate in postmodernist theory about the collapse of categories and to new historicist suspicion of poststructuralist tendencies to reduce all to indeterminate interpretations. Categories of religious orientation and political affiliation, I would argue, though shifting, exist and have powerful impacts. These impacts can only be dealt with by recognizing the nature and level of complicity of all individuals involved, for these will be considerably different, for example, for Rochelle Isaacson and District Attorney Feuerman.

Doctorow says he did not actually research the Rosenberg case, and indeed he may have been able to gather sufficient information by closely following news reports or casually reading sources. Such material embedded in the novel constitutes the documentary nature of texts discussed by Dominick La Capra as an important feature of historical works. Moreover, this kind of material in fiction is considered crucial by some theorists of the contemporary political novel: Michael Wilding for one argues, "The incorporation of documentary materials into the political novel is important to establish the texture of the created society, to provide the data for sociology" (10). Documentary material extends the realistic novel, actually plunging readers into historical situations and making them question their own interpretation of historical events and perhaps participation in them. The documentary material thus accomplishes what Doctorow has intended in his fiction, making literature a reflection of life rather than a rarefied artifact.

Throughout the novel Daniel extends the implications of his parents' case, making parallels between it and other miscarriages of justice, not just in the United States but around the world. He compares the FBI's early surveillance and tapping of the Isaacsons' phone to smoking as a means of torture used in sixteenth century Japan. His references to knouting in czarist Russia and Bukharin's outrages in the Soviet Union also indicate that throughout history governments have repressed their people. Astutely, Daniel analyzes that the ultimate force of law is the power to do physical harm to someone, even to go so far as to execute. Conversely, those who have this power are in effect the law or the rulers, as some urban areas besieged by gang warfare have learned. The Bad Man, similarly, is the law in a way that Blue is not; those who attacked the bus at Peekskill simultaneously were the law and invoked the protection of the law. By making these "connections," as Daniel would call them, Daniel reaffirms the cyclical nature of history as well as undercuts ideas of American exceptionalism.[17] The cynicism running through *The Book of Daniel* is thus very deep; the novel unflinchingly recognizes the degree to which people throughout history have suffered under repressive regimes.

Unlike Daniel, who reacts to his parents' conviction and subsequent execution with cynicism and enlightened false consciousness, Linda Mindish responds to her father's conviction with a Gatsbyesque attempt to begin her life anew. She changes her name, moves to Orange County, California, and cultivates a middle-class, conservative persona during the tumultuous 1960s. Daniel believes that in annihilating her former life she loses "the connection" she has as a survivor of the Atom Spy Trial; that is, the ability to make links between people's status in society (for example, the Isaacsons as working-class, left-wing Jews) and the way they are treated, as well as the ability to see cause and effect relationships between American foreign policy and anti-American sentiment abroad. In fact, Linda Mindish and her environment represent deliberate disconnections. While California is the refuge of the counterculture, its location at the extreme west of the United States also suggests it is the last refuge of 1950s America. Ultimately, California is a place of contradictions juxtaposed with one another. Here a bizarre representation of the world Sternlicht imagines actually exists in Disneyland.

The theme park Daniel describes can, as critics have noted, be seen as a Baudrillard-like simulation that substitutes for the real. In Disneyland people experience representations of their culture's key stories (Twain's Mississippi, the tea cups from *Alice in Wonderland*) without ever having read the original works. Thus Daniel concludes: "What Disneyland proposes is a technique of abbreviated shorthand culture for the masses, a mindless thrill, like an electric shock, that insists at the same time on the recipient's rich psychic relation to his country's history, language, and literature . . . this technique may be extremely useful both as a substitute for education and, eventually, as a substitute for experience" (351). The experience of Disneyland might then be seen in Sloterdijk's terms as a cynical ritual involving enlightened false consciousness. People in this theme park know they lack familiarity with the actual sources, but accept the substitutes without ever feeling deprived.

Opposed to a numbing simulacrum is an authentic ritual, a re-enactment of a significant event that kindles rather than obliterates ties with an actual experience, that sensitizes rather than deadens. Daniel's participation in the March on the Pentagon is such a ritual intended to pay back a debt he owes, and perhaps to exorcise the demonic visions he repeatedly refers to as being in his head. In the section of his account subtitled "Looking for Sternlicht" Daniel refers to going to the March as "driving into the heart of darkness" (306), aligning both the New Left and government oppression with this darkness. At the March he burns his draft card, giving his name as Daniel Isaacson, even though the name on the card is Lewin. When violence erupts, it is eerily reminiscent of the attack on the bus at Peekskill ("One could examine the mandarin faces. God was on their side," [311]), showing that the progressive 1960s are not truly different from the 1950s, and that the McCarthy era was not an aberration in American history. The assailants' seemingly inhuman qualities are emphasized in Daniel's description of the "many-helmeted beast of our own nation, coming through our flesh with boot and club and gun . . . My country. And it swats and kicks, and kicks and clubs . . ." (313). Though he is savagely beaten, Daniel has no sense that he accomplished a ritual re-enactment of his parents' ordeal. In prison, he surmises that being a revolutionary is much easier than it used to be: he is, after all, still alive.

This seemingly failed ritual highlights the almost exclusive power of oppressive experiences. It is nearly impossible for someone else to reenact a drama of injustice and death; thus these experiences are difficult to expiate. In a sense, Daniel's parents' death is like the suffering that Molly experienced from the Bad Man. But although Blue could not feel the suffering Molly endured, he was changed by his attempts to draw close to her and understand. Similarly, the March on the Pentagon marks the beginning of changes in Daniel; when he senses there will be violence he sends his wife and child away, protecting instead of brutalizing them.

Throughout the novel Daniel contemplates the meaning of complicity and fears that he is indeed implicated in perpetuating the evils of corporate liberalism. Again, Barbara Eckstein's argument comes to mind. In recognizing the complex web of relations between contemporary individuals, she sees the difficulty of assigning absolute guilt or innocence in many (not all) cases. What Daniel and readers of *The Book of Daniel* have experienced has made them aware of their complicity in evil which, "perpetuate the stereotypes and which, in turn, rationalizes the suffering. The self is an accomplice in this complicity. But in the web of complicity the self also suffers" (32–33). Eckstein's model is especially pertinent to Daniel's somewhat puzzling analysis of and reaction to Mindish's testimony against his parents. After reviewing six books about his parents' trial which reach widely varying conclusions as to the couple's innocence or guilt, Daniel acknowledges that he hated Mindish even before his parents' arrest. Yet he expresses a willingness to consider Mindish's innocence, that an ambiguous "they" would not be willing to entertain: "But only because he would have suffered more at the time. But only because he has suffered more since. Innocence is complicity" (277). In characterizing innocence as complicity, Daniel is acknowledging the web of relations and denying the possibility of a category "innocent" outside the web. His reference to an ambiguous "they" further collapses categories of distinction between historians of the case, those involved in the trial, etc. Barbara L. Estrin believes that when his birth parents were taken from him Daniel learned the futility of innocence (200). In acknowledging the possibility of Mindish's innocence, Daniel removes the villainous stance from him, but also robs the word "innocence" of its guilt-free connotation. His sophisticated analysis recognizes a web of connection rather than an absolute split between good and evil, but this recognition does not free him from bitterness, for Daniel is still pleased to imagine Mindish suffering. Implicitly this analysis of complicity recognizes that no one is completely innocent in the sense of being untainted. Daniel can choose to be cynical, not to be a cruel radical like Sternlicht, or to remain politically detached. He cannot choose to remove himself from the political world, for this world encompasses his life and, to a lesser extent, everyone's. But while the web encompasses all, some suffer more than others and some are more guilty than others (a point Eckstein perhaps does not sufficiently stress). The United States public is complicit in tolerating the outrages of the McCarthy era, but they are not all as guilty as true McCarthyites.

Whatever tentative resolution there is in *The Book of Daniel* can be found in the three endings that together and/or consecutively complete the novel. Linda Hutcheon interprets this kind of ending as a reflection of the postmodernist suspicion that closure is arbitrary and forecloses interpretive powers (*Politics* 69–70). Neither the demise of the childhood home Daniel knew, nor the death of his sister, nor the rebellion at Columbia University can be said to capture and totally sum up the discourse of *The Book of Daniel*. Politically, the inclusion of three endings is perhaps a break with the determinism characteristic of Marxism in which the ending would be predictable. Indeed, rather than being a book about the search for the truth, as it initially appeared to be, *The Book of Daniel* is in the end a novel about the act of searching itself. Yet the search is not completely open-ended, for Daniel's example suggests it is possible to reach some tentative truths.

Although none of the three endings closes the novel, each resolves an emotional issue for Daniel. As Paul Levine states, "the multiplicity of endings suggests both the process of self-realization and historical continuity which the survivor must work through" (*Doctorow* 70). The first ending in which Daniel walks away from the Bronx home that is now occupied by poor African-Americans suggests his ability to let go of his past, as well as the seemingly inevitable shuffling of poor people through this neighborhood. The second ending buries his sister but resurrects Daniel's own emotions, for Daniel pays the old men to pray for all the deceased members of his family, lovingly squeezes his wife's hand, and actually begins to cry. While nothing can erase the pain of his having lost his parents, his bitterness is mitigated. A cycle of violence is possibly broken, for perhaps Daniel will now be less likely to inflict the pain he experienced on others. This healed self reflects one aspect of Doctorow's vision of the revolutionary expressed in an interview with Paul Levine in which Doctorow evokes early Reichian psychology as an attempt to bridge "Freudian insight to Marxist sociology": "Reich came to believe that there is no hope for political progress until people can be freed from their neurotic character structures" ("Writer" 64). Cantor voices a similar view in stating that the road to permanent revolution is a state of consciousness where the ultimate goal is not outside the self but is created as one creates the self, as one continually remakes and reformulates the self (13). It is a version of the self strikingly different from the cynic whose mode of operation is detachment.

Even if Daniel has gained some knowledge through his ordeals, Doctorow's novel certainly does not rationalize suffering. In fact, his characterization of Daniel undercuts sympathy and easy formulations that people are ennobled by suffering. *The Book of Daniel* fully recognizes Daniel's pain and the injustice of the United States government, while refusing to paint a simple picture of victimization. Ultimately, the novel makes us question our complicity in American injustice and in politics in general. The third ending in which Daniel is forced to halt writing his account because radicals have taken control of Columbia University is particularly fraught with ambiguities. It is doubtful Daniel feels liberated, but he leaves nonetheless. His account is "sealed for all time," but we are reading it, perhaps as helpless "secret sharers" of Daniel's insights, perhaps as complicitors in his socially enforced silence.[18]

The Book of Daniel is then a powerful political novel because in it Doctorow has found the style and voice to convey political, social, and historical concerns exemplified in the Rosenberg case. Daniel's sophisticated voice and frequent genre-crossing reflect a highly intelligent and educated, if deeply scarred, narrator. The postmodern indeterminacy of meaning and the various endings effectively represent the complexities of a controversial trail, while its faithful representation of Daniel's plight and political, ethical themes make it an effective work of midfiction. *The Book of Daniel* certainly accepts that indeterminacy is a permanent feature of modern life, but nonetheless shows that there are some certainties. One may not be able to ascertain the Isaacsons' guilt, but one can certainly surmise they were treated unfairly in politically volatile climate that was particularly unfriendly to left-wing, working-class Jews.

Moreover, *The Book of Daniel* is provocative in that it is densely packed with themes other than those discussed here, some of which are touched upon briefly but not fully explored. One of these is the position of African-Americans, who are represented as more politically astute than other groups, in the United States. Artie Sternlicht believes African-Americans are the only people in the United States who know they are enslaved; the janitor Williams informs the Isaacson children of their mother's arrest. In his next novel Doctorow will investigate the situation of African-Americans and show their similarities with and crucial differences from other ethnic groups.

Notes

1. In other interviews Doctorow has referred to this book as his *Mardi*.

2. See Doctorow "The Bomb Culture," "The Bomb Lives!," "Orwell's *1984*"; Levine "The Writer as Independent Witness."

3. See McCaffery "A Spirit of Transgression," Weber "The Myth Maker," Fowler *Understanding E. L. Doctorow*.

4. The novel was praised by many reviewers for its handling of complex historical material and its characterizations. See especially Lehmann-Haupt, "No Handwriting on the Wall" and Richmond "To the End of the Night." Critics who gave negative reviews often disliked the novel's ideology or believed its experimental techniques were ineffective. See Bell "Guilt on Trial" and Catinella Rev. *Saturday Review* 54.

5. Postmodernism has been extensively examined and debated. Natoli and Hutcheon *A Postmodern Reader* provides a good survey of important early postmodern essays and current debates. In particular, Zygmunt Bauman, "Postmodernity, or Living with Ambivalence" offers a thoughtful discussion of the differences between modernism and postmodernism. Jameson *Postmodernism, or the Cultural Logic of Late Capitalism* views postmodernism as not just as aesthetic movement but one intricately tied to economics and culture. Hutcheon *The Politics of Postmodernism* argues that postmodernism has a political impetus while Eagleton *The Illusions of Postmodernism* argues that though it has some strengths, postmodernism is seriously flawed, primarily by its indeterminacy and inability to enable agency.

6. See Levine "The Writer as Independent Witness," Doctorow "The Beliefs of Writers," "Living in the House of Fiction," "The Passion of Our Calling."

7. A prime example of historians' investment in their research is illustrated in work on the Rosenberg case itself. Walter and Miriam Schneir wrote *Invitation to an Inquest*, long considered the definitive defense of the Rosenbergs. Passions ran high when Ronald Radosh and Joyce Milton published *The Rosenberg File*, which drew upon FBI files made available by the Freedom of Information Act and which concluded that Julius Rosenberg was guilty. Numerous other historians and cultural critics have written on this case. For a select bibliography see "Selected Supplemental Bibliography" in Tokarczyk *E. L. Doctorow: An Annotated Bibliography*.

8. The actual Rosenbergs lived on the Lower East Side, as did David Greenglass, Ethel's brother who testified against the couple. The harshness of conditions in this area is revealed in a horrible accident Ruth Greenglass had when she was several months pregnant. A kerosene heater used to warm their bitterly cold apartment was knocked over, and Ruth suffered serious burns.

9   The Isaacsons are not, I argue, depicted as tragic martyrs to their own political ignorance, as Fowler claims (6). Rather, I agree with Paul Levine who in his book concludes that the couple are guilty of self-deception and thus accomplices (complicitors) in their own demise (43).

10 For a discussion on survival in this novel see Tokarczyk "From the Lions' Den," Levine "E. L. Doctorow: The Writer as Survivor."

11 Certainly there are numerous episodes in United States history that show how the nation fell short of its promise of justice—most notably in its treatment of African and Native Americans. The McCarthy Era is noteworthy for its insistence on political conformity and its persecution of white Americans who held left-wing views. John Parks sees Daniel's account as refusing exceptionalist ideas of American justice, as an account written in the tradition of Poe, Melville, and Hawthorne, "challeng[ing] the glib certainties of Franklin and Emerson with the 'power of blackness'" (41).

12 Daniel's account itself offers two interpretations of Paul Isaacson's action. The first sees it an act of heroic martyrdom; the second, which Daniel endorses, believes that Paul Isaacson was trying to secure a policeman's help. In either interpretation Paul Isaacson functions as a scapegoat.

13 While Sternlicht's view of the past might be excessive it echoes some of the controversies in new historical criticism: the idea that all history is a construct clashes with the idea that there are tangible lessons to be learned from concrete historical events. See Thomas, "The New Historicism."

14 Joyce Nelson has posited that there are important similarities between the development of the atom bomb and the development of television. Most notably, they had similar corporate sponsorship; General Electric was heavily involved in the Manhattan Project. See "TV, the Bomb, and the Body."

15 See Jameson *Postmodernism* and Hutcheon "Beginning to Theorize the Postmodern" for a discussion of the importance of mass media and culture in postmodernism.

16 The jury in the actual Rosenberg trial was likewise devoid of Jews and progressives, and included an examiner, an auditor, two bookkeepers, an accountant, and an estimator. It has been argued that people who choose such professions often have authoritarian personalities, which are characterized by deference to authority, intolerance for non-conformity, and suspicion of outgroups. See Wexley *The Judgment of Julius and Ethel Rosenberg*.

17 The notion of American exceptionalism has been hotly debated by scholars since the 1970s. For an overview of how some positions have evolved see Kammen "The Problem of American Exceptionalism."

18 In the movie *Daniel* the main character actually joins the protestors in the end, supposedly embracing political action.

Chapter 4

The American Dream, Insiders and Outsiders: *Ragtime*

In *Ragtime* we find many of the themes that mark the rest of Doctorow's fiction, but they are expressed in some notably different ways. Like Doctorow's earlier work, *Ragtime* is a historical novel, representing approximately the years 1902 until 1914. It focuses on three families and includes a wide array of historical personages. But as critics have noted, *Ragtime* is as much about the era itself, a period of rapid change, as it is about any families or individuals. Partially for this reason, the position of the narrator is far less defined than in other Doctorow fiction; though the narrator is generally believed to be the Boy, he is never clearly identified as such.[1] This ambiguity in narration leads Christopher Morris to conclude that *Ragtime* is the first in a series of Doctorow novels (the others being *Loon Lake*, *Lives of the Poets*, and *World's Fair*) in which the narrator cannot be determined as omniscient or as a clearly identifiable character. In detaching language from a source, *Ragtime* and other novels in this series, "show[s] in new ways the delusion of the self as the autonomous manipulator of language" (*Models* 98). Implicitly, Morris suggests, the novel shows the constructed and indeterminate nature of history, a continual concern of Doctorow's.

As striking as the narrator's ambiguous identity is his distance from the narration; the novel's prose and Boy's relative detachment from the stories he narrates sharply contrast with other Doctorow narrators' pained engagement. These narrative choices themselves reflect another strategy on Doctorow's part to indirectly express his political and social concerns. The artist figures are separated from the narrators (in a move that prefigures a split between the artist and his psychic twin in *Loon Lake*) facilitating more ambiguity and indirection. Furthermore, in *Ragtime* Doctorow actually does "compose" history, as he has often said novelists do. The use of history in this novel is unlike anything Doctorow has done previous to this novel, and perhaps something no novelist has yet replicated. Rather than imaginatively render a historical event, as *The Book of Daniel* does, *Ragtime* mingles actual historical events (such as the strike in Lawrenceville, Massachusetts) with historical characters in fictional situations (Freud and Jung in the Tunnel of Love), and invented characters. La Capra's distinction between documentary and worklike aspects of texts thus collapses in this novel. This collapse, as well as Doctorow's imaginative use of history, undoubtedly reflects his skepticism about the dividing lines between history and fiction as expressed in "False Documents" and his distrust of claims of fact.

Ragtime's style of fictionalizing history is described by Linda Hutcheon as "historiographic metafiction," work that is both metafictional and historical in its echoes of past texts and contexts. Such work situates readers within historical discourse without surrendering its authority as fiction, and thus satisfies a desire for grounding while querying the very basis for that grounding ("Historiographic" 3-4). Like *The Book of Daniel, Ragtime* does establish some tentative truths, and thus may be seen as another work of midfiction. *Ragtime* is, in fact, a highly playful midfiction book. The novel's short, sometimes humorous, and highly accessible prose might be called "mock historical" writing that mimics the prose of history texts. Consider, for example, the following passage: "Everyone wore white in the summer. Tennis racquets were hefty and the racquet faces elliptical. There was a lot of sexual fainting. There were no Negroes. There were no immigrants. On Sunday afternoon, after dinner, Father and Mother went upstairs and closed the bedroom door"(3-4).

The apparent simplicity here is deceptive, for the excerpt raises questions about the typicality of the life being described, the relationship between individual families and larger society, and society's blindness to racial problems. Moreover, while the novel begins with the vision of white middle-class America (no Negroes, no immigrants) it quickly revises itself to state that there apparently were Negroes and immigrants. In a sense, *Ragtime* is a revisionist historical novel including the stories of women, immigrants, Labor, and others excluded from standard histories until very recently. Because the novel so often subtly prompts readers to reread their own sense of history, it is useful to keep in mind the quotation from Scott Joplin at the beginning of the novel, "Do not play this piece fast. It is never right to play Ragtime fast."[2] The apparent ease of reading *Ragtime* coupled with the complex themes and social commentary that are subtly introduced are likely what account for the commercial and critical success of the novel.³ Yet the epigraph on ragtime music is worth keeping in mind when pondering the meaning of this novel. The book is indeed a "good read," a quick one, yet the message lingers.

In *Ragtime* Doctorow uses an array of literary devices and genres in addition to postmodern techniques to comment not only on the era itself but the realization of the American Dream in this era. The blend of historical and fictional characters along with the experimental prose allows Doctorow to make a detached, but nonetheless powerful critique of American society and the possibility of true progress in an era of rapid and apparent advances. Doctorow's adaptation of the midfiction subset of postmodernism in *Ragtime* radically disrupts the surface elements of history, chronology, and believability, but it does so while clearly suggesting that there are definite, observable incidents of injustice.

Throughout the novel two distinct image clusters recur, images though seemingly in opposition to one another, actually complement one another. The first is the Boy's fascination with stories from Ovid's *Metamorphoses* and with the possibility that anything could become something else. The second are the images of repetition suggested in Ford's assembly line, Morgan's fascination with reincarnation, and the baseball game that intrigues the narrator because the same action recurs. Together these two kinds of images suggest the historical process: the progress (or illusion of it) that demands constant adaptation and the tendency of historical patterns to repeat, most markedly along issues of inequity. The images of repetition also suggest Newman has called the "wave motif" in American literature and history: because of continual immigration waves over time the motif is repetitive rather than linear and chronological. The novel's patterns of repetition and metamorphosis converge in the figure of one of *Ragtime's* most compelling figures, Coalhouse Walker, Jr. He wants to progress, but the force of American racism ultimately destroys him.

The fates of Coalhouse Walker and other characters in this novel—some highly plausible, some requiring suspension of disbelief—are rendered through adaptation of the romance genre.⁴ While scholars of the American romance, most notably Richard Chase, once saw the genre as one that evaded direct engagement with sociopolitical issues, new Americanists have seen a political enterprise in the American romance.⁵ In her study of this genre Emily Miller Budick argues that the tradition's emphatic rejection of mimetic modes of representation coupled with its equally strong insistence on specified settings in place and time gives the novel a double consciousness. Her analysis of romance writers is particularly applicable to Doctorow, for she claims, "From the late eighteenth century to the contemporary period a remarkable lineage of American writers produces a fiction that acknowledges the force of skepticism and yet allows writing to commit itself to history and society" (ix–x). Similarly, Wilding argues that in romance fiction the confrontation of the hopes of romance with the realities of realism arises from the nature of political fiction, of which the romance is a subgenre. Essentially, what Budick and other revisionist scholars of the American romance see in the form is its ability to grapple with seeming polarities. As this chapter will reveal, oppositions abound in *Ragtime*. Romance hopes are realized in the lives of Tateh and Mother; the actualities of realism are represented in figures that disappear, such as Evelyn Nesbit and Mameh, as well as in those that are oppressed for their political positions, such as Emma Goldman and Coalhouse Walker. Readers' stance toward the "romance" characters might be compared to their stance toward the American Dream: they remember and focus on the characters who have achieved an unlikely happiness rather than the more typical ones who do not.

The juxtaposition of unlikely characters and events in *Ragtime* represents a mosaic in which the lives of different kinds of Americans are placed next to one another. Evoking the image of the mosaic implicitly undercuts the idea of America as a melting pot, complicating ideas of assimilation. Although the lives of characters from diverse backgrounds intersect, they meld unevenly. Evelyn Nesbit disappears from Tateh's life; Ford and Morgan have no sustained interaction; Emma Goldman has little influence outside her radical sphere. Yet when some characters interact with others from different backgrounds, lives are permanently changed: most notably when Sara and Mother interact, and Tateh and Mother meet. Hence, *Ragtime* represents the complex, unpredictable nature of interaction in a multicultural society.

The novel's pastiche quality and the many varied personages within it also thwart impulses to totalize history and raise questions about the depictions of periods in other historical texts. The complexity of characters' motives thwarts simple analysis; for example, we are uncertain whether to admire Tateh for his adaptation or scorn him for betraying his ideals; we condemn Walker's terrorism but admire his uncompromising self-respect. To the extent that any character's actions are predictable, they are expected only if we understand determinism, with Raymond Williams, as not only the setting of limits but also the exertion of pressures, pressures I would argue often specific to given individuals and situations (87). The accidental nature of many events, such as Mother finding the baby, makes it highly unlikely they would recur, so they could not be predicted. In contrast, Coalhouse Walker's response to society's refusal to treat him justly—although it is extreme—might be predicted, given his character and the racial climate of the times. Hence, although *Ragtime* depicts many contingencies and certainly acknowledges that some events may be beyond human control, the novel as a work of midfiction affirms some degree of causality.

The sometimes fantastic contingencies in the novel are part of the romance tradition. In addition to adapting conventions of this genre, *Ragtime* utilizes, and indeed disrupts, the genre of proletarian fiction, a genre that has been overlooked until recently (but will be thoroughly examined in the next chapter). In her study of 1930s fiction, Barbara Foley defines the proletarian social novel (a kind of proletarian fiction) as one with multiple protagonists from various social classes as well as using realistic modes of representation. The novel employs juxtaposition and interaction to illustrate significant patterns and forces in the class struggle. Typically, a work focuses on a strike or some similar key event, and readers are prompted to identify with protagonists who have chosen the correct sides. While some features of this genre—realistic representation, singular focus on class struggle—are not applicable to *Ragtime*, there are nonetheless striking similarities in the function of multiple protagonists (undercutting a bourgeois focus on individual identity), in the juxtaposition of characters, and in the sympathy *Ragtime* evokes for minority characters. The proletarian social novel can thus be seen as another genre that Doctorow skillfully revises in *Ragtime*, in the process revising the genre itself.

Like many traditional novels, and in the spirit of much recent political debate, *Ragtime* foregrounds individual families. These families represent different ethnic groups and socioeconomic classes: the WASP Mother and Father's family, the Jewish immigrant Tateh and Mameh's, the African-American Coalhouse Walker and his girlfriend, Sara. One way to situate the individual families is to examine their members' responses to the rapidly-changing society—in the novel's terms their ability to metamorphosize. This focus has its basis in the romance tradition, for as one scholar notes, the action of historical romances (such as James Fennimore Cooper's) often "turns on the failure of a character or a class to understand that attitudes and behavior recently appropriate are tenable no longer" (Dekker 15). These words describe Father, a successful, relatively affluent businessman curiously unable to adapt to his changing society, especially its increasingly multicultural character. The beginning of his decline is suggested in what should have been the pinnacle of his success, his journey with Admiral Peary to the North Pole. The white explorers are contemptuous of the natives: Peary says the Eskimos are children and must be treated as such, and the narrator reporting Father's sentiments says, "There was no question that the Eskimos were primitives. They were affectionate, gentle, emotional, trustworthy, and full of pranks" (62). These condescending perceptions, coupled with Father's revulsion at his Eskimo lover's open sexuality, indicate he, like the characters in *Heart of Darkness*, sees the natives as Other and is disoriented by his encounter with them. Yet his sense of superiority as a white male cannot compensate for his body being unsuited for the harsh Arctic climate; the tendency of his extremities to freeze suggests his intrinsic inflexibility, his inability to adapt to new circumstances. Sensing that he is losing his privileged position, Father is threatened by minorities who may surpass him. Although he recognizes the soundness of Peary choosing the African-American Henson (an actual explorer on the mission) as a companion to the North Pole, he resents Henson's presumption he would be the choice, very likely resenting self-confidence in an African-American.

As an explorer and successful businessman, Father represents the limitations of American visions of Manifest Destiny as suggested by Turner and similar frontier theorists. Through him, *Ragtime* scrutinizes the mythology of self-discovery, suggested in works such as Tennyson's "Ulysses," that accompanies narratives of adventure or exploration. Rather than providing Father with an opportunity for discovery and achievement, each exploration further alienates him from himself and his home. Upon his return from the Arctic voyage, he does not even know how to behave in a domestic setting: "The family stood around and watched him on his knees. There was nothing he had to tell them" (92). This novel's examination of a man's decline is also part of the romance tradition, for many American historical romances focus on patriarchs and recount not only the circumstances which alienated them from their society, but also their eventual decline and fall (Dekker 109). Working in this tradition, *Ragtime* depicts three patriarchs, revealing not only who can adopt appropriate attitudes and behavior, but also who is allowed to change.

Father's condescending attitude toward nonwhites in the Arctic predicts his attitude toward Coalhouse Walker. Although Father tries to negotiate with authorities on Walker's behalf, Father clearly dislikes him, undoubtedly because the musician is not subservient, and indeed will fight for his rights. That Walker's terrorist gang is alien to Father may at first not be surprising, but on reflection one realizes that at the time of his death Father was smuggling armaments on the *Lusitania*, engaging in the illegal transport of weapons for what he believed to be a just cause, which is not so different from Walker's actually using weapons for his cause. As Daniel would say, Father cannot see the "connection"; as Emma Goldman would say, he cannot see the "correspondence" between his life choices and those from other racial groups. The description of his death makes the resemblance between Father and the other characters, a resemblance forgotten by him, clearer: "Poor Father, I see his final exploration. He arrives at the new place, his hair risen in astonishment, his mouth and eyes dumb. His toe scuffs a soft storm of sand, he kneels and his arms spread in pantomimic celebration, the immigrant, as in every moment of his life, arriving eternally on the shore of his Self" (269). As Linda Mindish lost her own past, Father lost the connection to the struggles of his own immigrant ancestors and their ability to change as needed. He is, as Christopher Morris suggests, a perpetual beginner (*Models* 98–114). But unlike other characters, Father cannot choose a new beginning appropriate for the time. Rather, his "beginning" is continual repetition of previous actions in new guises, futile attempts to reassert his old status. Ironically, his temperament will not allow him to progress.

In contrast to Father, Mother's ability to cope with change is suggested by her unofficially adopting an African-American baby, and marrying Tateh. Moreover, unlike Father, she is courteous to Coalhouse Walker and sympathetic to him both as he courts Sara and seeks recompense for his car. Her open-mindedness is likely the result of the changes she underwent during Father's absence, taking more responsibility for the household and becoming more aware of her own sexuality, a subtle transformation that on a personal level reflects "momentous change coming over the United States" (69). Part of this change is, of course, in the status of women that would close the First Wave of twentieth-century American feminism with the passage of the Nineteenth Amendment to the Constitution granting women the right to vote. As Mother develops, she longs for a "life of genius" beyond what the predictable Father could give her. Her desire might be viewed as typifying the "American Dream" reinterpreted by some contemporary scholars as not only or even primarily upward mobility, but rather the chance to live in freedom and reach one's individual potential. Mother does not, as more radical women might, attempt to live independently, but she is receptive to social changes that give her access to a more rewarding life. In fact, she is first willing to become involved with someone whom she believes is displaced nobility, and nonetheless willing to marry him when she learns he is a self-made member of the *nouveau riche*. (She is perhaps also fortunate in that her first husband happens to die, freeing her to remake her life in a second marriage.)

Mother represents but one possible response of a woman to the changing times. Evelyn Nesbit's role as a sex goddess whose face appears in every paper sensationalizing the Harry K. Thaw trial represents women as repositories of male dreams, a role women have always had but which was intensified by photography's ability to capture and reproduce images of desire. Mameh is significant in that, like Nesbit, she disappears after Tateh abandons her for giving in to her employer's sexual demands, illustrating the vulnerability of working women. Sara, who tries to intercede in Coalhouse's struggle, is, in her naive attempt to approach politicians, even more vulnerable than her future husband. Emma Goldman, the lifelong anarchist and advocate for women's rights, is finally exiled from the country, "disappeared" like Mameh and Nesbit. Taken together, the female characters represent the relatively narrow range of options available to women and the high price of transgressing boundaries. In depicting the way political change affects various women, Doctorow is again suggesting that, to use the cliché, the political is personal, and that the personal ramifications left out of history texts provide another example of how history is constructed.

The interrelationships of these various characters' lives are described by Emma Goldman speaking to Evelyn Nesbit as correspondences, "our lives correspond, our spirits touch one another like notes in harmony, and in the total human fate we are sisters" (52).[6] Goldman's words suggest the interrelationship of all characters in this novel with a metaphor appropriate to music that the title itself suggests. The literary precursor for Goldman's sentiment, however, is John Donne's "For Whom the Bell Tolls" suggesting people's interdependence. Correspondences in *Ragtime* also signal the book's affinities with some proletarian novels in which there is a strategic juxtaposition from lives of characters who may or may not know one another, leaving readers to hypothesize why they belong in the same novel (Foley 271). In essence, readers are forced to make the same connection the speaker of the Donne poem does, but also to ponder the dynamics of this connection in the world of inequity the novel depicts.

Some of the inequity in this novel results from the social conditions in urban areas during this time. As Paul Levine notes, *Ragtime* depicts the United States's movement from a smalltown society to a metropolitan one, and much more than *The Book of Daniel*, represents the diversity of this landscape (*Doctorow* 54). One of the energizing prospects of these rapidly growing urban environment was a release from small-town enclosures and the possibility of spontaneously, accidentally interacting with very different people.

But while there is potential in rapid industrialization and urbanization, there is also considerable suffering. Many historians have found increasing inequality in America as the nation became more urban.[7] Roy Lubove argues that urban slum problems had their roots in the same ethos of greed that shaped western land development: the counterpoint of the speculator in western lands, represented in *Welcome to Hard Times*, was the urban jerry-builder, eager to expand opportunities and move on. Tenements resulted from rapid growth and poor planning. To some extent, they were also the by-products of acculturation to urban life, a nation's inability to cope with the rapid change from a rural to an urban environment (3). The poor and dangerous conditions Tateh endures—poverty so stark his wife succumbs to her employer's sexual advances and streets so dangerous Tateh works with his daughter tied to him so she will not be kidnapped—are the results of industrialization, as is the poverty depicted in Charles Dickens's novels. In their insensitivity to human needs, the cities are similar to the town Hard Times in Doctorow's first novel. Furthermore, during the period between the Civil War and World War I, the urban rich in New York moved uptown while the poor stayed downtown in the slums, a development that intensified class stratification (O'Connell 83). Yet the rich were geographically not that far away from the poor. Such proximity explains the impoverished who in *Ragtime* peer into the banquets of the wealthy, separated by a glass window they know they will not penetrate. Because of the visibility of the slums and the glaring distinctions between owners and workers, cities embarrassingly exposed the falsity of a classless society in America, revealing divisions by race and nationality as well (Lubove 42).

Cities also have been the points of arrival for new immigrants, and between 1890 and 1910 over one million immigrants settled in the United States (McCormick 28). Immigrants who came to this nation in search of a better life were often shocked at their exploitation and pitiful living conditions. As some scholars point out, in 1893 when Turner offered his thesis on the frontier, millions of European immigrants were living in poverty. His thesis was thus problematized: why such appalling social conditions in this apparently progressive nation (Appleby et al.). Of course, immigrants were supposed to be able to rise from poverty, or at least see their children achieve better lives. Indeed, Tateh himself achieves the

American Dream. But his and many other "metamorphoses" in the novel are at least partially attributable to privilege associated with a character's gender, race, and ethnicity.

Tateh is particularly interesting for the kinds of people he represents: an artist trying to make a living from his sketches, an entrepreneur, and, importantly, an impoverished Jewish activist.[8] The account of Tateh's participation in labor struggles vividly illustrates the class struggle, noted by urban scholars such as Lubove and O'Connell but erased in the textbook accounts of American history, and strengthens *Ragtime's* resemblance to the proletarian novel. But while in a proletarian novel, especially a proletarian *bildungsroman*, strike involvement might be a turning point in which a character would become more committed to radical action (Foley 327), here it is the point at which Tateh abandons his labor affiliation, even though the strike was successful. When the strike ends, Tateh realizes the essentially conservative goals of American Labor, "The I.W.W. has won . . . But what has it won? A few more pennies in wages? Will it now own the mills? No" (109). Since he now perceives the Labor movement as tied to the status quo, and has often been at odds with labor leaders who wanted "inspirational art," it is not surprising that Tateh decides to "point his life along the flow of American energy" (111), to become an entrepreneur. One might read the seeds of Tateh's decision in his leaving New York City, "the city that has ruined his life" (76), hoping for a more comfortable life on the urban outskirts, as did many who fled the cities after World War II. His decision is further suggested in his fears for his child's future, "Every once in a while he would look at his child, and seeing the sure destruction of her incredible beauty in his continuing victimization, he would clutch her to him and tears would fill his eyes" (75). His desire to provide his daughter with a respectable bourgeois life is further reflected in his revulsion for Emma Goldman's views, as well as in his abrupt rejection of his sexually exploited wife. His radical sympathies do not extend to women's rights, and from his perspective his radical cohorts might have negative influences on his daughter. Consequently, he metamorphosizes or recomposes himself and his art.

Tateh's decision to sell his silhouettes to the Franklin Novelty Company has a few important components. First, it raises the question of how a socialist cause might deal with individual talent. Factory workers are interchangeable in their work; an artist presumably is not and thus must be involved in a different kind of struggle for justice. Also, commodification of art becomes an issue. In a capitalist nation, some commodification is necessary and Tateh commodifies the kind of art that he can effectively market because it is right for the time. Sketches on the street attract little attention. Silhouettes, on the other hand, are appropriate for the age that is discovering how to create the illusion of moving images and that itself might be represented as a rapidly changing image. As Sternlicht said he would blow the American government apart with images, Tateh transforms his future by manipulating them, eventually making motion pictures. Although he is a self-made man in the Gatsby mold, he senses he must remake his identity to be accepted in some segments of society. Hence, he becomes Baron Ashkenazy (the surname, a tease or clue since it indicates one of European Jewish origin), a displaced noble rather than formerly penniless Jewish immigrant.

Ironically then the former socialist activist epitomizes the problem for radicals that Emma Goldman saw embodied in Evelyn Nesbit as an object of desire: "I am often asked the question How the masses permit themselves to be exploited by the few. The answer is By being persuaded to identify with them. Carrying his newspaper with your picture the laborer goes home to his wife, an exhausted workhorse with the veins standing out in her legs, and he dreams not of justice but of being rich" (71). Tateh's upward mobility gives validity to the dream.

Despite his transformation into an affluent entrepreneur, it is unclear whether Tateh has completely abandoned his radical sympathies. He adopts Sara's baby and plans the Little Rascals series in which race and class tensions are erased, and visions of brotherhood are delivered in a palatable form to Americans (Bevilacqua 103). Whether his liberal deeds are a pragmatic adaptation of radical sympathies or a sell out is as difficult a question as whether Tateh adapts or sells out his art. Doctorow himself has stated that he sees Tateh as an example of how a man can succeed in the very system he is criticizing, and yet retain a sense of himself as a radical by giving to political causes, and so forth. (McCaffery 45). The liberal as opposed to radical stance toward social change is consistent with Doctorow's stance of skeptical commitment. Since he is passionately committed to social justice, yet ambivalent about the efficacy of sweeping social movements, his position toward change is cautious.

While Tateh is successful in transforming himself into Baron Ashkenazy—a personage more acceptable to wealthy Americans than a Jewish immigrant—Coalhouse Walker is destroyed partially because he does transform himself. Upon first meeting him Father assesses, "Coalhouse didn't seem to know he was a Negro . . . Walker didn't act or talk like a colored man. He seemed to be able to transform the customary deference practiced by his race so that they reflected his own dignity rather than the recipient's" (134). Furthermore, aside from the fact that he comes from St. Louis, we know little of Walker's past: he seems Gatsbyesque in that he comes from the Midwest with a firm sense of himself.[9] The source of his dignity is thus very different from Booker T. Washington's, the esteemed African-American leader who tries to persuade Walker to surrender, for Washington preached "the Negro's advancement with the help of his white neighbor" to provide vocational training and the resulting opportunity for hard work (235). (Interestingly, Walker tells Washington that they are both "servants of [our] color" demanding respect [238].) For Walker, dignity rests upon his identity as a musician, his desire to be with Sara and his child, and his sense of justice. Like Tateh, he is an artist and a family man, but unlike Tateh he cannot change his appearance and name to change his social standing. His refusal to play the part of a servile, timid black man causes whites either irritation (Father) or outright hostility (Willy Conklin). In the personage of Coalhouse Walker, Doctorow thus suggests the depth of discrimination against African-Americans—they cannot even try to assimilate into the white middle class (not that doing so is necessarily desirable) because their skin color marks them as different, and many whites will not tolerate deviation from race-assigned roles.

Walker's self-made status is represented in a number of ways—through his fine clothing, his self-assured manner, and his calm assessment of situations. This previously law-abiding man becomes a terrorist only after the law proves unresponsive to him and after his fiancee is accidentally killed by authorities. When Walker resorts to violence, the violence itself is carefully planned, thereby undercutting stereotypes of black men as impulsive and uncontrollable.

Given his rationality, it is both interesting and puzzling that Walker goes to such lengths to get his Model T restored. A band of African-American men (and Younger Brother) do support his cause, but the reaction of an African-American lawyer is probably typical of many African-Americans who have seen far greater miscarriages of injustice than what Walker endured: "I want justice for our people so bad I can taste it. But if you think I would go to Westchester County to plead on a colored man's behalf that someone deposited a bucket of slops in his car, you are very much mistaken" (154). Walker's attitude toward his car can be understood only by considering the importance Americans assign material goods to signify identity as well as status. While Doctorow is likely unaware of it, the persecution Walker suffered because of his car has a historical basis. In the first volume of his autobiography Chester Himes recalls how his

African-American family offended white neighbors in rural Mississippi by, shortly after World War I, being the first family to own a car. The townspeople were so incensed that they drove Himes's father from his job and eventually forced the family to leave the state (Lipsitz). In addition to suggesting relative affluence, the automobile represents an affinity with progress, allying African-Americans such as the Himes family and Coalhouse Walker with figures such as Mother and Tateh rather than Father. According to Neumeyer, Walker's attachment to the car is also consistent with the repeated themes of manufacturing and production in the novel and the implication that those who manufacture are crucial to progress. Furthermore, in the United States especially, the car has become a symbol of mobility and freedom, and geographic mobility itself has often been associated with upward mobility.[10] Immigrants coming to the United States to escape poverty (rather than to escape political persecution) best exemplify this association.[11] Hence, an African-American who owned a car in the early 1900s was signaling his desire to better his socioeconomic status.

Nonetheless, the question still arises as to why someone as individual as Coalhouse Walker would choose to express his identity through a commodity such as an automobile rather than through his music.[12] Marshall Bruce Gentry in "*Ragtime* as Auto Biography" posits that references to Henry Ford and his assembly line suggest associations between the interchangability of parts on Ford's assembly line and the interchangability of people who purchase cars. One might argue that Walker acts because his dignity is affronted; the item itself is not crucial. Yet Walker has made a very deliberate purchase at a time when Model Ts were not common; it seems more likely that Walker is using the car to express his individuality as people in capitalist countries especially often use material possessions such as clothing or cars to distinguish themselves. Thus through his demeanor, possessions, and the values they imply, Walker signifies his comfort with progress and his desire to gain the trappings of bourgeois society. Walker is resisting his assigned status as an African-American male, but he is resisting in ways that possibly reinscribe existing inequities (although perhaps along class rather than race lines). It is then not surprising that, as he probably realized, he is co-opted as Gerald Graff defines the term: his avenues of resistance are themselves limited by those in power.

To understand Walker's actions and the significance of his car in the novel, we also might consider a comparison Malcolm X made between cars and racism. According to him, racism is similar to a Cadillac: every year General Motors changes the contours of this car, but a Cadillac is a Cadillac despite these modifications. Likewise, racism might take on different guises, but it is racism nonetheless (Lipsitz 701). *Ragtime* indeed represents racism in various guises: from the working-class hatred of Willy Conklin, to the opportunistic ruthlessness of the District Attorney Whitman, to Father's smug condescension.

That Walker responds to racism with terrorist acts is jarring not only because his actions are violent, but also as critics have noted, because they are anachronistic, characteristic of the period when the novel was written rather than the one in which it is set. They might be viewed as a warning for the age reading the novel that if races are not treated equally and fairly eventually there will be violence (Fowler 78). It is also possible to read this warning in the light of the American romance genre, which often transcends time. Such a reading is reinforced by other occurrences of time sequence being thwarted in *Ragtime*, most notably when the boy urges Houdini to "warn the duke" about the assassination years ahead. Hence, the jeremiad tendencies evident in *Welcome to Hard Times* and *The Book of Daniel* have been adapted in this novel in a subplot that functions like a parable. According to Alan Wilde, midfiction often resembles parable, the advantage of parable being that it challenges the passivity of reader responses and ultimately raises questions about the moral effects of literature on us ("Strange Displacements" 183–184). Particularly because the Coalhouse Walker story is the most developed subplot in the novel, it prompts readers to consider the relationship between surface and deeper meaning, between the fictional story and the reality of racism in America that make it plausible (perhaps more plausible than Mother's or Tateh's fates).

Ultimately, Walker's terrorism may be best understood by considering the source of this subplot, Heinrich von Kleist's story, "Michael Kohlhaas" (1808) (which was itself based on a chronicle, again suggesting interplay between fact and fiction). In this tale situated in the sixteenth century, Michael Kohlhaas refuses to pay an unjust toll to cross a junker's road. His prize horses are confiscated and mistreated, and the man demands justice. Finally, after his wife is killed in an attempt to intercede, Kohlhaas becomes an outlaw, setting castles and even parts of cities afire. Finally, his horses are restored and he is summarily executed. David Emblidge argues the extended allusion to "Michael Kohlhaas" suggests that injustice in twentieth-century America is comparable to that in sixteenth-century Europe. However, the failures of American justice are already suggested in Harry K. Thaw's trial and Mameh's sexual exploitation.

Doctorow's choice of the Kleist tale does not itself represent or even significantly extend the theme of injustice. Walter L. Knorr believes that by drawing so heavily on a somewhat obscure foreign tale Doctorow creates an anxiety of critical reception in readers that balances his own anxiety of influence. While Knorr's point is valid, what is more important is that in alluding to the Kleist tale Doctorow establishes a literary dialogue around issues of injustice, prompting readers to question if there are other literary works dealing with these themes that they have failed to notice. This nod in the direction of literary forefathers; along with the adaptation of romance, proletarian, and postmodern genres; is an earmark that Doctorow is creating an aesthetically fine political novel. Finally, "Michael Kohlhaas" is a story of class injustice and persecution; alluding to it revives questions not only about the racial struggle Walker is fighting, but also about the class injustice suffered by Tateh and Evelyn Nesbit (who is from the working class).

Indeed, the Coalhouse Walker subplot raises questions as to who actually holds power and influence in the democratic United States. Instead of seizing an elected official's home, Walker takes J. P. Morgan's library. According to the narrator, Morgan is "at the top of the business pyramid"(114). To Walker, he is understandably the most powerful man in the United States. Indeed, Morgan bailed out the United States government with a loan during the panic of 1907. He, more than any government agency or official, profoundly affected the nation's welfare. The scope of his actions, coupled with his belief in reincarnation and conviction that he must be descended from great rulers, indicate both his power and elitism. Alan M. Winkler describes Morgan as a man of supreme confidence; a man who, in response to a question about what his yacht costs, replied if one had to ask one couldn't afford it (106). Such self-assuredness and conspicuous consumption are traits shared by Coalhouse Walker. In seizing Morgan's library, Walker is challenging the epitome of white power as an equal. Moreover, that Walker is satisfied to hold Morgan's property rather than the man himself hostage again indicates the importance of material possessions.[13] (His seizing the building is applauded by Emma Goldman, who sees it as a first step toward toppling the status quo.) Morgan's own advice to law enforcement officials, while ruthless and pragmatic, also acknowledges the importance of recognizing property rights: "GIVE HIM HIS AUTOMOBILE AND HANG HIM" (242).

Morgan's advice suggests the full force of the law delivering the kind of justice that Michael Kohlhaas ultimately received (his horses restored and a swift execution). Yet Coalhouse Walker becomes a terrorist because the law is unwilling to protect him (as it failed to protect Kohlhaas). His treatment may be contrasted with that of Harry K. Thaw—a man who committed premeditated murder and who physically abused Evelyn Nesbit, yet who, while awaiting trial in prison, is given conjugal privileges with Evelyn Nesbit. Coalhouse Walker is shot down before even being formally charged. As Daniel would say, "law protects privilege," but perhaps at a cost to society as a whole. Michael Kohlhaas's words to Martin Luther might as easily be applied to Coalhouse Walker, "I call that man an outcast who is denied the protection of the law! . . . Whoever withholds it from me drives me out into the wilderness among savages" (152). Significantly, Walker is often referred to as a savage by the press and by law enforcement officials.

Walker ultimately is destroyed because he is an African-American man trying to assimilate into American society. The representation of different fates for Tateh and Coalhouse Walker suggests, especially after *The Book of Daniel*, an examination of the different position of Jews and African-Americans in the United States. Furthermore, while Walker certainly receives the harshest treatment in the novel, some other characters also fare badly: Younger Brother is killed in the Mexican revolution, Evelyn Nesbit disappears into obscurity, Emma Goldman is deported, Father sinks on board the *Lusitania*. Taken together, the fates of the characters who endure as compared with those who do not suggest first that the ability to adapt to change is crucial. As I have already stated, differences in this ability explain the differences between Father and Tateh. Furthermore, the enduring landscape of *Ragtime* is like the enduring landscape of American political debates: it is composed of families with middle-class values. Those on the periphery—anarchists, radicals, sensational beauty figures—eventually disappear from the novel. And finally, in the figures of J. P. Morgan, Henry Ford, and Harry K. Thaw, the power of money to buy influence and justice is depicted. Harry K. Thaw marches in the Armistice Day Parade long after Coalhouse Walker has been shot down.

In a number of ways then, *Ragtime* exemplifies how, according to the views of the new Americanists, the romance accommodates political views and social critique, especially with the incorporation of postmodern elements. It has been argued that there is a tendency for literary critics [and I would add for many others as well] to see American politics as operating on a consensus model free of major conflicts (Harris 43–44). Coalhouse Walker's terrorism, Tateh's union activities, and Emma Goldman's radicalism all show that there is serious disagreement in a society that seems committed to the same goals and values.

Ragtime's ending envisioning the Little Rascals series has been justifiably criticized as sentimental.[14] However, this ending might better be read as any one of the three endings of *The Book of Daniel* is: as one possible, incomplete closing. The fates of all the characters in the novel must be considered for *Ragtime* to suggest how progress and social change might be accommodated, as well as to suggest the serious limitations, especially along race lines, as to who is allowed to progress.

While Morris is certainly correct in stating that the ambiguity of the narration as well as the continual reversals and changes in the plot complicate a simple reading of history, I argue, as I did in discussing *The Book of Daniel*, that *Ragtime* consistently raises questions about the nature of power and inequity, and prompts readers to consider them.[15] Coalhouse Walker's apparent desire to assimilate as well as his terrorism will likely be continually debated by readers, as will Tateh's metamorphosis into Baron Ashkenazy. In considering the fates of the various characters, perhaps especially the "disappeared," readers may ponder not only their history but their complicity in current political and social problems. Houdini, lamenting that unlike the manufacturers and leaders of his time he cannot produce a "real world" act, has been seen as an artist figure, but *Ragtime* does not lament the illusory quality of fiction. Rather, in the romance tradition it uses illusion to raise questions about what is considered reality.

In her work on the political aspects of postmodernism Linda Hutcheon sees intertextuality in novels such as *Ragtime* as drawing attention to the impossibility of constructing rigid boundaries between art and the world, and the impossibility of knowing either. As she and other critics, especially Barbara Foley, have noted, *Ragtime* has affinities with Dos Passos' *USA*; yet Dos Passos seems to believe that historical reality is knowable, while Doctorow emphasizes that history and identity are continually composed and recomposed. Doctorow emphasizes the artificial nature of such composition while simultaneously rendering the connection between life and art.[16]

In *Ragtime* Doctorow playfully explores the continuing promise of the American Dream. In an era of rapid change and urbanization, the dream is more available to those who can metamorphosize themselves, both by transforming their talents into something the era appreciates and by transforming themselves into acceptable personages. Tateh is able to make the latter transformation; Coalhouse Walker is not permitted to aspire to this dream. His and Sara's deaths reflect the many, often unrecorded lynchings and similar murders of African-Americans who aspired to upward mobility. *Ragtime* is Doctorow's most playful, amusing novel. It is most marked by the ironic distance that characterizes postmodernism. Yet in this novel Doctorow consistently suggests the problems associated with progress—namely that the progress of a few often coexists with the misery of many, that technological progress (Ford's assembly line), and that the rewards of progress are not available to all. The distinction between fact and fiction, between worklike and documentary texts are thoroughly jumbled. Even so, readers are able to make important distinctions between the fates of those allowed to progress and those who are disappeared or annihilated. The novel's panoramic scope particularly implies that it is impossible to remain outside the web; everyone is complicit in the fates of all the characters. Readers will thus very subtly realize their own position in American society and thus come to reflect on the nature of their complicity. *Ragtime* is then a highly effective piece of midfiction. While it may appear to be all surface (as some critics charged), it actually critiques the very surface it represents, beginning, for example, with the mock-factual statement, "There were no Negroes," and then focusing on an African-American family. The novel gives a powerful, yet distanced representation of injustice in America, thus exemplifying Doctorow's preference for indirection in fiction.

In *Ragtime* the achievement of the American Dream, which Father had attained and Walker so strongly desired, is embodied in Tateh. Although his decision is to abandon or at least modify his socialist ideology is somewhat problematic, there is nothing sinister in his upward mobility. Yet the callousness of the wealthy at the balls and of J. P. Morgan in particular suggests a much darker side of the American Dream—one that will be thoroughly examined in Doctorow's next novel.

Notes

1. While most critics have surmised that the Boy is indeed the narrator, some have argued that the narrator is anonymous. See in particular Cooper "The Artist as Historian," King "Between Simultaneity and Sequence." Morris in his notes on *Ragtime* supplies convincing textual evidence for the Boy as narrator (*Models* 239). In the musical *Ragtime*, on which Doctorow collaborated and which he views as more faithful to the novel's vision than the film *Ragtime*, the narrator is clearly the Boy.

2. Many critics have analyzed the novel by applying the structure of ragtime music, in which there is an insistent bass played against improvisation. Josie P. Campbell, for one, sees Coalhouse Walker's story as the insistent bass; the other stories are the improvisation. See "Coalhouse Walker and the Model T Ford." Other critics have seen the historical background as the insistent bass, the families as improvisation.

3. *Ragtime* is unusual in that it was both a critical and a popular success; it was a bestseller and it received the National Book Critics Award. The book's aggressive promotion by Random House has been examined in articles such as Fremont-Smith "*Ragtime* Jackpot: How to Make a Million Bucks in Just One Day" and Glueck "A Solid Gold Jubilee for Random House." As critics have noted, the novel initially received some rave reviews, then reservations were voiced. Charles Berryman "*Ragtime* in Retrospect" discusses this critical shift and posits that critics have misunderstood the novel. *Ragtime* has been criticized for many of the qualities that others have seen as strengths. Some critics find the panoramic quality highly innovative and engaging, while others find the prose style and sketchy characterizations dull. Kermode "Those Were the Days" finds the novel superficial. Kramer "Political Romance" faults the novel for a perceived left-wing bias. Reviews that saw the novel as truly remarkable include "Birth of the Blues" *Economist* 258 and George Stade *The New York Times Book Review* (6 July 1975). Doctorow also collaborated on the musical *Ragtime*, which received generally favorable reviews. The film *Ragtime*, on which Doctorow consulted, was generally seen as a failure.

4. Doctorow has repeatedly acknowledged a debt to Hawthorne. Kramer faulted *Ragtime* as a romance that lacked the veracity of a novel.

5. See in particular Emily Miller Budick "Sacvan Bercovitch, Stanley Cavell, and the Romance Theory of American Fiction" for a new Americanist critique. Other recent studies of the romance include Samuel Chase Coale *In Hawthorne's Shadow: The American Romance from Melville to Mailer*, "Hawthorne and Two Types of American Romance," and John McWilliams "The Rationale for 'The American Romance.'" While Richard Chase's seminal *The American Novel and Its Tradition*, in which he makes the distinction between novel and romance, has been faulted by new Americanists for a failure to perceive a political enter-

prise in the romance, it should be noted that this "failure" is an outgrowth of the times during which Chase wrote, when political issues in literature were barely discussed. Even in discussing the novelists Herman Melville and Frank Norris, there is scant attention to political themes.

6. For a discussion of correspondences in literature see Williams *Marxism and Determinism*.

7. See Veysey "The Anatomy of American History Reconsidered."

8. Cushing Strout argues that Doctorow's Jewishness is key to interpreting his fictionalized history: his concern for Jewish immigrants (Tateh, Houdini, Emma Goldman) is reflected in his giving them names, unlike the generic WASP family of Mother, Father, and so forth. See "Twain, Doctorow, and the Anachronistic Adventures of the Arms Mechanic and the Jazz Pianist." The African-American characters, Coalhouse Walker and Sara, are also named. Hence, if Strout's point is valid, it would imply Doctorow has affinity or concern with African-Americans.

9. Maria Diedrich "E. L. Doctorow's Coalhouse Walker: Fact in Fiction" sees two American sources for Coalhouse's last name. George W. Walker was a minstrel who caricatured whites who caricatured African-Americans in black face. David Walker was a free black man who worked for Civil Rights in the early 1800s.

10. According to some historians not just in the U.S. but through much of the western world the belief persists that it is possible to improve one's life chances by relocating. See Veysey, "The Autonomy of American History."

11. Houdini, the immigrant who repeatedly threw off implements of bondage, escaped, and achieved acclaim also represents upward mobility. In the musical *Ragtime* this association is more sharply drawn than in the novel.

12. Budick *Fiction and Historical Consciousness* argues that Walker's insistence on his car being returned to him in perfect condition reflects a private vendetta rather than a social consciousness of African-American struggle. Diedrich "E. L. Doctorow's Coalhouse Walker " argues that in calling himself President of the Provisional Government and forging a group identity among his followers, Walker does exhibit a political consciousness. My own view is that Walker is fighting for justice and for his right to attain the accouterments of the American Dream—a less lofty aim than liberty and equality, perhaps, but one that is extremely important to most Americans.

13. Morgan is on a trip to Egypt when his home is taken.

14. The ending in the musical is far more sentimental, for there is no mention of Harry K. Thaw's questionable release from a home for the criminally insane or of his marching in the Armistice Day Parade. Rather, the musical ends with a scene of Tateh, Mother, the Boy and Girl happy together as Tateh plans the Little Rascals series.

15 There is, however, a tension in *Ragtime* between the novel's implication that history is indeterminate and its implicit revision of history. Again, see Thomas "The New Historicism."

16 Hutcheon "Historiographic Metafiction," Foley "From *USA* to *Ragtime*."

Chapter 5

Fathers, Sons, and Class Injury: *Loon Lake* as a Revision of the Proletarian Novel

In *Ragtime* Tateh and Evelyn Nesbit represent the nemesis of proletarianism in the United States: Working people often dream not of justice for workers, but of becoming rich. This problem is worked out with a vengeance in Doctorow's next novel, *Loon Lake*.[1] Class issues involve issues of inheritance. Upper-class fathers pass on a name, traditions, and wealth; working-class fathers pass down the story of their struggle.[2] In *Loon Lake* the father-son relationship itself is a contested site: a man is given an option to remain a proletarian, avenge injustice perpetrated by the wealthy, and identify with a father figure from the working class. Instead, he chooses to become the heir to a man who has been his oppressor and to enter the oppressor class. For the left, the problem is specifically why he does so, and the complexities of the answer are suggested in the prose itself. In *Loon Lake*, as critics have noted, Doctorow continues the experiments with narration begun with *The Book of Daniel*; its openenedness coupled with its strong moral message marks it as a piece of midfiction. Furthermore, *Loon Lake* is a historical novel, depicting the 1930s, an era that, as Parks says, represents a turning point in United States history, a time when socialism was perhaps seen as more viable than it has been before or since this period (71). Again, Doctorow's stance toward Joe's upward mobility and toward the American Dream itself is expressed indirectly through the narrative techniques and through the complex portrayals of the characters themselves. Harter and Thompson see Doctorow's ability to engage reader sympathies with the least proletarian of characters as evidence that Doctorow is as interested in artistic and epistemological questions as he is in politics. I argue that Doctorow's political vision is integral to his view of art and epistemology, and part of his political vision is a recognition of how loaded the promise and cost of the American Dream are. It is a recognition that readers themselves experience in the text and thus recognize their complicity. As a historical novel, *Loon Lake* is tied less directly to history than Doctorow's earlier works. It depicts a past era and includes actual events such as the Ludlow mining disaster, but it does not include actual figures as *The Book of Daniel* does, and certainly does not playfully include historical personages as *Ragtime* does. Furthermore, in *Loon Lake* the recording of history is far more complicated than it was in Doctorow's earlier fiction; documentary aspects in the forms of biographies, computer printouts are left for readers to decipher: we are also given Penfield's poems with require more interpretation, and thus are more worklike. Integrating these elements with the complex, interwoven tales of the two protagonists is challenging, sometimes frustrating for readers.

Partially because of the novel's experimental challenge, its critical reception was mixed; some reviewers praised its ambition and treatment of the Depression, while others found the postmodernist style contrived and the ending unbelievable.[3] What is perhaps most interesting is a comment made by Diane Johnson: that readers' reactions would likely depend upon their class background. While *Ragtime* suggested class inequity and tension, especially in the description of the strike in Lawrenceville, Massachusetts, *Loon Lake* depicts the power and brutality of wealthy industrialists, as well as the connections between wealth and organized crime. Although its main character leaves the working class, *Loon Lake* is in many ways Doctorow's most class-conscious novel. That there is not, as John Parks notes, a socialist alternative as there is in *Ragtime* further reinforces the power of the American Dream on working-class consciousness.

Critics have described *Loon Lake* as an inverted Horatio Alger story. They have also noted a number of literary allusions to F. Scott Fitzgerald and Wordsworth, and affinities with John Dos Passos. They have not, however, commented explicitly on this book as a proletarian novel.[4] A novel that depicts the metamorphosis of a poor hobo into a wealthy man would not be considered proletarian under many definitions of the genre, but *Loon Lake* is indeed a highly provocative, if unconventional, proletarian work. A careful reading reveals that *Loon Lake*, like *Ragtime*, shares many characteristics with this radical form, a fact that may signal Doctorow's desire to recuperate this frequently disparaged genre. Barbara Foley, asserting in *Radical Representations* that conservative critics have dismissed proletarian fiction's shortcomings as the result of its ideology, has called for a "critique from the left," one in which Marxist critics would cease applying bourgeois standards and entertain the possibility that 1930s leftist fiction often failed because it was not radical enough—not because it was too radical (168). Although *Loon Lake's* plot would irritate many leftists because it apparently reinforces bourgeois values, the novel is actually radical in its attempt to represent class issues through an experimental form coupled with proletarian themes and to represent the often exceedingly high cost of upward mobility.

Barbara Foley argues that proletarian writers of the 1930s (the era in which proletarian novels flourished) struggled to reconfigure bourgeois genres, such as the *bildungsroman* and the autobiographical novel, and to find a form amenable to proletarian concerns. Quoting from Eva Goldbeck, she emphasizes the promise of proletarian themes as literary material, "The class-struggle opens up a new world, factually and psychologically: That is why it is a great literary theme. The bourgeois writer has to criticize and conserve; the proletarian writer must destroy and construct. He [sic] is a pioneer, with a pioneer's necessity to be creative" (62–63). For many of the proletarian novelists of the 1930s, this pioneer spirit did not extend into literary form. Frequently, proletarian novelists and critics equated proletarian fiction with realistic fiction. As Michael Wilding notes, Irving Howe for one assumed that the political novel—any form of political novel—was a form of nineteenth-century realism (4).[5] Some proletarian novelists were biased against forms that might not be accessible to the widest possible audience, while the literary community disdained strictly realistic forms, creating what Barbara Foley terms the implied dichotomy between bad realism and good experimentalism (54). This dichotomy has all the dangers of any other, and there are many reasons why a modern proletarian novelist might want to use experimental forms.[6] Jay Cantor, like many contemporary Marxist theorists, has argued that it is necessary for radical intellectuals to shift from the certainty associated with orthodox Marxism (7). His views have some affinity with Barbara Eckstein's, for she employs deconstructive techniques because she believes they disclose "complicities," "whereas a will to knowledge, a desire for certainty, creates only more oppositions, the binary mythology of politics as it is usually understood" (24). A departure from linear narrative would be a way out of the expectations of certainty and the predictable dead-end results they produce as exemplified in two-party politics. To represent the complexities of problems associated with class and mobility in the United States, a new form and new version of the Oedipal story is created in *Loon Lake*. The novel is thus a distinct example of the postmodern genre of midfiction discussed earlier: fiction that both in form and content rejects the certainty associated with realistic representation, but that nonetheless asserts some truths.

An experimental proletarian novel might also encourage a way of reading advocated by some neo-Marxist critics, one that not just verified Marxist preconceptions (the goal of some earlier critics and writers), but made them more complete; that is, actually fleshed them out for readers (Cantor 4). Leftist writers and critics have tried to prompt readers to revision Marxist theory and—when aiming at a wider audience—the American Dream. To do so, the form and content of the traditional proletarian novel would have to be modified and the contemporary political realities would have to be addressed. In his interview with Richard Trenner, Doctorow expressed his view that since Franklin Roosevelt's time the political debates in this nation have been between the right and the center; the left has had no voice (55). *Loon Lake* gives voice to the left-wing view of Labor and Depression history while simultaneously suggesting the possible causes for the left's demise: the lure of wealth, the difficulty of building true solidarity among many workers, and the wide corrosive reach of money and power.

As Doctorow's most experimental novel, *Loon Lake* includes shifts in chronology and point of view. Repeatedly, the novel expresses skepticism of and disdain for sequential narration. Perhaps this sentiment is most clearly expressed in Joe's words at the end of the novel: "You are thinking it is a dream. It is no dream. It is the account in helpless linear translation of the unending love of our disynchronous lives" (254). Because *Loon Lake*—even more than *Ragtime* and *Welcome to Hard Times*—is intensely preoccupied with class and power relations, this skepticism about language and narration itself might profitably be tied to economics. David S. Gross's analysis of language in *Welcome to Hard Times* is, I believe, particularly applicable to *Loon Lake*: "In a world where only economic relations matter, as social critics since the Enlightenment have been telling us, all other values are eroded and distorted, and the real, viable connections of community will not be present. For language not to be deceptive and obscuring, some sort of basis of trust must exist. If the "circuit of speech" is only a vehicle for self-interest, such trust is continually being destroyed. Language does not connect; it deceives, it controls, it manipulates" (135–36). *Loon Lake* implicitly addresses the problem of language as manipulative tool by consciously "manipulating" it and leaving so many loose ends for readers themselves to "manipulate" or use to "connect." The novel further undercuts the linear rendition (translation) with its juxtaposition of seemingly unrelated material. Furthermore, as critics have noted, the image of the lake with its circularity and reflective properties, "reflects" the parallel lives of characters in the novel, and may even suggest a cyclical rather than linear model of history: "The loons they heard are the loons we hear today/cries to distract the dying"(54). Again, there is an implicit critique of the notion of progress suggested in the images that recur throughout this book and a postmodern suspicion of linearity itself.

The text is further complicated by the presence of poems written by Penfield and short biographies that are supposedly computer printouts. The inclusion of both poems and objective biographies is itself notable, representing an attempt to link the objective information that is incomplete because it offers no interpretation with something more subjective and, in a sense, more human. This novel is thus dealing with some of the same questions that are raised in *Welcome to Hard Times*, but here rather than having a narrator struggle to separate data from their interpretation, the raw material is provided for readers to do so. For example, the biography/poem on Bennett tells us, "Countervailing data re his apparent generosity to/worthless poet scrounge and likely drunkard Warren Penfield" (158). We may speculate on Bennett's motives, but they remain unverifiable speculations.

Penfield describes his poetry as an expression of human sorrow, some of which is indeed reflected in lines such as the ones about the loons' cries. Much of it, however, appears to be the story of life at Loon Lake; for example, "Well, anyway in the summer of 1936/ a chilling summer high in the Eastern mountains/ a group of people arrived at a rich man's camp" (55). The banality of these lines suggests the artist's difficulty in writing narrative poetry when he has no engagement with the story being told. It is the absence of strong feeling altogether that makes Penfield's poetry sad because it marks Penfield as an artist who fails because he cannot find a subject or a community for his art. The fragmentation in *Loon Lake* might thus be seen as reflecting the absence of a strong controlling narrative voice such as the Boy, even though never identified as such, was in *Ragtime* and Daniel was in *The Book of Daniel*.

In many respects *Loon Lake* is a romantic novel, both in the sense of having characteristics of the Romantic movement and in being about romantic love. Penfield writing on a lake evokes images of Wordsworth; the lake also alludes to Thoreau.[7] Furthermore, Joe and Penfield share a passionate longing for a girl they glimpsed years ago who now seems to be embodied in Clara. Yet the cost of this romantic existence is pain so extreme that, as is suggested in what is apparently a poem at the end of the novel, one might wish to eliminate it,

> Given wars before wars after wars genocides
> and competition for markets cloning will eliminate all chance
> and love will be one hundred percent efficient
> No *Sturm and Drang* German phrase no disynchronicity
> but everyone will have seen everyone else somewhere before (255)

These words express hope for a scientific solution to the vicissitudes of human passion. However, the novel itself offers an alternative to such passion in the various planned lives—Sandy James agrees to love and marry Joe, Bennett lives a civilized if passionless marriage. Harter and Thompson argue that, in the world vision implied by Doctorow, human possibility is continually frustrated by political failures, human psychology, and the very nature of things. In essence, human life seems like a mistake (10). Cloning here suggests a deliberate duplicating as opposed to the chance synchronicity between Joe's and Penfield's lives, the possibility of order, but at great cost to human spontaneity and creativity.

The novel depicts such passion as beyond human control, thwarting any systematic response. Arguing that Doctorow's preoccupation has always been with narrative, Geoffrey Galt Harpham sees imaginative possibilities suggested in the computer. According to Harpham, Doctorow's work shows that "the self is historically contingent and inconstant as the technology it appropriates" (81). Yet the concept of a Depression-era self being represented by the computer is anachronistic—as some hostile critics might charge that writing a proletarian *bildungsroman* in 1980 is. Through these seemingly anachronistic choices, Doctorow is again suggesting the affinity with political novels that transcend time boundaries. A peculiar kind of duality then exists in *Loon Lake*; the novel is both specific to the 1930s and timeless in its boundaries, evoking a sense that its themes are universal, much as the Coalhouse Walker subplot in *Ragtime* does.

Issues of history and sequence are further complicated by the image of the lake, its circularity implying that while people necessarily perceive and narrate sequentially, life is actually much more synchronous in a way history as story cannot capture. The skepticism about the nature of historical understanding expressed in *Welcome to Hard Times* and *The Book of Daniel* thus takes an intricate turn in *Loon Lake*. There are many ways in which this novel thwarts the expectations of straightforward narration, partially in imitation of tropes in the proletarian novel. When first beginning the book, the reader is immediately struck by the parallel lives of Penfield and Joe: both are poor boys who are estranged from their parents. The young Joe angrily reports: "They were hateful presences in me. Like an old couple in the woods, all alone for each other . . . I only wanted to be famous!" (3–4). Here Joe expresses a typical child's fantasy of having other, exceptional parents. Penfield, in comparison, is derided by his father for being chosen Boy of the Year and admonished to come into the mines to learn the experiences of ordinary men. As a budding poet, Penfield, too, would like to achieve some renown. Taken together the men represent two generations of workers during the Depression. Joe of Paterson also stands for the urban Northeasterner while Warren Penfield represents the mines of the West. In fact, the parallel lives are representative of much proletarian *bildungsroman* writing that was discussed in the previous chapter. In *Loon Lake* as in *Ragtime* the juxtaposition of incidents from the lives of seemingly unrelated characters prompts readers to ponder the characters' connection, and in doing so ponder the collective experience of the working-class rather than the individual personalities of bourgeois characters. If novels succeed in so orienting readers, they will be deemed successful proletarian *bildungsromane* that reject the conception to selfhood, personal development, and social accommodation that mark classic *bildungsromane* (Foley 284). *Loon Lake* functions as a proletarian novel by rejecting selfhood and to some degree personal development, but illustrating the process of accommodation by suggesting, through Joe's and Penfield's decision to stay with Bennett, complicity is a component of accommodation.

In the proletarian *bildungsroman*, certain parallel experiences will emerge as crucial in defining characters. The most significant experience shared by the two protagonists is being attacked by Bennett's dogs. Both men stay, though Joe for only a little while. Penfield becomes a dispirited, failed poet, physically overweight, symbolically weighed down by his failure to write about the lives of common people, the legacy his own father bequeathed to him. While Penfield's life at Bennett's estate is alienated from the working class, his failure as a writer might nonetheless suggest the failure of the proletarian writers in general, who many people believe never found the right voice or genre.[8] Joe, in contrast, begins to envision a way to rebuild his life by appropriating what is Bennett's.

Although they share similarities, Penfield, born in 1899, is old enough to be the father of Joe born in 1918. Both men share the birth date of August 2, as does Bennett, born in 1878, implying there is some bond among the three. The three men represent three generations. Penfield (a highly suggestive name for a poet) is a spiritual father for Joe because he has the ability to create much as a mother would. Perhaps more important, as one who vividly recalls a mining disaster, Penfield is a potential father to the proletarian Joe, for the mine workers were in the forefront of the union movement. It is significant that the potential solidarity between Joe and Penfield is that between father and son rather than between two brothers, for brotherhood implies shared responsibilities and perhaps an acknowledgment of sibling rivalry while a father-son relationship suggests that one must have control or authority over another in order for the relationship to succeed. Similarly, for a grown man to be looking for a father implies a dissatisfaction with the father he had.

While some dissatisfaction might be attributed to Joe's and Penfield's specific families, some of it is also class based. In their *The Hidden Injuries of Class* Richard Sennett and Jonathan Cobb note that working-class children (the focus is on boys) get particularly destructive messages from the mainstream society and even from their own families. Because popular American mythology holds that anyone with a modicum of ability and perseverance can achieve at least middle-class status, those who do not are deemed lazy or failures. Working-class parents, wanting their children to have better lives, participate in their society's judgment of themselves. In essence, they tell their children "whatever you do don't be like us." We might consider Joe's thoughts while recuperating from the attack of Bennett's brutal dogs on Bennett's estate. As he dreams of fine clothes, he thinks, "And I felt again my child's pretense that those two grey sticks in Paterson were not really my parents but my kidnappers! Who knew whose child I really was!" (82). Working-class youths such as Joe are perpetually in search of father figures who are successful middle or preferably upper-middle class men. "Brothers" also looking for affection are rivals. Hence, solidarity with peers, requisite for organized labor, is difficult. Joe, however, realizes his own evil deeds and recognizes an affinity with Bennett. In thoughts that might have been Daniel Isaacson's, Joe in the police station imagines he and Bennett are "complicitors": "We're both against them. And, having made this up, [being Bennett's son] I cannot make it work unless I believe it" (253). Rather than Sloterdijk's enlightened false consciousness, which enables people to go through the motions of, perhaps, behaving as though the wealthy capitalists' interests were their own while knowing the two groups' interests were at odds, Joe manifests a more common form of false consciousness: actually believing the lies one tells oneself and actually "performing" them. The figure of the orphaned or alienated son, so common in Doctorow's fiction, in *Loon Lake* takes a very dark turn in a man's choice of a surrogate father.

Significantly, Penfield says in a note to Joe, "You are what I would want my son to be" (177), and indeed bequeaths Joe his notes and books. Joe's taking Clara away from Loon Lake is thus an Oedipal move of a son taking away his father's lover. The proletarian poet recognizes that it takes more grit than he has to survive and admires the scrapping, albeit ruthless Joe. For this reason, Penfield bequeaths his notebooks—his entire life's work—to Joe. Joe, however, has no more desire to become Penfield's "heir" than Penfield did to go into the mines and become a working poet. Rather, Joe prefers Bennett's emotionally empty life to Penfield's economically dependent one, and thus chooses Bennett as a father figure. The choice is somewhat ironic given that Penfield indirectly rescues Joe: when Joe is being interrogated by police he is inspired to say that he is Bennett's son because, he tells us, he had learned the art of narrating his own life from Penfield, even though Penfield's narrations are often unproductive. Penfield, a failed writer, is in a sense a failed Gatsby: he sprung from the platonic conception of himself, but having enacted his own creation finds it, as does Gatsby, missing some essential component. Joe as Bennett's son likewise recreates himself, by some measures more successfully.

The importance of parallel lives might be related to the prevalence one scholar sees in the specter of the "Other" in 1930s life and literature. Alan M. Wald argues that many writers and activists were forced to keep their identities secret in order to protect their jobs and personal lives (15). Such an analysis has resonance in considering the identity Joe created while working at the automobile plant, as well as in suggesting the disjunctures in many characters' lives (for example, Penfield's years in Japan). Penfield might then be seen as an actualization of an "Other" life, one of a more gentle if beaten poet that a ruthless hobo might try to suppress or eventually discard entirely, as Joe renounces his affiliation with Penfield.

While the parallel between Joe and Penfield has been recognized, the doubling between Clara and Sandy James has not been commented upon. Like Joe and Penfield, the two women represent different poles of lower-class life. Clara is urban, glamorous, drawn to the fast life. In contrast, Sandy James is from Appalachia, simple, a competent settled mother at the age of fifteen. (In the context of Doctorow's fiction, it is significant that Sandy James is a child who has been deprived of her childhood.) Barbara Foley points out that in proletarian novels kernel events, such as the effects of poverty, are often repeated (295). The pairing of Joe and Penfield, Sandy James and Clara, has the effect of complicating the representation of poverty's effects. While the two men have had some remarkably similar experiences, they are fundamentally different people, as are the two women. But despite their differences, the two women get along well, reflecting perhaps class affinity. Clara expresses admiration for Sandy James, and repeatedly protects her interests after Red is killed. Indeed, what Clara perceives as Joe's callous treatment of Sandy after her husband's murder—Joe's pressuring her to make decisions and taking her insurance money—is likely a factor in Clara's leaving Joe. Of course, it is evident that Clara cannot resist the pull of the fast life with Tommy Crapo, perhaps especially when it seems that some working-class cohorts behave no differently from gangsters.

The glamour and wealth of Bennett's life is an obvious reason for Clara's departure as well as for Joe's affiliation with him. When convalescing at the estate, Joe perceives he has entered an inner sanctum whose ways are mysterious to him. He looks at the guest book and ponders, "If only I could understand the significance of the notations, I'd have what I needed. I'd know what I always dreamed of knowing—although I couldn't have said what it was . . . some mysterious system of legalities and caste and brilliant endeavors" (70). For Joe, these words are the equivalent of the poor peering into windows where banquets were held in *Ragtime.* They are also the equivalent of Fitzgerald's insistence that the rich are different from others. Class markers are firmly inscribed, yet may seem incomprehensible to outsiders; that they are so firmly inscribed emphasizes the strength of these distinctions in a supposedly classless society.

These distinctions are maintained not through talent or hard work, but, the novel repeatedly illustrates, through brutality. Furthermore, this brutality cannot easily be contained. As in *Welcome to Hard Times* and *The Book of Daniel,* a crucial theme in *Loon Lake* is that evil corrupts. One of the manifestations of this evil in *Loon Lake* is the dogs' vicious attacks. Penfield responds by remaining at the lake, a beaten poet. Joe, in contrast, begins to spy upon Bennett and masquerade as one of the rich. Significantly, when Joe is bitten by the dogs he is walking into the woods, an action reminiscent of Shakespearean comedy in which characters disappear from society into the forest and emerge with their problems resolved. The bizarre twist on the nature/culture relationship results from Bennett's owning nature. One who emerges from his woods may be tainted by his evil. When reflecting upon his attitudes and behavior, Joe speculates that he has been corrupted by the dogs' attack. Like many other survivors in Doctorow's work, he acquires his oppressor's characteristics. The tendency of survivors to do so has important implications in the United States where people who have suffered economic deprivation may, like Tateh, pass for persecutors.[9] Or they may even become persecutors. This phenomenon might be understood by applying Foucault's theory of "repressive hypothesis": that power operates not by repressing dissident forces, but by organizing and channeling them, ultimately rendering them ineffective or actually supportive of the status quo (Foley 169). Anger in Penfield and Joe is organized into envy, which makes the men want to be like those they hate, a response that some have argued is common among many working-class people in the United States who may, for example, vote for Ronald Reagan.

This rather straightforward cause-and-effect analysis is complicated by the circular, reflective nature of the book that repeats and elaborates upon themes. The brutality of the dogs' attack and its ramifications are prefigured in the episode in which Fanny the Fat Lady at the carnival is gang raped. The rape is engineered by the carnival owners because they sense the woman is ailing and, in the words of Magda Hearn, they want to give regular customers "something special at the end of the summer, a grand finale" (128). As in *The Book of Daniel* and *Ragtime*, sexual torture is a dominant form of control in *Loon Lake*; in addition to the Hearns' staged gang rape, Red James spanks his wife for foreplay and makes embarrassing sexual comments in front of guests. Power over others is then, in Doctorow's work, Foucauldian; it is based on the ability to punish and humiliate, especially in vulnerable areas such as sexuality. (Indeed, Daniel says all power is based on the ability to harm physically those who transgress.)

Sickened by the brutality of the rape (to the point of beating one of the rapists) Joe takes his revenge on Magda. Capitalizing on his youth and Magda's sexual appetite, he brings her to a hotel room and repeatedly has sexual intercourse with her until she is exhausted. As Joe explains, "I had actually caught evil as one catches a fever . . . I wanted to do to her what had been done to the Fat Lady" (130–31). David S. Gross notes the prevalence of excremental images linked with money in much of Doctorow's fiction, but in this section in particular: the cheap hotel room smells of feces, Magda Hearn spills a stream of coins on the bed, Joe runs out on the exhausted woman and throws dollar bills to the winds. These images emphasize the corrosive power of money which is, according to Gross drawing on the work of Norman O. Brown, equated with excrement because of its "absolute worthlessness," because it is earned by making unnecessary commodities, essentially waste products (126).

The carnival itself might be seen as a wasteful, superfluous entertainment, but it is also an indirect representation of 1930s life. Rather than signifying a bizarre world, the carnival episodes in this novel may be understood through a Bakhtinian model of carnivalization in which two seeming opposites are engaged through an imaginative parody or recreation. Bakhtin cites the elite's enjoyment of Rabelais's bawdy work during the Renaissance; Dominick La Capra, discussing Bakhtin's ideas, points to pageants, national holidays and the like (52).[10] The Hearns's carnival, while seemingly the opposite of Bennett's estate and certainly very different from the factory town Jacksontown, is actually a mirror image of these societies. First of all, Joe notes that many of the carnival players are immigrants, as are Americans in general. In characterizing the carnival members as "freaks" and "pilgrims or revolutionaries" Joe again invokes the portrayal of characters such as Tateh as a street artist and Coalhouse Walker as a terrorist, as well as the literary type of the grotesque. If the carnival performers parallel the proletariat, the owners parallel the ruling class such as Bennett, who are willing to sacrifice lives for their own profit and amusement. The carnival then becomes a microcosm and a trope. Brian McHale notes that grotesque body imagery from the carnival is common in postmodern fiction, so in using this imagery Doctorow is once again employing postmodern literary techniques to express proletarian themes. His use of grotesque imagery in this novel is similar to that in *Welcome to Hard Times* and "The Leather Man": in all three cases the grotesque imagery is, like Sherwood Anderson's adaptation of the grotesque, a symptom of a world of gross exaggeration—one in which desire for material comfort on someone such as Joe's part could turn into ruthless greed.

While the carnival is then a reflection of the larger society, it is also an escape from it—not for those who work there but for the many spectators. One of the features of 1930s, popular culture is a split between, on the one hand, an awareness and need to confront the nation's serious economic problems; and on the other hand an effort to escape from them through lighthearted entertainment, such as Gene Kelly's *Singin' in the Rain* (Dickstein 226). Joe's participation in the carnival then emphasizes the serious divides in the Depression: not only between the unemployed or marginally employed and the wealthy, but also between the unemployed and those just a notch or so above them who can still afford to laugh at the carnies' misfortunes and antics. Yet paradoxically much of the 1930s popular entertainment, such as Shirley Temple movies or Little Orphan Annie comic strips, depicts people being rescued from adversity. Hence the carnivalization and escapism are as circular as the lake, reflecting back to the social problems from which there actually is no escape.

The carnival is also noteworthy for its strict divisions between insiders and outsiders; outsiders are rubes, fools who are easily conned. "Rube" becomes a defining word for Joe; he identifies people as such and conceives of himself as one who cannot be taken in. However, as his interaction with Red James—a hillbilly who fools him—illustrates, the division is not always so clear cut. There is no "inside" where one is safe from being conned, unless perhaps, one is wealthy and powerful. To be a rube is perhaps only one other manifestation of being poor and vulnerable.

Joe had, of course, never been an innocent; he begins the novel by telling of robbing a church poor box and kicking a priest in the testicles. Although there are significant differences, in some respects he fits Sloterdijk's profile of the modern cynic as an urban figure who maintains a cutting edge (4). Rather than being from the upper echelon, he is poor and something of an outsider. His cynical qualities indicate that he may have the necessary ruthlessness and acumen to move from his class of origin. Yet as we saw with Daniel in *The Book of Daniel*, even a high degree of cynicism is not equivalent to utter ruthlessness. Joe's sentiments toward Fanny and Clara show he is quite capable of tenderness. It is one of the ironies and strengths of the novel that the boy who initially appears so brutal is made to appear relatively scrupulous in a world dominated by Bennetts and Crapos. Critics have noted similarities between Edward Bennett and J. P. Morgan and Henry Ford in *Ragtime*. Bennett owns automobile plants; like Morgan, he is intrigued by monuments and great men of the past, and quickly turns his whims into operational ideas (Saltzman 103, Friedl 38). But while ruthlessness (which could be justified) is only suggested in Morgan's response to Walker, Bennett's is vividly depicted. Unlike Morgan though, Bennett often does not directly assert power, but rather uses others ranging from wild dogs to industrial spies, which suggests both the elusiveness and proliferation of evil.

The corrosiveness of Bennett's actions is best illustrated in the fate of the factory town to which Joe and Clara flee. The auto factory, while the antithesis of the natural lake, is an image of repetition. But the lake's repetition is seamless, without beginning or end, part of a natural cycle. Factory work, in contrast, is continual repetition of the same meaningless tasks—alienated labor, perhaps also representative of the dead end of a historical cycle such as that represented in *Welcome to Hard Times*. The lake is quiet, a place of nature, a private refuge for a wealthy man; the factory is constantly filled with the noise of production. Furthermore, the production line is linear (one piece logically must follow another) and unending. Joe gives a realistic, frightening picture of life on the assembly line: "the sun came through the mesh windows already broken down, each element of light attached to its own atom of dust and there was no light except on the dust and between the black space, like the night around stars . . . And all around me the noise of running machines, conveyer belts, the creaking of pulleys, screeching of worked metal, shouts, the great gongs of autobodies on the line, the blast of acetylene riveting, the rattling of moving treads, the cries of mistakes and mysterious intentions" (163–64).

The horrendous noise is expected, but the lack of light is surprising and hearkens back to the darkness of the coal mines mentioned earlier in *Loon Lake*. In this passage implicitly evoking Penfield's father, Joe reports he thought of his own father as a "fucking hero" for enduring this kind of work. Apparently, Joe previously had no direct knowledge of his father's work, which is plausible because if children do not value their parents' jobs they will not be motivated to learn about them. Knowledge of blue-collar work is a form of what Foucault describes as discredited knowledge: it is devalued because the people who have it are devalued.

The above passage is but one of many indications of Joe's attempt to become an ordinary working-class man. In Jacksontown, he tries an inverse Gatsby transformation: he buys Clara a wedding ring, rents an apartment in town, gets a job at Bennett's auto plant, and socializes with his co-workers. As he puts it, he believes he can "wrest life from a machine," (168) the machine being both the actual factory and Bennett's corruption. Like Gatsby (and like Penfield) he is obsessed with a certain woman. Clara is at the core of Joe's dream; he wants to marry and build a life that would move him from the marginal hobo class to the struggling industrial class. The hollowness of his plans for a new beginning is indicated in his desire to settle in California, the deceptive promised land of this era. As Gross notes, money and sexual/romantic love constitute central concerns of realistic fiction (121); hence, for all its experimental features *Loon Lake* deals realistically with the concerns of people's lives, which might be stated as the way money determines whom and how one loves.

Clara is significant as one manifestation of a figure about whom Penfield and Joe repeatedly dream: a girl urinating "golden water" in the streets. Gross notes the connection between love/attraction and excrement, but does not go far enough in developing it. If we reflect on the role of Evelyn Nesbit in *Ragtime*, we recall her as the personification of all desire; the working man dreamed of having her as an equivalent to having money. In *Loon Lake* this equation of Clara with an object or desire or what Christopher Morris might call a white goddess is ironic in light of her biography: born in a New York City slum, raised by the Sisters of Poor Clara until being expelled at age fourteen, worked as a counter girl at Kresge and receptionist at a funeral parlor, and, most compellingly, had been a gun moll. Like Nesbit, she is not a privileged beauty queen but a poor girl from the working-class. Her status as object of desire suggests her attractiveness is in her ability to use her sexuality as a commodity to gain wealth; it is her mobility as much as her beauty that attracts. Since she inspires a dream of mobility more likely unattainable rather than sexual desire that might be fulfilled with another partner, the desire she creates is, in Gross's terms, excremental.

Joe's fantasy of a life with Clara is undone by the reality of the world she embodies—Crapo's/Bennett's Industrial Services. Red James's treachery and role in union busting is representative of a devastating chapter in organized labor's history, and his role as a "double agent" leading a "double life is yet another variation of the doubling theme. His role is a particularly strong example of coopting, representative of a world, as Gross's analysis of money and language indicates, in which nothing can be trusted. Like a lake full of reflections, the novel *Loon Lake* reflects a world in which nothing is as it appears and everything is permeated with the power of the wealthy.

Yet in considering this novel's status as a revised proletarian novel, especially its potential for praxis, it is essential to consider whether *Loon Lake* leaves open the possibility of imagining another fate for both the union and for Joe. According to Barbara Foley: "In order for a text to suggest a 'way out,' . . . it does not need to depict the insurgent proletariat as an empirical fact, but only to signal that, while the consciousness of the proletariat is an admixture of bourgeois and revolutionary tendencies, aspects of this consciousness which are currently secondary will in time become primary and essence-determining" (116). In *Loon Lake* perhaps the way out is suggested through Joe's consciousness as well as through the circumstances of his life, through his desire to have a productive working-class life. *Loon Lake* is then not a novel that suggests it is inevitable that Joe would betray the working-class; in other circumstances more revolutionary action might be possible.

As previously mentioned, Joe certainly has the intelligence to imagine and remake his life. What he does not have is power and money behind that intelligence—and these are precisely the things that Bennett has, and what make Bennett's influence so pervasive. The wealthy man is described as elusive and impermeable with "[a] manic energy [of his], a mad light in his eye. . . . That was what free men were like, they shone their freedom over everyone." "All the intelligence I had of him . . . had not prepared me for the impersonal force of him" (106–7). According to these descriptions, Bennett is, like the Bad Man in *Welcome to Hard Times*, almost a force of nature. When Joe and Clara try to run from Loon Lake they run right back into his territory, like a couple attempting to flee a storm that is on a specific course. There seems to be no escaping him. Likewise, there seems to be no way to outsmart such power and remain on the outside, no effective resistance. Joe thinks he will be able to con Bennett; instead, in a circular motion reminiscent of the lake, Joe ends up running back to him. Even after Bennett has destroyed every dream of Joe's, Joe, like Penfield, decides not to kill him. The possibility of resistance from the outside is similarly thwarted. As Joe observes, no one has to buy the police in a company town; the police are already "in." The forces against the union are so great and the actions of "operators" have such dire consequences that in this particular struggle the union cannot prevail.

Union activity permeates Penfield's life as well as Joe's, albeit less extensively. In 1919 Penfield is in Seattle during the General Strike, expressing optimism about the action and about human nature itself ("you take away men's fear and be surprised how decent they can be" (224)). Yet moments later Penfield is sharing his landlady's skepticism, speculating that if the strike prevails the organizers will probably become as evil as those presently in power. Despite being a poet with romantic leanings Penfield is then, in Sloterdijk's terms, capable of a cynical critique that inevitably reveals an "embarrassment of ideas confronted by interests underlying them" (19). Furthermore, he is acutely aware of cycles of repetition in human life, particularly the one in which victims become victimizers; his pleas to God are pleas to end all forms of repetition.

Throughout the novel the distinct life of Joe's psychic twin, Penfield, is recounted in juxtaposition with Joe's. While Joe searches for material security, Penfield embarks on a spiritual quest partially intended to resolve his material deprivation. As a child he would "transform" reality rather than "apprehend" it; when his family is evicted "the pitiful pile of his family's belongings on the wagon bed is represented [by him] as a vision of high civilization" (38). His impulse is typical of many working-class intellectuals who want to escape into art; yet unlike the popular entertainment of the era, Penfield's art at least partially reflects suffering even as it transforms it. Penfield's body straining to attain the meditative positions of Zen Buddhism graphically suggests his efforts to comprehend human pain. In addition to following an Eastern ideal of the importance of self, Penfield is perhaps reaching for a reformed consciousness implied in *The Book of Daniel* and advocated by some contemporary

Marxist critics. To them, the road to permanent revolution is a state of consciousness where one's goal is not outside the self but is created as one creates the self (Cantor 13). This theory suggests a new notion of the self-made "man," one counter to the bourgeois Gatsbyesque idea. Penfield is possibly unable to fashion this self because he is always in exile—in Japan, at Loon Lake. Unlike Joyce's Dedalus who renounces home and family in search of art, Penfield, as a more typical contemporary working-class protagonist, leaves Colorado in search of a sanctuary where he can create. Unable to find a home, comrades, or an independent source of income, he flees the physical realities into worlds of meditation and art, continually reflecting suffering without being able to address it.[11]

It is fitting that one who was always searching for transcendence from the material world would die in a plane crash with Bennett's wife Lucinda, a woman who would have chosen life without a body if she had been able. Symbolically, Penfield, young enough to be Bennett's son and in some sense his adoptee, like Joe makes an Oedipal move in taking his surrogate father's woman. Lucinda, like Penfield, is searching for transcendence represented by the very loons whose strange cries permeate the lake. The two are thus spiritually in opposition to Bennett whom Joe conceives of as a "killer of poets and explorers," two kinds of people who suggest dreams that nourish the psyche. In *Ragtime*, for example, when Father stopped exploring he stagnated, dying emotionally, as the successful Bennett has apparently died emotionally, childless in a loveless marriage.

The end of *Loon Lake* hearkens to a biblical quote Doctorow once paraphrased in discussing this novel with me, "What profit a man if he gain the whole world, but suffer the loss of his soul." Harpham is certainly correct in stating that the "narrative production" Joe learns enables him to survive, but I would add to survive at a terrible cost (83). As Joe's final biography indicates, he is wealthy and powerful, but he has the same loveless, emotionally impoverished life Bennett did. His marital failure is more poignant because he could never recreate the passion he had with Clara. As Morris notes, after contemplating Bennett's murder, Joe leaps into Loon Lake in a baptismal gesture (*Models* 130). Joe is christened as Bennett's son; we learn of his adopted and actual identity at the same point in the novel. While Morris sees this leap as leading to the revelation of the character's true surname (Korzeniowski), it is important to remember that the computer printout on Joe's life follows Joe's act but is not in any way directly related to it. What is most important about the ending is that Joe has successfully assimilated into the world of the wealthy. While his factory work is acknowledged, his hobo years and tough childhood are absent from his biography. Joe then becomes representative of rich Americans who have come into wealth through scheming and ruthlessness. Their printed histories acknowledge neither their crimes nor their lower-class origins, which again signals Doctorow's skepticism about historical records that purport to be completely objective. *Loon Lake* illustrates that the powerful do not spring from the platonic conceptions of themselves, but as Herwig Friedl says, power keeps reincarnating itself on human and political levels (41).

Harter and Thompson's theory that the name Korzeniowski, evoking Joseph Conrad, suggests both a man who has had many identities and the novel's *doppelgänger* theme is persuasive (85). I would extend their interpretation by adding that Conrad was a writer whose parents were exiled and undoubtedly killed prematurely for their Polish-nationalistic activities, perhaps like Joe's working-class forebears. Edward W. Said believes Conrad's background made him highly self-conscious about his complicity in colonialism. Hence, *Heart of Darkness* cannot be read as "just a straightforward recital of Marlow's adventures; it is also a dramatization of Marlow himself" (23). Joe's position is even more ambiguous than Marlow's, for whatever guilt he may feel, Joe embraces Bennett as his surrogate father. Revealing Joe's name at the end of the text emphasizes why Joe has to reject the name, that legacy, to become Master of Loon Lake, and provides another clue as to his apparent spiritual emptiness as Bennett's heir.

Taken as a whole *Loon Lake* is a contemporary proletarian novel with clear markings of the genre as well as of postmodern influences. It is perhaps overambitious in its experimentation, making the prose at times seem awkwardly written rather than stylistically innovative. *The Book of Daniel* succeeds in its complexity because of Daniel's strong, guiding narrative voice; the ambiguous narration along with other experimental techniques makes *Loon Lake* a very difficult novel to follow. Nonetheless, it is a provocative revision of proletarian genres that suggests the connections between generational and class conflict. It is further a bold attempt to represent Doctorow's skepticism about the accuracy of historical (biographical) records and the possibility of straightforward narration. In a sense, *Loon Lake* is an effort to retell the story of the American people, their choices, and their losses in a crucial era; as Richard King said in his review, this novel might be called "Why There Is No Socialism in America." To tell this story, Doctorow both recuperates and revises a 1930s genre. Furthermore, as he did in *The Book of Daniel*, Doctorow reveals his skepticism about organized political activity in a very political novel.

In the classic proletarian *bildungsroman*, the plot trajectory must depict the protagonist's development of class consciousness. Furthermore, "Events and characters should exhibit patterns of redundancy embodying the dynamics of historical necessity" (Foley 328). But a contemporary author and audience would likely find this trajectory deterministic and simplistic. In order to deal with complexity and complicity, a new story and a new form would have to be written—one like *Loon Lake* that represents the tremendous power and lure of wealth while indicating possible directions for different outcomes, and clearly suggesting wealth does not equal happiness.[12]

Notes

1. Doctorow's only drama, *Drinks Before Dinner*, was published in 1978 and performed at New York City's Public Theater. The play depicts a seemingly respectable man, Edgar, who pulls a gun at a dinner party and forces people to listen to his apocalyptic visions of contemporary life. In the preface to the play Doctorow states that in *Drinks Before Dinner* language rather than plot or character is crucial, and the play may be seen as a "theatre of ideas" rather than one of dramatic action. Reviewers generally found the play dull, resembling an interior monologue or platonic dialogue rather than a drama. Coincidentally, I saw *Drinks Before Dinner* at the Public Theater before I'd even known of Doctorow's fiction. I found the play provocative and superbly acted.

2. I refer to fathers rather than parents because *Loon Lake* is about surrogate father-son relationships.

3. Critics who praised *Loon Lake* generally found its experimental style coupled with its political themes highly effective. Negative reviewers found the style pretentious and too difficult to follow. For positive reviews see Maloff "The American Dream in Fragments," Johnson "Waiting for Righty," and Robert Towers "A Brilliant World of Mirrors." For negative commentary see Atwood "E. L. Doctorow: Writing by His Own Rules," Burgess "Doctorow's 'Hit' Is a Miss," and King "Two Lights That Failed."

4. Paul Levine in *E. L. Doctorow* does note the affinities between *Loon Lake* and some proletarian fiction of the 1930s, perceptively arguing that many proletarian novels such as Richard Wright's *Native Son* and Henry Roth's *Call It Sleep* illustrate how allegiances based on race, religious, or ethnic identity often supersede class solidarity (71).

5. Wilding critiques this assumption and argues that in order to consider what imaginative prose might have to say about politics, we must move beyond the narrow confines of realism commonly associated with the political novel.

6. I use the term "proletarian writer" guardedly, for there has been considerable controversy over what constitutes a proletarian novelist. Should one currently be working-class, from a working-class background, or should one who writes about proletarian themes despite class origin and affiliation be considered a proletarian writer? In terms of background and current class membership, Doctorow does not qualify as proletarian, but I consider him a proletarian novelist because I place primacy on the themes themselves.

7. Paul Levine in his book also alludes to darker associations with the lake: It recalls Clide Griffith's crime in *An American Tragedy* (67).

8. While 1930s proletarian writing, and fiction in particular, had generally been dismissed as polemical, in recent years there has been an attempt to re-examine

and recuperate it. In addition to Barbara Foley's *Radical Representations* see Michael E. Staub *Voices of Persuasion*, Paula Rabinowitz *Labor and Desire*, and Constance Coiner *Better Red: The Writing and Resistance of Tillie Olsen and Meridel LeSeuer.*

9   For a full discussion of survivor characteristics and the tendency of some survivors to become oppressors see Tokarczyk "From the Lions' Den."

10   For Bakhtin's highly influential treatment of the carnivalesque in literature see *The Dialogic Imagination.*

11   The figure of Penfield contemplating suffering also marks the place where Doctorow's political speculations join philosophical ones. Like most serious thinkers, Doctorow continually questions the meaning of suffering, both that caused by human greed and exploitation and that without a clear cause.

12   See Eckstein on the political novel and complicity (35) and Hutcheon *The Politics of Postmodernism* on the political ambivalence of postmodernism (142).

Chapter 6

Gangsters, the 1980s, and Greed: *Billy Bathgate*

Doctorow's eighth novel, *Billy Bathgate*, is also a historical novel in that it is set in the 1930s. Like *Loon Lake* it includes some historical verities from the period: the character of Dutch Schultz and his mobsters, and the circumstances of Schultz's death. Indeed, the novel so accurately represents many facets of Schultz's life that one critic describes *Billy Bathgate* as a fictive retelling of a media story (Henry 39). Yet this novel is not concerned with the nature of historical understanding or, as *Loon Lake* is, the problems of narration itself. (Indeed, *Billy Bathgate* is far less experimental and more accessible than *Loon Lake*.) Rather, *Billy Bathgate*, like much of Doctorow's fiction, might be considered a *bildungsroman*—a *bildungsroman* of a criminal: *Billy Bathgate* represents a shrewd slum youth coming of age as a gangster. The boy Billy Bathgate is, like Joe in *Loon Lake*, another inversion of Horatio Alger's protagonists. Billy's father has deserted the family; his mother is barely sane, impoverished, marginally caring for herself and the boy. In these limited surroundings, Billy scrapes by and yearns for a better life. Through his intelligence, cunning, and luck he gets his chance at upward mobility, and indeed acquires a fortune. In contrast to the protagonists in Horatio Alger stories who advanced through hard work, good deeds, and luck, the men in Schultz's world advance by seizing power and instilling fear. The novel, in its depiction of cement bucket executions and gangland shootings, graphically represents the brutality of organized crime. Yet *Billy Bathgate* would be far less interesting if it were a novel only about organized crime, as some lesser crime stories are. Rather, while the gangsters' violence is specific to their crime world, its ethos is not. As Peter S. Prescott remarks, Doctorow is equal to F. Scott Fitzgerald and William Kennedy in his ability to understand and depict the relationship between criminality and the American Dream.[1] Too often it is greed and ruthlessness rather than virtues that bring success. This point is probably truer in some periods of American history than others. Although it takes place during the Great Depression, *Billy Bathgate* was written during the 1980s, a time like the Gilded Age depicted in *Ragtime* when a culture of greed—that is an acceptance and even glorification of greed—became widespread. While a number of critics missed the significance of this fact, some did comment on the connection between the values critiqued in *Billy Bathgate* and those of the period in which the novel was written.[2] In *Billy Bathgate* Doctorow continues his critique of a lack of community, and especially a lack of nurturance, that he began in *Welcome to Hard Times*. *Billy Bathgate* may be seen as a fable about the 1980s depicting the lure of crime to those locked out of the American Dream.

Like *Loon Lake*, and to some extent "The Writer in the Family," *Billy Bathgate* is about a boy searching for a father. The protagonist is attracted to a disreputable man who is, for Billy, an idealized version of the father he never had, the kind children will imagine when they fantasize, as did Joe, that they have been taken from their real parents. It may be difficult to conceptualize a crude mobster as an idealized parent. However, for young people growing up in poverty, there have been two relatively quick routes out—crime and sports, and Billy, who shows no signs of being athletic, chooses the former (Koenig "Billy"). It is not that "losers" are drawn to crime; according to crime boss Dutch Schultz and our own reading of Billy's actions, Billy is "a capable boy." To him, the rackets, not the school, are the institution of learning. He "worship[ped]" their "rudeness of power" (3) because such power enabled gangsters to perform what we know to be an outstanding feat—move from the working to the upper class.

The upward mobility of men such as Dutch Schultz makes them local heroes. As Billy explains, "The quality of my longing was no more specific than anyone else's, it was a neighborhood thing . . . it was the culture where you lived" (29). Minako Baba notes that the attraction of gangsters in the 1930s was phenomenal due to the depressed economic conditions. Indeed, the image of Billy and his mother strolling down the Bronx's Bathgate Avenue with its numerous stands of fruits and other goods for sale captures the sense of his name, a boy from the slums in a country that seems to promise abundance. Interest in mob figures, however, extends far beyond the confines of 1930s Bronx. In an interview with Michael Frietag after the publication of this novel, Doctorow pointed out that the American public has a fascination with gangsters, and that he himself was interested in their mythic dimension (in Tyler "American Boy" 46).³ In analyzing the genesis and quality of modern myths, Roland Barthes claims that although they always have a historical foundation, myths are emptied of history: "What the world supplies to myth is a historical reality, defined, even if this goes back quite a while, by the way in which men have used and produced it, and what myth gives in return is a *natural* image of this reality" (142). Barthes's analysis helps to explain the appeal of violent gangsters: It is not the actual, often historical, criminals who are appealing, but the "mythic," or recurring popular representation of them as brash outlaws and daring entrepreneurs that enthralls. The public is then in love with the idea of gangsters, not their actual personalities and deeds. *Billy Bathgate* effectively engages gangsterdom on two levels: the mythic level through Billy's admiration of Schultz and the real level through the incorporation of the actual Dutch Schultz and scenes of gangland violence. The novel thus represents the public appeal of organized crime and the dangerous implications of this appeal.

One indication of this appeal is the continued popularity of crime novels, a popular genre Doctorow once again adapts. Critics have distinguished the detective from the crime novel by stressing that the former, in its implicit faith in reason and capture of the criminal, upholds bourgeois values of law and order, while the latter reflects a more cynical society, some might say a more degenerate bourgeoisie. An essay by successful crime writer Mario Puzo asserts, "as society becomes more and more criminal, the well-adjusted citizen, by definition, must become more and more criminal" (qtd. in Mandel 101).⁴ Similarly, in his study of the crime novel Ernest Mandel claims that the history of the crime story is intertwined with social history "because bourgeois society in and of itself breeds crime and leads to crime; perhaps because bourgeois society is, when all is said and done, a criminal society" (135).

Because it takes place during the Depression and examines the lure of the disreputable to a lower-class boy, *Billy Bathgate* is, like *Loon Lake* a highly class-conscious novel. Moreover, it is a novel that holds up the past like an imperfect mirror, showing how gangster sensibility reflects even if it distorts the prevailing ethos of the 1980s. Many theorists and policy makers in various disciplines have warned that economic disparity is an increasingly serious problem in many nations. Indeed, Barbara Eckstein argues that economic inequity is one of the most serious issues confronting the late twentieth century.⁵ Numerous studies reveal that in the United States particularly the disparity between the very rich and the very poor increased significantly during the 1980s. Doctorow certainly shared

Eckstein's alarm, and in essays criticized the Reagan Administration's values and policies. For example, in "For the Artist's Sake," purportedly an address to the subcommittee of the House Appropriations Committee in defense of funding for the National Endowment for the Arts, he asserted, "The truth is, if you're going to take away the lunches of schoolchildren, the pensions of miners who've contracted black lung, the storefront legal services of the poor who are otherwise stunned into insensibility by the magnitude of their troubles, you might as well get rid of poets, artists, and musicians." He concludes by expressing concern that a nation cutting back on everything but defense would be devoid of social and cultural resources, little more than a vast armory (Trenner 13–15). In essence, the United States would become like the gangsters who devote a great proportion of their resources to protecting their booty.

Critic John Leonard sees *Billy Bathgate* as a fairy tale about capitalism, with Schultz's brand of capitalism representing a form of social Darwinism (451). If one recalls some of the policies of the 1980s, in which social services were cut and corporate criminals often thrived, one can see the comparison between Schultz's world and contemporary America.[6] Given the passion of Doctorow's views about the Reagan Administration, we might wonder why Doctorow did not choose to write a book depicting this era's greed. In a sense, *Lives of the Poets* is such a book, though it focuses on the malaise of writers rather than that of the nation as a whole. But more important, Doctorow's fondness for presenting jeremiad in the form of allegory dates back to *Welcome to Hard Times*. The technique was effective in raising questions about self-interest and community in 1960, and it is perhaps more aptly chosen in the 1980s. Probably it would have been difficult for Doctorow to write a novel about greed and corruption in the 1980s that did not sound polemical. So he returned to an era with which he is fascinated and in which one could easily find stark poverty as well as enduring dreams of upward mobility.

To understand criminal elements in 1930s society, we must look at the gang's marginal figure, the initiate Billy, and scrutinize his development as a criminal. Even given that Billy is highly aware of his lower-class status and the advantages those more privileged than he have, it is striking how often the word "class" appears in the text. Billy's perceptions can be analyzed by theorizing that Billy is attuned to class as a method of vision as well as division.[7] Not only do he and Drew's husband share a common rung in society, for example, but they also have an outlook shaped by similar forces. Hence, when Billy meets Harvey in awkward circumstances, he is relieved to discern the man is from the working class. Furthermore,

Billy refers to "class act" and fears he is not in Mr. Schultz's class (39). Perhaps most telling, the rackets' appeal is graphically represented when Billy, in an apparent initiation to gang life, watches Bo Weinberg with his feet in cement and sees in this doomed figure "the glamour and class of a big racketeer" (12).

While Billy maintains a guarded ease with the gangsters who likely share his background, he is uncomfortable with the upper-crust Drew with whom he is simultaneously enamored. Critics have pointed out that she may be viewed as a mythic figure, part siren, part Aphrodite.[8] Her first appearance in the novel is emerging from the bottom of Schultz's boat, "her marcelled blond head, and then her white neck and shoulders, as if she was rising from the ocean" (15). In the context of this novel, Drew's mythic status is tied to her being from the upper class, a status that has mythic proportions to Billy. Thus though a dream figure, she is situated very differently from Clara, Joe's beautiful, unattainable woman in *Loon Lake*, or from Evelyn Nesbit as object of desire in *Ragtime*. When Drew and Billy are together, she tries to gentrify him, and he reacts with the ambivalence typical of working-class people realizing income itself does not bring higher socioeconomic status. Wholly at ease at the racecourse where the two have been sent to keep Drew out of the limelight, Drew cannot perceive how alienated Billy feels in what he describes as "the impregnable kingdom of the privileged" (224). In Berman's terms, she is an "x" because, like Bennett's home in *Loon Lake*, she represents the ambiance of the wealthy that is unknown and seemingly impenetrable to the lower classes.

Furthermore, although Drew is comfortable in this environment, she is far from trapped in it: she has an ability to adapt unmatched even by the shrewd Billy. At home in the woods, on a boat, in the city, she is described as someone who "took on the coloration of the moment"(152). This ability is another trait that prompts Berman to label her as the "X" quantity; she is an unknown figure whose worth or liability to the gang cannot be determined. Schultz may be able to "erase" his personality, but Drew can mold it to the moment as easily as she can go from one man to the bed of his executioner. While she seems to be Dutch Schultz's captive, she behaves like an honored guest, even giving the gang advice. Utterly confident, she does not seem to realize gang members are plotting to kill her. Of course, Billy rescues her, and it seems likely that she is repeatedly rescued by men enthralled with her.

In addition to leaving Billy a child, she had a marked effect upon his life by indeed gentrifying him in some respects. Upon viewing her surroundings, Billy expresses amazement at what people need when they are wealthy, and what presumably he will learn to need. His use of the word "need" here evokes the Marxist concept of false needs—capitalist-induced desires that people become convinced they must satisfy. In this respect the image of Bathgate Avenue, Billy's taken name as well as neighborhood, is particularly significant. Fruits, vegetables, etc. are foods that are needed, but not needed in the quantities that exist on the shopping avenue. (When Billy sees barely stocked shelves in Onondaga, he is sorely disappointed.) Bathgate Avenue represents a forerunner to the modern supermarket, where everything is available in variety and abundance.

Billy's desire for plenitude may be shared by many in his neighborhood, and indeed by many Americans, but Billy has specific qualities that make him a more likely gang recruit than many of his cohorts. Significantly, he is a juggler, an actor who is very conscious of his performance and who, as Wills says, is always simultaneously inside and outside his own action. The magical elements of juggling hold no fascination for Billy; dexterity counts (Wills). Juggling becomes the governing metaphor in the novel; repeatedly the word "weight" is used—most notably in his referring to the weight of his ambition—recalling one of Billy's prime acts of juggling objects of unequal weight. By performing challenging feats he draws attention from one of Dutch Schultz's men, in effect launching his career. Finally, the juggling represents Billy's ability to balance his safety and ambition, in essence manage the volatile gangsters while proving his bravery and avoiding trouble with the law. To Billy, America is a "big juggling act" that could, through the right combination of skill and luck, keep him and his cohorts up in the air (95). The word "juggling" is often used by harried professionals and business people who try to balance many different family and work demands; that Billy is a juggler then underscores his being an ordinary person who strives to perform his tasks well rather than a ruthless criminal who might be viewed by average citizens as a different breed. Like many successful performers in all fields, Billy has the ability to manipulate his audience's reactions. This aptitude differentiates him from the freaks in *Loon Lake*, continually manipulated by the owners and the audience.

In conceiving of Billy as a performer, the figure of Ronald Reagan comes to mind. Reagan was an actor-president who was able, among other things, to balance the often conflicting demands of social and fiscal conservatives in his party. Additionally, he was always attuned to his surroundings, and, like the characters in *Billy Bathgate*, continually able to mutate in response to them. He changed from a divorced man to a proponent of family values, from a union representative to the president who broke the air traffic controllers' union. That Billy shares traits with Reagan is further evidence of Billy's typicality as well as the similarity between gangster and 1980s values.[9]

Furthermore, Billy is quintessentially an urban youth, so acclimated to the streets that he is perplexed by small-town Onondaga quiet. If he is troubled while in the city, he will stare at the structure of its buildings or survey its landscapes, knowing the urban environment had always been reassuring. After returning from Onondaga, he fears the country has damaged his senses—his street sense—and strives to get back into the rhythm of New York life. As a juggler he seeks to maintain his rhythm and balance. An urban figure sharpening his cutting edge in the metropolis, Billy fits the portrait of the modern cynic, seemingly conforming to avoid being conspicuous (Sloterdijk 4). His discomfort with the outdoors, shared by Dutch Schultz (as well as Jonathan in *Lives of the Poets*) suggests the agoraphobia some social critics saw rising as the populations of cities grew. These critics diagnosed the ailment as reflecting a generalized social estrangement (Vidler 20). As Billy grows older, he becomes more adept at the cynic's pose, attending college and serving in the armed forces, never believing that participation in these institutions will bring him success. He has gone beyond or perhaps unconsciously rejected enlightened false consciousness, having replaced it with a criminal consciousness.

While Billy's talents and temperament may predispose him to organized crime, his family structure is also crucial.[10] A close reading of the novel reveals that Billy's seemingly insane mother has an enormous effect on him and indeed on the novel itself. In "Motherhood and Postmodernism" Terry P. Caesar argues that in many novels by contemporary males mothers are unsettling, disruptive figures because in the face of technology and postmodern theories of simulation, "their very experience persists in being so authentic and singular" (120). In the course of his argument, Caesar states that the mother's job in a patriarchal society is to police her son; having a criminal son merely literalizes her relationship to him. But despite these policing functions, mothers are cherished figures. Dutch Schultz and Bo Weinberg both call for their mothers when they are dying, and Billy himself after Schultz's murder (but before he retrieves the money) expresses a sense that he failed his mother. Caesar's strongest evidence may be a quote from Doctorow's interview with Christopher Morris in which Doctorow states that Billy's mother (who, Caesar points out, has no name) is definitely a counter to the world of Dutch Schultz and furthermore, "[Billy] could have done none of this unless she was the way she was. In a certain sense, he was doing it *for* her" (134).

While Caesar's argument is provocative, it ignores the class dimensions and related family dynamics that "compose" Billy and his mother. According to Parks, Doctorow's novels often are disruptive or subversive of regimes of power, in part because they restore neglected or forgotten voices. Although she seems out of touch with the world, Billy's mother is perceptive about her son's activities and perhaps about the possibility of redeeming him by helping Billy father his own son, breaking the cycle of paternal neglect that plagues many families. Given these facts, we might see Billy's mother as having a kind of subjugated knowledge, a discredited knowledge common among mental patients as theorized by Foucault ("Lecture 1"). By the end of the novel, however, more than her forgotten voice is restored; the forgotten, non-functioning personage of the mother is restored as the son symbolically takes on Schultz's position. Her role as a single mother is familiar in many low-income households in which men often weary of the seemingly impossible task of supporting families and simply leave. In an environment where shrewdness, agility, and quick wits are essential, youths often have more power than adults, especially adults who have never recovered from traumas, as Billy's mother has never gotten over the father's departure. Literally, Billy does act for his mother because he is the man who must provide for her, physically and emotionally. His mother's words while gratefully taking Billy's gifts, "I hope he knows what he's doing," mirrors the experience of many poor parents who suspect/know their offspring are involved in crime, but take the profits because they need money.

Billy's love for his mother may spur him to illegal acts, but it is rewarded in the novel. For one, the mother's carriage acts as a protective amulet when Billy uses it for camouflage while shadowing Thomas Dewey (Baba 37). In the end the mother enables Billy to reclaim symbolically the carriage by helping him raise his child. Her own sanity is apparently restored after Dutch Schultz is murdered, the symbolic and literal father both having been "x'd" out (312). The "x factor" then takes on another meaning, representing those parts of one's past one may discard as one's circumstances change and one changes with them. Caesar sees Billy at the novel's end as being capable of only replacing his father since he could not confront him, but indeed he had replaced his father throughout the book. True, Billy was absent from his mother while with the gang, but Schultz tells Billy that all the gang members have families whom they must leave for business.

Billy is typical of Doctorow's male characters looking for a father figure. With his picture x'd out by his wife, the father is an unknown quantity in the boy's life, as absent fathers often are a gap in their children's psyches. So Billy finds another father figure whose impact he (and we) can measure. Significantly, he attaches himself to a man who, like his own father, is apart from his family, but whose absence Billy can more easily rationalize. As important, Billy attaches himself to a man whose experience and temperament are very similar to his own. The actual Dutch Schultz's father deserted his family, leaving the wife to support his son. Facing economic difficulties, Schultz dropped out of school in the sixth grade, but nonetheless impressed people with his intelligence. He was a voracious reader and, due to his business acumen, thrived while running an illegal saloon during Prohibition. In the novel Dutch Schultz solidifies Billy's identification with him by presenting himself as a successful "juggler," almost a Gatsbyesque figure who beat the odds: "Christ, I had to earn everything I got, nobody gave me a thing, I came out of nowhere and everything I done I done by myself" (67). In seeing himself as a victim, Schultz justifies his actions as well as his occasional paranoia (Sanoff). As the law and gang rivals close in on him, Schultz bemoans his fate and rhetorically questions when a man can collect the fruits of his labor, alluding again to the fruits represented on Bathgate Avenue, the fruits of the American Dream. Initially, it seems ironic that Billy is so drawn to Schultz at the demise of the gangster's career. However, if Schultz were at the height of his power, he would not worry about finding a successor. When he senses his power is waning, he grooms an adopted son, much as the aging Bennett groomed Joe.

The actual Dutch Schultz is known for having talked a long monologue on his deathbed, and the fictional Schultz does the same. Doctorow's adaptation of this speech is another example of a technique used in *The Book of Daniel*, and to a lesser extent *Ragtime* and *Loon Lake*—intertextuality between actual history and fictive characters. While many facts about historical figures are invented or altered in *The Book of Daniel* and *Ragtime*, according to Charles Clerc all but one fact in *Billy Bathgate* is, according to one scholar, verifiable as true to the actual Dutch Schultz story. More than many other of Doctorow's historical characters Schultz thus has what Brian McHale, drawing on the work of Umberto Eco, describes as a transworld identity: Dutch Schultz has a fleshed out identity in his own life or "work" as represented in historical documents, in his deathbed monologue, and in *Billy Bathgate* (57). This complex identity again suggests a blurring of the lines between history and fiction and an implication that this novel may be as "true" as more seemingly objective documents are.[11] Because he has left such a full account of his thoughts, the gangster resembles a mentor in the proletarian *bildungsroman*, who often articulates the dialogue informing the text, further suggesting his influence on Billy who will likely carry these words with him throughout his life (Foley 305). Two other male figures, Weinberg and Schultz, speak on their deathbeds, suggesting not the end of their speech but its resonance. Bo Weinberg tells Billy he will never forget how the execution was enacted, and Billy expresses a desire to give words to Schultz's inarticulate rage. The surrogate father's half-formed speech—inarticulate, primitive, perhaps half feminine as dying men symbolically return to the womb from which they emerged—informs Billy's ideals, finalizing his initiation as a gangster.

While *Billy Bathgate* can be seen as an inversion of Horatio Alger novels, it is also an inversion of the proletarian *bildungsroman* in which a young working-class protagonist acquires a militant or revolutionary class consciousness (Foley 327). Clearly Billy acquires a gangster consciousness, one better understood by considering a characteristic of the proletarian *bildungrsroman*: the protagonist comes to a recognition of his place in social relationships, a realization that entails seizing what is rightfully his (Foley 284). In *Billy Bathgate* what is rightfully one's own is whatever one is primed to take, what one can steal or con away from another and use to increase one's own wealth. For Billy, it is the gang's money, his adopted father's legacy to him.

Schultz himself is something of a juggler or, to use another cliché description, a man who wears many hats. On the one hand, he sees himself as a shrewd businessman managing as no one else can; on the other hand, he has the violent, irrational temper typical of gangsters in many Hollywood films.[12] Billy reports that he and the other gang members lived by Schultz's moods and tried to elicit good ones, suggesting a child's attempts to manipulate a volatile parent. Possibly Billy feels unsafe with Schultz if the two are separated because Billy cannot manipulate the leader's moods from a distance. Yet Schultz himself is not necessarily captive to his moods. While in power, he can, when desirable, exercise control over his temper: for instance, he shows no emotion at Bo Weinberg's pleas or insults, but appears like a "silent author of the tugboat, a faceless professional, because he had let Bo's words erase him" (14). Schultz has not, of course, had his personality erased, but rather camouflaged it, temporarily turned himself into someone else as so many of Doctorow's characters (Linda Mindish, Edgar in "The Writer in the Family") are prone to do. Indeed, his very name suggests a transformation of identity; the actual Dutch Schultz's name was Arthur Flegenheimer; he was nicknamed "Dutch

Schultz," the name of a former neighborhood bully, at age seventeen. Hence, taking the bully's name suggests the survivor's paradox that runs through Doctorow's fiction: the man who becomes Dutch Schultz both vanquishes and becomes what he feared. The alias "Billy Bathgate," in contrast, evokes a more complex fate because his name suggests the richness of Bathgate Avenue, a legitimate place of consumption. While Billy's name suggests a transition from organized crime into the world of the (somewhat suspicious) *nouveau riche*, Schultz's name represents his membership in the crime world.

More than an adaptation to the world around him though, Schultz's mutability is a device to extend his influence. Repeatedly he notes that the organized crime business is changing and attempts not only to change himself but also to groom young Billy to take the mantle. In converting to Catholicism and taking refuge in rural Onondaga, he attempts to appropriate other values and regions, appearing to assimilate them. In a sense, his fall is correlated with his diminishing ability to control his personality; when his tax case goes badly, he impetuously kills a fire inspector and man in a barber shop, disrupting the gang plans in the process.

Disrupting the gang plans is not a small matter, for organized crime has a ritual aspect (such as its cement bucket executions) that functions as other rituals do; they hold the group together. To a boy from a dysfunctional home, the planning, rules, and the peculiar stability of gang life are a refuge and an integral part of the gang's appeal. Indeed, Billy specifically wants to maintain the "harmony," the order of gang life (186). He loses his father figure and the entire gang, but in retrieving the money he retrieves an inheritance. In his unstable world, Billy comes to see money as the antithesis of the unknown "x factor," the one constant, the known quantity that can be passed down though people may die. Personalities may mutate, but money's power never changes. Money's stable quality explains its psychological as well as practical appeal to an underprivileged boy. It is the logical inheritance in a late capitalist society in which rapid change and developments in technology quickly make traditional values antiquated and the wisdom of elders outdated. Funds may diminish with inflation, but a large bag of money will always be worth something.

Taken together the psychological appeal of money, potential of crime for upward mobility, and family dynamics constitute the building blocks for a boy's attraction to organized crime. *Billy Bathgate*, I stated earlier, is a novel about the 1980s as well as the 1930s. The dynamics discussed help explain the continual appeal of gangsters to the American psyche, but there are elements in the novel that refer specifically to the 1980s. In

"A Gangsterdom of the Spirit" Doctorow indicts the greed and corporate crime that characterized this period. Evoking Sherwood Anderson's *Winesburg, Ohio*, he characterizes the excessive individualism of the Reagan years as grotesque, an ideal of individualism gone awry, and indeed describes the era's political conservatism as a "gangsterdom of the spirit" (349–54). In essence, politicians and businesspeople who embraced Reagan's political philosophy and practiced *laissez faire* capitalism were, in Doctorow's view, behaving like gangsters. Though *Billy Bathgate* is set in the 1930s, it is a book critiquing 1980s values, particularly in financial institutions.[13] While Dutch Schultz is the crime syndicate's leader, one of its most powerful figures is the financial manager appropriately named Abracadabra Berman, able to manipulate numbers in ways reminiscent of 1980s speculators such as the film *Wall Street*'s Gecco. Similar parallels between organized crime and the financial world abound. Many people uninterested in financial matters might ponder Billy's lines, "When crime was working it was very dull. Very lucrative and very dull"(58). Likewise, when Hines informs the gang that Schultz's prosecution is too advanced to be reversed, Billy is awed that the flow of money has no effect, fearing its impotence puts an entire system in jeopardy. Such fear, like the novel itself, looks back to the thirties and into the eighties, suggesting both the Depression's collapse of financial institutions, and the Wall Street and Savings and Loans scandals of the 1980s. In this context, we might reflect on the extent to which Billy's juggling has the illusion of magic as the financial world often has the illusion of magic to the people outside it. Laypeople are dazzled by mergers and numbers, hope that the stock market will maintain steady growth or "balance," and understand little of the dexterity behind the manipulations.[14]

In many respects, *Billy Bathgate* is a novel about what happens behind the scenes in the organized crime business. While the novel certainly depicts violence, Koenig is correct in stating that its thrust is not on the violent events themselves but on the process leading up to them, on the genesis of violence (63). After all, Billy does not enter the crime syndicate because he is enthralled with violence, as some young criminals are. Rather, in his pursuit of a better life he tries to achieve an American ideal for which he apparently has the makings. The characteristics necessary for achieving this ideal are suggested in a number of classic works of American literature and/or criticism. For example, according to R. W. B. Lewis in *The American Adam*, at the heart of the American myth is, "an individual emancipated from history, happily bereft from ancestry . . . an individual self-reliant and self-propelling" (5).[15] Implicit in this myth is the concept of the exceptional character, one who is not only fortunately deprived of ancestry, but who also has the strength and vision to be self-reliant. While the individualism here is specific to myths that may be associated with American exceptionalism, the exceptional hero is characteristic of both the traditional autobiography and the proletarian *bildungsroman*. Typically, the proletarian hero is exceptional for the choices he makes, the autobiographical hero for his natural aptitudes. Doctorow's hero is a combination of both, exceptional in his streetwise sense, his cunning, and his almost instinctive choice to work for Schultz.[16] His decisions are so bold partially because Billy is a typical youth who does not see himself as making lifelong choices, but rather believes he can escape from Schultz and the gang if he desires. He is unaware that in viewing Bo Weinberg's murder he has endured a rite of passage into a life of crime.[17] As Dutch Schultz sadly tells him later, once in the rackets, always in the rackets. Billy's sense that his life is charmed—a belief that his life is out of his hands—is in part a freedom from having to make choices, because the gang chooses. There is no escape from gang life, and gang protocol is strictly dictated.[18]

That we never see Billy become violent or harm another suggests the basic goodness Doctorow sees in the boy (Tokarczyk "City" 34). If he has any desire to atone for his gang activities, Billy does so when he takes in Drew's and his child and renews family life with his mother. Terry P. Caesar argues that the presence of mothers in much male literature stands for a more familiar fear of fathers, a fear resulting in an alliance between mothers and sons that is doomed to failure (133). Billy's alliance, however, has not failed; family life resembles what it had been before his father left. The novel then is an Oedipal story with an acceptable twist in that Billy's actual mother is the symbolic mother of his child and his symbolic father's woman is the actual mother of his child. When Schultz is killed, the shadow of Billy's literal father is finally X'd out and a new family is formed.

Given the specificity of the Great Depression and the organized crime of the period, it is useful to examine further how *Billy Bathgate* represents the 1980s. We might reflect on Eva Goldbeck's claim, discussed in the chapter on *Loon Lake*, that the proletarian writer must destroy and then construct, making his/her job far more challenging than the bourgeois writer's, who simply maintains the status quo. Applied to this novel, destroying might be seen as unpacking or deconstructing the myth of gangsters as outsiders: Billy finally blends into American society, becoming quite acceptable and successful; reflecting on his assimilation into more respectable society, he remarks that in school he realized he was in "even greater circles of gangsterdom" (320), again indicating the criminal essence of bourgeois society. Cantor's proposition that Marxist critics want to find a way of reading that not only verifies Marxist preconceptions, but makes them complete may be productively applied to *Billy Bathgate* (4). Billy's story does not verify traditional Marxist preconceptions, but it certainly supports a left critique of capitalist excesses. If we view determinism in Raymond Williams's revisionary way, as not just setting limits, but also exerting pressures, we can see the limits of Billy's world, the scant choices available to him as a slum child with a mentally ill mother growing up in the Depression. The burden he feels as an ambitious and intelligent boy not only to provide for himself and his mother, but also to excel and gain recognition, coupled with the fact that the only people from his neighborhood to succeed are organized criminals, are pressures that sway him toward gang life. In a sense, Billy's criminal career is overdetermined.

Donald Pease's reading of Schultz's behavior recognizes what Doctorow calls the grotesque turn in 1980s American society. According to Pease gangsters were, "Firm believers in the spirit of capitalism, even in the era of Depression, [who] constructed an underworld that released Americans from the economic virtues they produced in their everyday lives. Here a different ordering of the relationship between needs and their satisfaction prevailed, transforming the need for thrift into the wish to get rich quick at the numbers" (458). This desire for instantaneous wealth has come to be seen as characteristic of the 1980s, by no means typifying even the majority of the population, but certainly characteristic of an obvious, wealthy minority primarily in business, politics, and the arts.

In reading *Billy Bathgate* as a novel about class, we see that as in *Ragtime*, characters' mobility is tied to their mutability. For example, Billy perceives that because people go through so many changes in life all identification is temporary. As was suggested earlier, Schultz's conversion to Catholicism, as well as some other characters' changes, indicate life is essentially protean (Freedman 39). Not surprisingly then, Billy is able to become renowned and successful, presumably by blending in with his surroundings, camouflaging his gangster personality into a more acceptable corporate variety. The changes in *Billy Bathgate* are quite believable and part of what gives the novel its power in representing the past and throwing a light on the present. As has previously been discussed, the novelist's world, in contrast to the historian's fixed, some would say monological, one, is always being formed and reformed with each reading, and thus constantly engaging readers in dialogue (Rosenberg 385). To inspire this response in readers, the characters and events have to be as volatile and subject to interpretation as life itself. And in a society described erroneously as classless, the characters have to be able to migrate between classes as inconspicuously as illegal aliens cross the border, being able to live simultaneously in two worlds.

The disappearance of both Billy Bathgate's and the actual Dutch Schultz's father, along with data on the prevalence of single-parent families in poor neighborhoods, indicates that the family structure is possibly disintegrating or at least being reconfigured. Political theorists have speculated that when the status of a society's deep structures becomes problematic, the issue of political or intellectual response becomes extremely difficult.[19] Clearly Billy is ambivalent about the institution of the family, devoted to his mother but also angry about being returned to ordinary family life after the excitement of being with the gang. In words we might expect of some 1990s anti-government groups, Billy expresses admiration for Dutch Schultz's living in defiance of institutions, particularly a government that: "did not like you and did not want you and wanted to destroy you so that you had to build your own protections for yourself with money and men, deploying armaments, buying alliances, patrolling borders, as in a state of secession, by your will and wit and warrior spirit living smack in the eye of the monster" (67). In the midst of Schultz's worsening legal battles, Billy is disturbed that something as ordinary as government justice could disrupt his destiny, suggesting the boy's lack of respect for the power of legitimate authority as opposed to that of violent criminals.

If we consider again Eckstein's theory that good political fiction makes the reader feel complicit with the evils portrayed in it, we see how *Billy Bathgate* prompts us to reconsider our situation in contemporary society and the extent to which our society accepts and reflects criminality. The mythic quality of the fiction thus takes on new dimensions, for, as Greenblatt argues, great art is great partially because it is a cultural register. From numerous talented writers in any given period, we seize upon a few not only because of their literary flair, but also because their work contains what readers need to understand or appreciate in their own era (ctd. in Lentricchia "Foucault's" 233). While *Billy Bathgate* is certainly specific to the period it depicts and indirectly addresses the era in which it was written, if we assume the novel will endure, we might speculate that the book contains themes that pertain to many eras, albeit more literary and cultural work might be required of an era or culture in which greed and ruthlessness were less prevalent. While standing in a bar shortly before Schultz's murder, Billy reports, "I am facing the walls with my back to the doorway leading to the bar, but I have an advantage because the tarnished mirror allows me to see farther down the transverse corridor into the bar than someone sitting under the mirror and looking out. It is the peculiar power of mirrors to show you what is not otherwise there" (300).

In Doctorow's conception of writing discussed in "A Spirit of Transgression" the writer also has the power to accurately perceive personages and events and to depict them for readers (McCaffery). Rather than the mirror held up to reality though, this writer's mirror may be a tarnished, seemingly distorted one that allows people to see things otherwise veiled. One does not necessarily see class inequity in the United States because it is veiled by ambiguous physical class markers (many middle- or upper-middle-class people wear torn clothing) as well as by denial. Seeing class inequity and one's class status in this reflection is part of recognizing complicity. The image of the tarnished mirror also complicates the traditional view of art as representation, as a mirror held up to nature. Such complication "reflects" the paradox inherent in Doctorow's work and in much political criticism as well: that authorial perceptions of, for example, greed or class inequity, bear witness to suppressed truths, yet all texts are interpretations.[20]

Finally, *Billy Bathgate* is, like much of Doctorow's fiction, a commentary on the failure to nurture. Billy is drawn to Schultz in part because this gangster is the only one to take Billy under his wing. And like Molly of *Welcome to Hard Times* Schultz trains Billy to be an outlaw and a fighter because he believes that is the only possibility for survival, to say nothing of prosperity. Doctorow's commentary during the Gulf War that the honor of a nation is that of a father and/or mother caring for children, not grooming them for war reflects his view of such warrior training ("Open Letter"). While some critics have faulted the ending of Billy and his mother strolling with the baby carriage, the presence of Billy's child underscores that there is a new generation to be brought up by those who have never been adequately nurtured; this generation's fate is another "x factor."

In *Billy Bathgate* Doctorow has examined the character of an inherently decent boy drawn to crime and the forces that make his criminal life almost inevitable. The novel represents Doctorow's view of political and social reality in a specific American era and implicitly suggests the possibility that if Billy's life circumstances had been different, he might have evolved differently. It does not, however, depict any effective action to alter the course of events.

Notes

1. *Billy Bathgate* was on the whole well received by reviewers. See in particular Anne Tyler "An American Boy in Gangland," Donald Pease rev. in *America*.

2. See in particular Richard Eder "Siege Perilous in the Court of Dutch Schultz," which sees the book as a dialogue between two eras.

3. While many critics note a widespread fascination with organized crime figures, there is some dissent. Merle Rubin "Bathgate Technique Surpasses Tale" believes Doctorow is wrong to depict Billy's attraction to Dutch Schultz as a phenomenon as universal as Faust's attraction to knowledge. Michael Wood "Light and Lethal American Romance" acknowledges the power of the myth Doctorow seemingly debunks, but worries that readers may not be able to resist the myth's power and consequently shrug off the violence in the novel.

4. The crime novel has received little scholarly attention, although in the last few years it has attracted more study as the investigation of popular genres has become more acceptable in the academy. In addition to Mandel's work, see especially Tony Hilfer *The Crime Novel: A Deviant Genre*.

5. The other great issues, according to Eckstein, are nuclear weapons and ecological mismanagement.

6. Of course after conservative Republicans took control of the House and Senate in the 1994 elections there was a return to what might be called social Darwinism, with some representatives even proposing orphanages for the children of young unwed mothers.

7. The concept of class as a means of vision as well as division is derived from Marx's claim that class determines consciousness, a claim that has been adapted by a number of literary and cultural theorists. See Jameson *The Political Unconscious* and Bourdieu *Distinction: A Social Critique of the Judgment of Taste* in particular for a discussion of class status as visionary lens. For a discussion of Bourdieu's concept of class see Richard Terdiman "Is There a Class in This Class?"

8. In particular see Minako Baba. I am indebted to Baba for many insights on the class dynamics between Drew and Billy.

9. For insight into Doctorow's view of Reagan's life and character see "Ronald Reagan" in *Jack London*.

10. There have been many studies and theories on the effects of family structure, particularly single parent families, on temperament, but for a recent case study see Gulenson, M. D. "The Effect of Paternal Deprivation on the Capacity to Modulate Aggression." The study focuses on boys, especially boys in poor areas.

11. Morris in his book notes that this novel shares a title with one of Doctorow's earlier works consisting of seven short prose pieces, "The Songs of Billy Bathgate,"

which features a rock singer with the titular name. Morris sees the characters of both the short prose collection and the novel as stand-ins for the writer (200–01).

12 See *Goodfellas, Bugsby, Donnie Brasco* and to some extent *A Bronx Tale*. Gangsters in *The Godfather* series are portrayed quite differently, often concealing anger and plotting an appropriate revenge.

13 When asked about the relationship between "A Gangsterdom of the Spirit" and *Billy Bathgate* Doctorow responded, "I suppose there's a connection. It's not the kind of thing you can afford to think about in the writing. But it's a fact that the book about crime came to me in the 1980s." (Tokarczyk "The City" 34).

14 The culture of the Wall Street robbers and Savings and Loans criminals extends to lower socioeconomic classes as well. In the 1980s the crack epidemic hit a high in many cities, destroying neighborhoods, ruining many lives, and making some people very wealthy. The leader of a crack operation in *New Jack City* is the modern day equivalent of Dutch Schultz, having become even more ruthless.

15 For further discussion of Lewis's theories as they relate to Doctorow's work see Claridge "Writing on the Margin: E. L. Doctorow and American History."

16 Rhoda Koenig finds Billy's sexual exploits and daring highly unlikely for a boy of his age. While his character and actions are unusual, I do not find them unbelievable. We often read of urban youths whose crimes and sexual exploits sadly belie their ages.

17 However, Billy reports he did not feel confident during this execution. Perhaps he senses it is a turning point for him, or perhaps he is uneasy witnessing murder for the first time.

18 A recent interview with Crips and Bloods gang members reveals many similarities between the appeal of organized crime in *Billy Bathgate* and the appeal of contemporary street gangs. See Li'l Monster, Rat-Neck, Tee Rodgers, B-Dog, Leon Bing "When You're a Crip (or a Blood): Gang Life in Los Angeles." The most important difference between Billy Bathgate and contemporary gang members is the role of race in shaping the attitudes of the latter.

19 See in particular Chaloupka "Cynical Nature: Politics and Culture after the Demise of the Natural."

20 See Thomas "The New Historicism" and Morris *Models* for discussion of this point.

Chapter 7

Postmodernism Reconsidered on an Urban Landscape: *The Waterworks*

Even more than *Billy Bathgate*, *The Waterworks* has been called an allegory of the Reagan era.¹ Both works deal with the nature of greed and depict societies in which there is little community; rather, a Darwinian ethos of survival of the fittest prevails. Yet *The Waterworks* might as easily be seen as an extension of, or even an answer to, themes in *Welcome to Hard Times*. If *Welcome to Hard Times* is at heart a city novel championing the values of civilization against the savage energies of the countryside (Fowler 10), *The Waterworks* is a quintessential city novel exploring the sensibility of an urban environment specifically during the beginning of the Gilded Age (O'Connell 34).² Roy Lubove has argued that the urban slum problems had their origins in the same values that guided western land development (3), the values of greed, self-centeredness, and rabid individualism depicted in *Welcome to Hard Times* and railed against in "A Gangsterdom of the Spirit." While *Welcome to Hard Times* is set against the harsh, empty plains, *The Waterworks* is filled with descriptions of the dense urban architecture and population. New York City and the Gilded Age (the latter part of which is depicted in *Ragtime*) represent intensified, exaggerated versions of the United States. The metaphor operating in *Billy Bathgate* is a gangsterdom of the spirit attributable especially to the Wall Street barons and speculators of the 1980s; the metaphor of *The Waterworks* is a collusion among science, government, and wealth (Tokarczyk "The City" 35).

The echoes of Hawthorne (the treatment of science, nuptial ending, fantastic elements) particularly bring to mind the American romance novel and its political orientation. Again, as we see in *Ragtime*, "The confrontation of the hopes of romance with the actualities of realism runs throughout political fiction. It is a pattern that arises from the nature of political engagement. The formal polarities arise from the situation, the politics, the character choices" (Wilding 8). In *The Waterworks* the harsh urban scenes and historical veracity of Boss Tweed's corrupt power constitute realistic actualities; the nuptial ending and demise of Sartorius, the hopes of romance. Doctorow is thus able to use the romance genre, as he did in *Ragtime*, to suggest the depth of social problems and, in *The Waterworks*, the possibility of change. Harter and Thompson argue that both *Welcome to Hard Times* and *Ragtime* enact fables of the repeated undoing of hope; depending on how the ending is read, we might see *The Book of Daniel* as enacting the same fable (Harter and Thompson 71).[3] *The Waterworks*, in contrast, can be interpreted as enacting a fable of hope, a story of battle against evil in which, unlike in *Welcome to Hard Times*, the "good guys" win. Considering Edmund Donne and McIlvaine's relentless search for Martin Pemberton and the truth about his father, Augustus Pemberton, the novel could be read as a detective novel in which, as is typical of the genre, law and order prevail.[4] Ultimately, *The Waterworks* fulfills the promise of Doctorow's midfiction brand of postmodernism.

According to Alan Wilde in "Strange Displacements": "Midfiction seeks to affirm in the face of the void, although its assent is 'local, limited, and temporary.' In other words it seeks positive knowledge . . . without ever losing sight of the fact that knowledge in any absolute sense . . . is completely out of reach" (192). In *The Waterworks* positive knowledge is discovered and utilized to end evil deeds, thus suggesting the possibility of praxis. The novel might be read as enacting an agency advocated by some cultural critics. New historical critics have argued that poststructuralism is of limited use to those who need not only to deconstruct discredited histories, but also to construct new histories in which they are represented.[5] *The Waterworks* is an imaginative reconstruction of history that restores forgotten voices and suggests positive change is possible. Unlike any other Doctorow novel, in *The Waterworks* an evil collusion is dissected and broken; unlike any other Doctorow novel, a way beyond the impasse of postmodern indeterminacy is suggested.[6]

Indeed, the sense of *The Waterworks* is close to Appleby et al.'s consideration of postmodernism, which finally insists, "upon the human capacity to discriminate between false and faithful representations of past reality and beyond that to articulate standards which help both practitioners and readers to make such discriminations" (261). While the novel does not articulate standards for determining truth, it certainly delineates the characteristics of "villainy." Sartorius represents a radical disruption of the categories of life and death, although these categories are continually reinscribed by the policeman Edmund Donne, who is described as bringing order to chaos, and by the narrator's own discoveries. As McIlvaine explains it, "There are moments in our lives that are something like breaks or tears in moral consciousness, as caesuras break the chanted line, and the eye sees through the breach to a companion life, a life in all its aspects the same, running along parallel in time, but within a universe even more confounding than our own. It is this disordered existence . . . that our ministers warn against . . . that our dreams perceive" (220). Such a state has been described by Hannah Arendt as the banality of evil: the sense that evil people often, like Sartorius, appear to be respectable, but violate society's norms of human decency and respect for life.

As does most of Doctorow's fiction, *The Waterworks* insists upon the importance of community through numerous suggestions that human lives and actions are interrelated. One of the central symbols of the novel is the newspaper as it was laid out during this period.[7] Each of the major news stories occupied one of the seven columns and each story ran beside the others. Symbolically, these stories juxtaposed with one another suggest that ". . . the sense is not in the linear column but in all of them joined together" (115). McIlvaine sees a symbolic importance in this layout, ". . . as if our stories were projections of the multiple souls of a man . . . and no meaning was possible from any one column without the sense of all of them in . . . simultaneous descent . . ." (115). In promising that the columns will ultimately be joined together, McIlvaine is first promising to put relevant stories in context and secondly suggesting that individual lives and occurrences are in fact more related than many of us imagine, a suggestion reinforced by the name of the investigating officer Donne, evoking John Donne's poem "For Whom the Bell Tolls," "ask not for whom the bell tolls/It tolls for thee." The double weddings of Sarah Pemberton and Edmund Donne, Emily Tisdale and Martin Pemberton, underscore how interconnected these lives have been. The fates of the exploited urchins represent those of all helpless residents for whom citizens should care. As one critic argues, the horror of Sartorius's experiments is in the extent to which they break ". . . the moral consciousness itself, revealing the darkness and chaos of a universe that negates the understanding and faith of the human bond" (Solataroff 788).

While *The Waterworks*' themes and plot signal a move toward determinacy, its experimental prose is characteristically postmodern. Stylistically, one of the novel's most striking features is the number of ellipses. Grimshaw's lines relating his conversation with Martin are typical:

"Yes. You know I have learned over the years . . . about souls in need of pastoring . . . how they often bristle, or present a superior attitude" (37). The use of ellipses and sometimes dashes has the effect of reproducing the sense of oral speech. Perhaps more important, it, like the novel's relatively long, often complex sentences, slows down the pace of an urban detective novel in much the same way as the thick descriptions of jungle landscape slow down *Heart of Darkness*, ensuring that readers take the necessary time to ponder the tale's meaning. And finally, they moderate the certainty of the tale's moral by underscoring the incompleteness of memory, leaving readers to ponder an alternate tale left out in the elliptical spaces.

As in much of Doctorow's work, the story is conveyed by a narrator who struggles to render a horrible truth he has experienced. In this struggle, Doctorow suggested in conversation, McIlvaine is similar to Marlow in *Heart of Darkness*.[8] Again, as did Blue and Daniel, McIlvaine represents the historical process itself. In this respect, McIlvaine's account may be interpreted as "recomposing" (in Doctorow's vocabulary) a part of the American political consciousness: the collusion of powerful figures and institutions.

The novel's efforts to involve the reader in constructing and understanding the city are suggested in McIlvaine's recollections: "I'm reporting what are now the visions of an old man. All together they compose a city, a great port and industrial city of the nineteenth century. I descend to this city and find the people I have come to know and for whose lives I fear. I tell you what I see and hear. The people of this city think of it as New York, but you may think otherwise. You may think it stands to your New York today as some panoramic negative print, inverted in its lights and shadows . . . a companion city of the other side" (59). As did Blue in *Welcome to Hard Times*, McIlvaine writes with a consciousness of future readers' ability to shape the past with their image of the present, and with a hope that they will learn from his lessons. The image of the inverted panoramic negative recalls the mirror image in *Billy Bathgate* and thus suggests the artist's role. McIlvaine's decision not to publish his story implies that by the time he has seen Sartorius defeated, McIlvaine is no longer interested in personal glory, but in community welfare, the kind of community welfare Blue consistently tried but failed to promote, the community welfare for which Jonathan yearns.

Reviewers have noted that *The Waterworks* is a prototypical city novel, that in fact the city is a major character.[9] Set in New York in the decade after the Civil War, the novel depicts a period in American history that is important to understanding the development of urban areas and their relationship to the American dream. At one point the narrator of *The Waterworks* states that he ignored the great story of the westward push to write about New York. Yet no less startling than the frontier's settlement was the rapid push toward urbanization in the late nineteenth century (Veysey 470). The 1870s were associated with accelerated industrialization as well as with westward expansion. In 1860 only nine U.S. cities had populations of 100,000 or more; by 1880 twenty cities did (Lubove 39–40). Urban centers were important not only for their size but, as *Ragtime* suggests, for their relationship to America's promises. In his book on New York, O'Connell argues that though much of America's mythology revolves around rural landscapes, "the real test of American democracy would occur in the cities, in particular in New York City" (13). He also asserts that New York City is both an intensification of the nation and its antithesis. With its large immigrant population dreaming of a better future, New York reflects the country's commitment to the ideal of individual potential to excel, "that the free expression of many individual wills can compose a great and unified nation" (xiv). (The word "composed" is, of course, charged in Doctorow criticism, and *The Waterworks* itself is in many ways a study of the composition of individual enterprise in the city.)

If cities in general and New York in particular are where American ideals are tested, they are also where these ideals break down. Cities expose the myth of a classless society through divisions, one scholar argues (Lubove 42). In essence, *The Waterworks* represents an urban equivalent of the western frontier evoked in *Welcome to Hard Times*—what Annette Kolodny refers to as a borderland of liminal landscapes on which distinct human cultures first encounter one another's otherness ("Letting Go" 9). While *Welcome to Hard Times* faintly suggests the clash of cultures between the Native American John Bear, immigrants such as Zar, and migrants from other sections of the United States, *Ragtime* evokes a city's multicultural landscape, and *The Waterworks* suggests the class conflicts between the Augustus Pembertons and the street urchins.

In addition to class differences, *The Waterworks* represents other ills of modern urban life such as overcrowding and impersonality, prompting one critic to call it a "gaslight romance" because it focuses on the dark side of the past (Kaverny 40). When McIlvaine ponders Martin's startling claim that he has seen his late father, McIlvaine interprets the words metaphorically to characterize the city that neither man could love nor bear to leave (8). Part of the city's attraction has often been attributed to its unparalleled energy, especially obvious in a boom time such as the 1870s. But much of this energy flows from the corrupt and/or opportunistic people who make money at the expense of others. In the decade following the Civil War there was in fact tremendous economic growth; many had acquired wealth in this war, and McIlvaine reports, in the postwar decade there was "nothing to stop progress" (12), or the advent of modernity. Throughout I have argued that Doctorow has been critical of notions of progress, and in this novel the trappings of progress in reservoirs, aqueducts, tunnels etc. are inextricably bound with Sartorius's instruments of destruction, prompting one critic to speculate Doctorow is implying ". . . that progress is a slippery matter, that change does not move in a straight line" (Sante 40). Ultimately, the question is what constitutes progress and at whose expense it is achieved.

In a short interview Doctorow remarked that in *The Waterworks* he was writing about the New Yorkers whom Edith Wharton left out, the ordinary people (Graeber 31). These include those whom we would call the disenfranchised. As McIlvaine describes the city "falling into ruins, a society in name only" (10–11), he mourns a lack of community. The narrator's sense of loss was likely shared with many of his contemporaries; as was stated in a previous chapter, a common and often explicit theme underlying the responses of writers and social critics in the nineteenth century is the estrangement of urban inhabitants from cities too rapidly growing and changing (Vidler 11). One consequence of such rapid growth in a community is that it becomes unable to account for its members. To McIlvaine, the newspaper is itself an urban artifact; in villages a newspaper is unnecessary because people can see what happens and quickly relay events to one another (87). The anonymity of the city is further suggested in McIlvaine's failure to notice that Martin did not come into the office for several days, "In modern city life you can conceivably experience revelation and in the next moment go on to something else. Christ might come to New York and I would still have a paper to get out" (25).

Swelling populations and densely-packed urban spaces, according to some critics, breed certain kinds of pathology. The notion of the spatial pathology of the city was first articulated in European romantic writing and later in the emerging social sciences and psychoanalysis. Georg Simmel, for one, in his "Metropolis and Mental Health" speculated that urban social relationships would be impersonal and that objective distance would replace subjective empathy (Vidler 20–21). According to some psychologists, the impersonality and crowded conditions of the city caused modern maladies such as claustrophobia and agoraphobia. Feelings of claustrophobia can be detected in McIlvaine's reactions to Sartorius's environs; viewing the reservoir as "unnatural," McIlvaine is ready to "believe in every dark vision if it appeared [there]" (57). The reservoir is further described as a windowless and gasless, resembling a hermetic undersea vault (203). In this world of water, McIlvaine feels oppressed, trapped, much as did the characters in the recent popular movie *Waterworld*, and in sharp contrast to the characters in *Lives of the Poets: A Novella and Six Stories* and *World's Fair*. *The Waterworks* transforms a life-giving, liberating image into a suffocating one.

Agoraphobia and claustrophobia were diseases primarily of the middle class in the nineteenth century, but *The Waterworks* represents maladies more commonly found among the unemployed and working classes in this period: "ambulatory automatism" (whose sufferers resembled the living dead) and hysterical amnesia (Vidler 26). Sartorius disappears, seemingly forgetting who he is, and eventually becomes one of the necropholictics so well described by Simon Schama in his review. Similarly Martin appears to forget his own life in pursuit of his late father, and later is enthralled by Sartorius's operation. The text is filled with characters who are exaggerated, urbanized versions of Selig Mindish: those who attempt to deny their pasts and their mortality, in the process losing their class privilege, and end up among the living dead.[10]

In the popular American imagination especially, the city has often been viewed as nature's antithesis, but *The Waterworks* calls this conception into question, depicting the city as, like nature, naturalistic and Darwinian. McIlvaine tells us, "I had always made a distinction what was nature and what was . . . City. But that was no longer tenable, was it? I longed to be back in my newsroom . . . not in this wild—I was not one for the wild" (224). The wildness associated with the city and nature is a state without controls, such as strict deadlines, formulas for composing news stories and the like. Sartorius and the city in which he thrives may, in Doctorow's terms, be viewed as grotesques only if nature itself never indulged in excess or propagated itself at the expense of others. McIlvaine himself describes nature as resembling the city by being spendthrift enough to produce great wealth for itself.

The narrator identifies himself as the penultimate urban dweller, "a street rat in [his] soul." For himself and his city, he dreams of revival, suggested in the image of new skin sprouting that from the pipes, tunnels and other underground apparatus (163). Throughout the novel the hope/

promise of redemption is repeated, most notably in the image of the Croton Holding Reservoir itself which, O'Connell argues, represents an ignored font of absolution (302) as opposed to the Roman bath that comes to McIlvaine's mind upon entering Sartorius's premises.

Contrasting with the images of redemption are the daily acts of sin and corruption in the city. Indirectly, McIlvaine suggests evil in comparing the sense of foreboding he has at Martin's disappearance with that he had at President Lincoln's death, commenting the audience must trust that this death "like everything I tell you, has a bearing on the story" (6). With Lincoln's murder, we may infer, the nation became vulnerable to carpetbaggers and profiteers similar to the Tweed ring in New York. Though Tweed is destroyed, the evil he represents still persists and intensifies during later "gilded ages." The narrator McIlvaine states that the inhabitants of New York practiced excess in everything from pleasure to death, that vagrant children slept in alleys while self-satisfied *nouveau riche* flaunted their wealth (12).

It is no accident that Sartorius's downfall coincides with Boss Tweed's, patron of the rich and corrupt. *The Waterworks* might be read as a parable of this boss's demise. One reviewer argues that Sartorius, though he has the trappings of villainy, is not truly evil. Instead, his scientific experiments function in the novel to put into relief two extremes of the New York population: the urchins and the wealthy, powerful men (Sante 11).[11] The novel's narrator spares no words in describing Tweed's "manifestly murderous," acts (10) claiming one could literally feel Tweed's force and comparing the man's hold on the city to a "vampire suck" (151). Having held so much power, Tweed could not conceive of the ultimate loss of power, his own death. Rather, "The Ring, with their vaulting ambition, would carry ambition to its ultimate form" (192), thus supporting Sartorius's research to ensure their own immortality. Hence, the relationship between Tweed and the novel's other villains is symbiotic. The narrator knows Augustus Pemberton was sustained by a culture; Tweed and his dignitaries in fact attended Augustus Pemberton's mock funeral. Sartorius freely admits that he chose his subjects not for virtue or intellect, but for their wealth, as they would endow his experiments. Though Tweed is a defining part of New York City at this time, his corruption is representative of corruption in general; when McIlvaine journeys from the city to Ravenwood he thinks of Tweed, juxtaposing him with the nation as a whole (222). The image of Tweed landing on Cuba, dreaming of the New York City where he believes immortality is now possible, represents the hubris of all the powerful men whom Sartorius courted.

The Darwinian essence of nature is personified in both Sartorius and his seeming victim, Augustus Pemberton. On the surface Augustus, a penniless immigrant who earned a small fortune and prominence among New York dignitaries, appears to be an American success story. Yet like so many Doctorow characters—Bennett from *Loon Lake*, Zar from *Welcome to Hard Times*, and Dutch Schultz from *Billy Bathgate*—Augustus has made his fortune at the expense of others' flesh, his "economic opportunity" is his capacity for ruthlessness. He not only sold shoddy equipment to Union soldiers (yet testified at the Senate Subcommittee on War Profiteering), but also likely participated in slave trading, even though slavery was abolished in New York in 1799 (O'Connell 13). His indifference to and contempt for others extends to his own family, whom he views as equivalents to Ravenwood: monuments to himself rather than human beings. So despicable is Augustus that when Martin first claims that his father is still alive, McIlvaine thinks the dramatic man is speaking of "the persistence of evil in general" (3).

Ultimately, Augustus Pemberton becomes a fool in Sartorius's hands. Sartorius himself is the novel's most formidable personage, embodying evil's complexity as well as villainy's tendency to "absent itself, even as it stands before you" (213), that is to be evasive, hard to pinpoint or confront. In his interview with me Doctorow agreed that Sartorius's scientific hubris has much in common with characters of nineteenth-century American novelists such as Hawthorne and Poe (36). Yet there are more modern roots for the skepticism toward scientific experimentation exemplified in this novel. In their history of science, Appleby et al. note that the generation of the 1960s, born in the shadow of the Bomb, had a more cautious attitude toward science than did its predecessors. Primarily the younger generation asked new questions in an effort to understand how specific ideologies and interests affected science (172).[12] Though not of the 1960s generation, Doctorow has in numerous essays commented on the pervasive if subtle effects nuclear weapons have had on the population as a whole and on writers specifically.[13] In addition to the Bomb, Doctorow in conversation has mentioned modern controversies around the use of science to alter life, particularly the Nazi experiments.[14] While we might be tempted to see Sartorius as an unscrupulous villain, he could also conceivably be viewed as "inanely excessive" (231), a grotesque scientist—and again here I refer to Doctorow's notion expressed in "A Gangsterdom of the Spirit" that a truth embraced fanatically often becomes a lie and/or a grotesque. Sartorius in carrying the ideals of his profession too far embodies this notion of the grotesque. His "noble lineaments of the grotesque" (130) include innovative and successful operations during the Civil War, as well as his belief in the germ theory and even heart transplants on animals. The picture of Sartorius is one of mental brilliance and emotional impoverishment. He is like the criminals who are often the subjects of modern detective novels: completely unable to empathize and extremely arrogant (Nickerson 102). That Sartorius was indifferent to the laws of society is suggested not only in his blatant disregard of them, but also in more subtle antisocial gestures, such as his lack of affiliation with any professional organizations. In trying to explain how someone so socially removed could marshal support for his work, Martin speculates that rather than actively seek support, Sartorius simply accepts what the disciples who gather offer him, "It's as if . . . there's an alignment of historical energies magnetized around him which . . . for all I know, is probably all . . . that makes him visible" (183). Here the word "visible" suggests making the work Sartorius imagines possible, and ironically, making it appear so that it can be discovered and stopped by McIlvaine and Donne.[15]

In a pre-modern ideal model of science, there was presumably a relatively tight fit between nature and human knowledge of it. That is, the clear scientific mind would be transparent as it faced nature rather than driven by personal interest, ideology, or some irrational force (Appleby et al. 29). Such an ideal is another dimension of positivism, and though *The Waterworks* is more determinate than some earlier Doctorow fiction, the positivist ideal is nonetheless questioned through the novel's depiction of scientific experimentation. As McIlvaine tells us, in Sartorius the scientific temperament produced a man who was unshockable, one for whom there was no sacrilege (199).

Sartorius is, like many Doctorow characters, a Gatsbyesque creation. His name itself is the composition of a self-made man. *The Waterworks* tells us that in the Middle Ages members of the German bourgeoisie who wanted to elevate their status took Latin forms of their names, hence, tailor became Sartorius; one who merely altered existing garments became a creator (128). Throughout the novel the image of a guided boat in the reservoir recurs, and finally McIlvaine imagines this boat being guided by Sartorius, suggesting his evil hand controlling all. (The image of the controlled boat is particularly chilling given Sartorius's associations with slavery.)

At one point McIlvaine says that he is haunted "not by ghosts, but by Science" (192), suggesting—especially with the capital "S"—that while Sartorius may be a grotesque he and his operations are terrifyingly characteristic of the discipline. Indeed, Sartorius, exploiter of orphans, tells the doctors examining him that he's no different from his colleagues in observing laws of selective adaptation (230). Martin Pemberton likewise describes Sartorius's home as filled with the "menacing furniture of science" (186), an obverse Eden reminiscent of Rappaccini's garden where the scientist, not God, is a dangerous creator. This image is, as I have already suggested, perhaps more terrifying in the twentieth century than it was in the nineteenth because science and technology have more power to destroy.

As was Rappaccini, Sartorius is a respected scientist who had generally worked within the bounds of his discipline. His orphanage, The Home for Little Wanderers, is scientifically managed according to the latest principles of child-rearing (153). What is lacking in this technically superior environment is any concern for the children's well-being. It is thus somewhat ironic when McIlvaine describes the orphanage as an "outpost of advancing civilization . . . like all our institutions at the edge" (156), indicating that the institution was part of what Doctorow might call the illusion of modernity, the sense that modern civilization fails to moderate nature's laws of survival of the fittest and meet human needs for community (Tokarczyk "The City" 35). Equally important, the men who approached Sartorius in the hopes of immortality are representatives of modern society, as McIlvaine says, hard-nosed realists turned "acolytes" (176). Sartorius's brand of charisma is best represented in the astonishing conversion of Martin Pemberton, who rather than being outraged by the nature of Sartorius's experiments, actually works for him, describing Sartorius's mind as "a field of gravity, drawing him to me" (198). In part, Martin is drawn in by the "aristocratic dominance" the scientist has over men who seemed impossible to dominate. Described as "recomposing" patients' lives, Sartorius behaves as an author who might recompose a literary character. The description of Sartorius swaddling his patients suggests he is infantilizing them, which he would have been unable to do had they not turned their lives over to him. Like a con man who chooses a mark by the person's vulnerability to extravagant promises, Sartorius plays upon the hubris of his victims, a desire to be immortalized perhaps especially prominent in the rich and famous. Their vulnerability is suggested by the frequent practice of having portraits created by artists such as Harry Wheelwright; Martin himself questioned who among the wealthy would refuse a portrait and "immortality." As Sartorius's subjects are recomposed, so too is Martin, for the intelligent investigative reporter denies the obvious evidence that children are being destroyed. Yet Martin's blindness to Sartorius is in a sense mirrored by the medical profession's unwillingness to fault the scientist because he was not *directly* responsible for the death of any child, suggesting the discipline's legalism which fails to acknowledge personal responsibility and to recognize the interrelationship of human lives.

Sartorius justifies his actions as consistent with contemporary science and even nature, claiming that nature is continuously profligate on its own behalf, immune to the agony of the species (240). In claiming that bodies have cycles and are subject to tides, he evokes the recurring image of the model boat in the water, here again suggesting he is a controlling creator. Equations between his work and natural processes are intensified in his statement that he is motivated by a search for truth about nature, which is reminiscent of nineteenth-century rationalizations such as Frederick Jackson Turner's that the displacement of Native American tribes was a result of natural forces.[16] Sartorius's grotesque pursuit of scientific truth is then not a personal deformity but a symptom of social malaise. For this reason, McIlvaine and Grimshaw yearn to expose and purge it through a public trial, through a report in which the newspapers could provide the beginning of a "spiritual chastening," "That we would . . . drop to our knees and gather our children to us" (236).

Evoking children is particularly significant since Sartorius's exploitation of them to perpetuate the lives of ailing old men evokes the theme of a society exploiting its children so aptly expressed in Doctorow's "An Open Letter to the President." Christopher Morris in *Models of Misrepresentation* notes that Doctorow frequently represents the writer as an orphan (138), but in *The Waterworks*, as in *Welcome to Hard Times*, the orphan characters are not creators at all, only vulnerable children. As Doctorow notes in his interview, in nineteenth-century New York there were "thirty to forty thousand vagrant children running around" (Tokarczyk 34). The novel represents these children as the failures of modern life: vagrant children who had, like Billy Bathgate, lost their family names, something that would never happen in a village society (83).[17] McIlvaine is familiar with one group of often-vagrant children, the "undersized" newsboys whose faces he describes as etched with "shadows of serfdom" (118), and who frequently die young. The narrator's sympathy for children is established in his fondness for the young Noah; hence, we can easily understand this bachelor's distress at their treatment. Again, the governing metaphor of the boat sailing at sea is compared to the child who drowned in the reservoir (58). More important, in McIlvaine's dream vision the child is a miniature like the boat, indicating children are seen as miniature adults rather than as developing beings with special needs.

Another representation of failed nurturance, again typical of Doctorow's fiction, is in Augustus and Martin's severed father-son relationship, and in the extent to which the narrator and Sartorius both become father figures to the symbolically orphaned Martin Pemberton. Donne quickly perceives the gravity of the Pembertons' differences, referring to a profound derangement of fathers and sons (238). Such an analysis helps to explain Martin's failure to resist Sartorius. As Schama notes, Martin is motivated to unearth the truth about his father not by filial love, as is Daniel Isaacson, but by hatred. Martin Pemberton is, in fact, a foil to numerous myths about men and ancestry. According to Friedman, for example, "The missing father is the link to the past that, for the protagonist, determines identity" (241). In contrast, McIlvaine says Martin had seen renouncing his father as gaining his own redemption (73). In forging his own identity, Martin rejects his father in every way, living by his wits rather than financial dealings, choosing a financially precarious life of a freelance, and even investigating his father as a Civil War profiteer. Yet Martin's renunciation of his father is no less problematic than Gatsby's reinvention of himself or Joe's rejection of his parents. It matters little whether Martin is motivated by love or hate; he is nonetheless driven to search for his father and is as altered by his discovery as Marlow in *Heart of Darkness* was.

Finding his father involved in such bizarre experiments is profoundly disturbing to the son who had viewed him as "merely a scoundrel and a thief and a murderer" (185). And as in *The Book of Daniel*, a man who seemingly embodies evil has become a vacant shell, not even recognizing his son, his face devoid of any human character, his body mindlessly dancing at Sartorius's balls.[18] Where we might expect the final break between father and son, a bond is forged: Martin comes to mimic his father's death-in-life state. Even after his rescue, Martin seems engrossed in a profound philosophic meditation that intrudes upon daily life, similar to Marlow in *Heart of Darkness* who after relating the story of Kurtz assumes a Buddha-like stance and otherworldly countenance. Martin, like Marlow, is altered, no longer the arrogant and often angry man he was before this episode, but rather someone who could speak of Sartorius "from some sort of peaceful resolution . . ." (179).

While Martin has rejected his biological father, he like Joe in *Loon Lake*, is given two surrogate fathers between whom to choose. Throughout the novel McIlvaine indicates that Martin belongs to a younger generation the narrator finds hard to understand. Part of Martin's recuperation involves his embracing McIlvaine after Sartorius has been defeated. However, his initial attraction to the scientist may be viewed as an Oedipal admiration for the man who is powerful enough to conquer his own father. In a sense Sartorius helped Martin to more completely reject his father by enabling the young man to see his father as only an impersonal subject for scientific experiments. When Martin himself is betrayed by Sartorius, he unlike Joe in *Loon Lake*, can renounce his evil surrogate parent and thus save his soul.

Despite the optimism inherent in Martin's choice and in the novel in general, Martin can never be completely released from the hold his father or Sartorius have had on him. Doctorow has said that one of the themes of *The Waterworks*, as in much of his other fiction, is the despair of being locked in history (Tokarczyk "The City" 35). Certainly throughout his fiction, especially in *The Book of Daniel* and *Welcome to Hard Times*, Doctorow has suggested that the burden of history cannot be negated. The narrator McIlvaine acknowledges this history in positing that perhaps the reason he never wrote the story was that it was part of Martin's patrimony, part of the young Pemberton's ongoing struggle toward resolution.

Martin's struggle, like the struggle against evil itself, is of course conveyed to us through McIlvaine's oral recounting of his memories.[19] Like Doctorow's other narrators, McIlvaine is a somewhat detached figure highly engaged in the act of narration itself: "I'm reporting what are now the visions of an old man. All together they compose a city, a great port and industrial city of the nineteenth century. I descend to this city and find the people I have come to know and for whose lives I fear. I tell you what I see and hear "(59). These words indicate the lifelong bachelor fits Sloterdijk's definition of the cynic as an urban figure who maintains a cutting edge in the goings-on of the metropolis. In reflecting on the writer's relation to his/her society, Budick states that writers do not/cannot break out of ideology, but may interpret or reformulate it by recasting it to make it explicit ("Sacvan Bercovitch" 81). That McIlvaine struggles for such an interpretation is suggested in the extent to which the story occupies him, "[has] grown into the physical dimensions of [his] brain" (219). In explaining his attempt to find Martin Pemberton, he underplays any fatherly or collegial concern, admitting that he "smelled a story" and was propelled. His desire to uncover the story is similar to Blue's efforts to keep the ledgers; McIlvaine's motives are apparently positivist, glorifying primary documents and newspapers as evidence of a stable universe. Yet he is simultaneously aware of the limits of his epistemology; for example, he says, "I want to keep the chronology of things but at the same time to make their pattern sensible, which means disrupting the chronology" (123). He understands the gaps between his understanding of Grimshaw's and

Martin's accounts and his rendering of them, and fears that readers may dismiss his stories as an old man's delusions.

In these concerns, he is also very similar to Blue moving away from positivism. Though a lifetime reporter, he is skeptical about recent claims for reporters' objectivity, calling it "a way of constructing an opinion for the reader without letting him know you are" (30). Significantly, he dreams of a story "the writing of which might transcend reporting" (113), indicating his desire to become a novelist or memoirist who would bear witness or as he says to give voice the events of his life and times (59). In the end, this is perhaps the story McIlvaine tells, one that conveys the importance of a historical event, but with the idiosyncrasies and gaps of an old man remembering and reflecting. Thus McIlvaine touches upon the idea that the novelist's world, unlike the historian's, is continually being created. The past has a "perpetual presentness" that is created in part by interpretation (Rosenberg 385). It is this fictionalized story—one that is filled with interpretations of Sartorius and Tweed, but unlike *The Book of Daniel*, one in which the interpretations are quite clear—that McIlvaine wants to tell. But unlike the Romantic writer, he does not have complete control over the story. Rather, he believes the story must almost tell itself in its own time: "Possibly it can't be rationalized . . . but there is some instinct that prefers the unintruded-upon meaning. That whoever tells our moral history . . . must run behind, not ahead of it. That if, in fact, there is meaning, it is not tolled out of the church bells but suffered into luminous existence" (207).[20] Such words are echoed in Sartorius's prediction that McIlvaine will not be able to write the story until the distant future, when the city is ready to hear it. (This possibility, which is reinforced by McIlvaine's own comment that there are limits to the use of words in a paper, provides another possible explanation as to why McIlvaine never publishes his exclusive.)

Unlike *The Book of Daniel* and *Loon Lake*, which tease readers' desire for closure, *The Waterworks* concludes with a romance ending of two weddings on a day when it seems the city might be forever captured, postcard-like "encased and frozen, aglitter and God-stunned" (253).[21] The almost artificial peace of this moment underscores its illusory and temporary qualities, much as the number of ellipses moderates a sense of certainty that marks the end of this novel. Sartorius and Tweed have been vanquished, but evil has not been finally defeated, and Martin has not and probably never will again be the person he once was.

While the narrator McIlvaine is, as previously mentioned, someone whom we might expect to have cynical traits, he, unlike the modern cynic, does not refuse optimism when he learns from experience and does not withdraw into mournful detachment after gaining disturbing knowledge. Rather, he seems to see Sartorius's downfall as he does the dual weddings: a precious triumphant moment to be cherished. Because of its optimism, *The Waterworks* fulfills some of the goals of the new historicism as expressed by Frank Lentricchia in "Foucault's Legacy": it offers a vision of effective action to free us from a world in which we are forced to become what we do not wish to become (241). That is, the novel suggests an alternative to cynicism and alienation. Readers of this novel not only become aware of their complicity in their society's evil, but they become aware it is possible to act against evil. Although such action may not free people from being complicit, it may mitigate the wrongdoings of which we are often unwittingly a part. If we draw upon Alan Wilde's theory of postmodern midfiction, we can see that *The Waterworks* in particular and Doctorow's work in general often exemplifies a postmodern vision, "If, as I have several times suggested, the defining features of modernism is [sic] its ironic vision of disconnection and disjunction, postmodernism, more radical in its perceptions, derives instead from a vision of randomness, multiplicity, and contingency; in short, a world in need of mending is superseded by one beyond repair" ("Horizons" 131).[22] But if the world is beyond repair, the community is not, and individual local actions are effective, if limited, against the powerful collusion of wealth, science, and government. In Foucauldian terms, *The Waterworks* is about truth and power; in their use of reportorial and police skills, Donne and McIlvaine produce truth that has the effect of producing power for agency. *The Waterworks*, like *The Book of Daniel*, has similarities to the detective novel, but while in *The Book of Daniel* the truth is "beyond reclamation" (360), in *The Waterworks* a truth that has ramifications for many lives is discovered. Moreover, all truths are not equal. Sartorius's relentless search for "scientific truth" is condemned. Like *The Book of Daniel* and Marxist critics such as Terry Eagleton,[23] *The Waterworks* indicates there are objectively verifiable categories.

The possibility of praxis was first suggested in the novella *Lives of the Poets* with Jonathan's decision to hide refugees and teach a young boy to type/write, a scenario some critics faulted as unbelievable. The ending of *The Waterworks*, in contrast, falls within the romance tradition and is thus not subject to the same tests of veracity. As in all romances, there are realistic elements, such as Sartorius's commitment to an asylum and Boss Tweed's fall. These elements represent a serious strike against injustice. The novel's optimism is all the more noteworthy given its gritty, historically-based representations of the nineteenth century city as ruthless and alienating. Indeed, *The Waterworks* implies the possibility and necessity of intervention against both harsh urban conditions and "nature's course," that is, survival of the fittest.[24] The novel implies that it is possible to go beyond merely recognizing one's complicity in evil to taking action that will mitigate, although never negate, evil. Like the newspaper's seven columns, the novel finally suggests that human lives are interconnected and can positively affect one another. For these reasons, the possibility of praxis in *The Waterworks* is more convincing and aesthetically satisfying than in *Lives of the Poets* with its image of the cautious writer sheltering illegal aliens or in *Ragtime* with its sentimental descriptions of the conception of *The Little Rascals*. *The Waterworks* stands as a fine development in Doctorow's work and a strong addition to the evolving American political novel.

Notes

1. See, for example, Stephen Fender,

2. For a discussion of Doctorow's views of the 1870s see "The Nineteenth New York."

3. I question Harter and Thompson's interpretation of *Ragtime* and point to Tateh, who not only achieves financial success, but also falls in love and marries. Tateh's decisions to abandon radical politics and fine art are problematic, but might represent an attempt to fulfill dreams within the American mainstream rather than an abandonment of them.

4. See Mandel's *Delightful Murder* for a discussion of this point. For treatment of contemporary detective novels, see Douglas Keesey "The Ideology of Detection."

5. See Brook Thomas "The New Historicism" and Linda Hutcheon *The Politics of Postmodernism*.

6. Ted Solataroff "Of Melville, Poe, and Doctorow" argues that *The Waterworks* ought not to be read as a cautionary tale in part because Doctorow's interests are metaphysical as well as political. While I agree, and have written about, dimensions of Doctorow's interest in the nature of evil that go beyond its political and social manifestations, I do not see reading this novel as a cautionary tale as necessarily erasing the possibility of metaphysical readings.

7. In conversation Doctorow said that he had considered naming his novel for the newspaper's seven columns, which to me suggests the newspaper layout is a governing metaphor for Doctorow.

8. In addition to the often-commented upon influence of American novelists, Conrad's *Heart of Darkness* echoes throughout the work. There is the motif of discovering evil and being altered by it, as well as the *doppelanger* theme. Certainly Conrad's influence has marked Doctorow's earlier work, especially in *Loon Lake*, in which Joe's surname might suggest that he, like Conrad, had many identities (Harter and Thompson 85). For discussions of affinities with nineteenth-century American writers, see in particular Solataroff and Michelle M. Tokarczyk reviews of *The Waterworks*.

9. *The Waterworks*, although generally praised, was not received as enthusiastically as *Billy Bathgate*. Simon Schama favored the book, while noting some prose excesses. Ted Solataroff ranked the novel among America's greats, while Merle Rubin found the story ultimately disappointing, and Luc Sante found the book filled with contradictions.

10. A state of living in death may be viewed as particular to modern society. One need only consider the debates about doctor-assisted suicide for the terminally ill, living wills to ensure people's comatose bodies are not kept breathing by artificial means, and so forth.

11 I disagree with Sante's analysis. Sartorius puts children in harm's way; whether he directly harms them or not evades the moral question, especially in the context of Doctorow's fiction in which nurturance is so crucial.

12 The generation of the 1960s refers to those in late adolescence or early adulthood during this period.

13 See "The Bomb Lives!," "Orwell's *1984*," "The Bomb Culture: It's a Cold World Out There, Class of 1983," and "Mythologizing the Bomb."

14 I had mentioned controversies over procedures such as surrogate motherhood and in vitro fertilization.

15 Doctorow has said that as a novelist he tries to make the invisible visible. Since McIlvaine does the same thing, he could easily be viewed as another of Doctorow's writer-narrators.

16 In addition to Turner's *The Frontier in American History*, see Appleby et al. 118, for a discussion on this point.

17 In considering McIlvaine's relative admiration for village society, one thinks of Hillary Rodham Clinton's book advocating societal rather than only familial responsibility for children, *It Takes a Village: And Other Lessons Children Teach Us*.

18 One might read the image of Augustus dancing in a Bakhtinian fashion as contributing to carnivalesque elements in the novel. In addition to Bakhtin, *The Dialogic Imagination*, see La Capra, *Rethinking Intellectual History*.

19 In his interview with me, Doctorow said he envisioned a stenographer taking down the account (36).

20 The last sentence certainly alludes to "For Whom the Bell Tolls" and further suggests the personage of Edmund Donne is meant to evoke this poem.

21 See Hutcheon *Politics* for a discussion of closure in *The Book of Daniel*.

22 For a discussion of this point and many other implications of postmodernism that relate to my study of Doctorow's work see Hans Bertens, "The Postmodern *Weltanschauung* and Its Relation to Modernism."

23 See *Illusions* for a discussion of this point.

24 In the context of the 1980s it is possible to see "nature's course" as the free market that many conservatives believe should be largely unregulated.

Afterword

In each of his books, Doctorow has reconfigured the genre of the American political novel. His depiction of important historical periods and issues digs at the nation's myths, such as the nature of the frontier and the opportunity for upward mobility. In his writing he has moved beyond the isolated privatist mindset he sees as characteristic of his generation, and done so in a way that fulfills goals he expressed in an interview years ago as he pondered ". . . is there some kind of new aesthetic possible that does not undermine aesthetic rigor? A poetics of engagement" (Trenner 48). This new poetics of engagement, I have implied, should make us recognize our complicity. That is, it should both "complicate" issues often sketched in broad ideological strokes and enable us to see ourselves as "accomplices" in our society's problems. As I complete this book, the United States has just concluded, what could more appropriately than the Harry K. Thaw or even the Rosenberg trial, be called the trial of the century. The United States Congress deliberated on two counts of impeachment, deciding whether President Clinton had committed crimes serious enough to warrant his removal from office. It determined he did not, and United States citizens are on the whole relieved that the process is over. Still, the Clinton scandal has taken a sizable chunk of the news since January of 1998 when the story broke, and is likely to be analyzed for some time. In some respects, this is an the kind of episode one critic identifies as a catalyst for Doctorow's writing: It is a moment of historical change demanding imaginative recreation (Claridge 11). In essence, it is a charged period. Consistently, Doctorow's novelistic depictions of such periods and events heighten reader sensitivity to the issues he sees as crucial—such as the nature of truth, the power of history, and the need for community. As readers attuned to our country's myths as well as to our own part in maintaining them, we might be able to take the insights learned from Doctorow's fiction and use them to shed light on contemporary events. Hence, at this odd, though important, juncture in American history, it seems appropriate to reflect on how Doctorow's work as good political literature might illuminate a particular political episode, the Clinton scandal.

From *Welcome to Hard Times* through *The Waterworks* Doctorow's work has grappled with the tensions between individual self-interest and communal welfare. His first novel depicts a town's demise because its citizens could not put the community good ahead of their own. *Ragtime* depicts the close proximity of the haves and the have nots and the resulting tensions. *The Waterworks* features a reporter who jeopardizes his job to locate a missing colleague, and ultimately save his city from unscrupulous people. Perhaps as important, Doctorow's most recent novel portrays McIlvaine's difficult decision not to publish his breaking story of Sartorius's inhumane experiments because he feared the public belief in goodness and decency would be undermined by the news.

Beneath the various public responses to the Clinton scandal is, I think, a perception that authorities are self-absorbed, whether in personal gain or in party politics, and unable to consider the national welfare. Unlike McIlvaine, the American media today seem concerned only with "breaking stories" without regard for how these stories might affect the public good. The nation's relative prosperity has likely muted the effects of the Clinton scandal, but one wonders if a comparison could be made with *Welcome to Hard Times*; that is, might the nation's current prosperity ultimately be undermined by people's inability to pull together, to consider community welfare rather than just individual pleasure or gain. In commenting on Doctorow's views of history and democracy expressed especially in *The Waterworks*, Mary P. Ryan says, "Indeed, Doctorow's jaundiced view of democracy is not too far off the mark of middle-class opinion in New York City in 1871, when many educated men and women lost faith in the political process" (325). The same conclusion might be reached of American citizens today, and it is as troubling as it was in 1871.

Part of the difficulty, of course, in balancing community welfare with personal gain is in knowing where to draw the boundaries between private and public life, boundaries that are perhaps especially fluid for a nation begun in revolution, distrustful of government, and admiring the rugged individual. *The Book of Daniel* shows how in a time of national postwar hysteria brought on by the end of World War II and the quickly escalating Cold War, individual rights were compromised through repressive legislation and blacklisting. According to Milan Kundera, quintessential totalitarian societies represented in Kafka's novels (and I have argued at times in Doctorow's) blur the distinction between private and public. Intimacy and secrets are not only forbidden, but also made impossible. The state's nature is to destroy the distinction between private and public; in Kundera's words, "you'll be taken unawares in your bed." One reason that the public is not more outraged by Clinton's transgressions is, perhaps, that it is appalled by the apparent disregard for private life and personal loyalty suggested by Linda Tripp's surreptitious taping of a friend's confidences and the Independent Prosecutor's badgering of Monica Lewinsky's mother to give information that might incriminate her daughter. These scenarios are eerily reminiscent of the fictional prosecution and execution of Rochelle Isaacson in an attempt to break Paul Isaacson's silence, and, some would maintain, the prosecution of Ethel Rosenberg in an attempt to pressure her husband into confession. True, it may be argued that Kenneth Starr seized upon the possibility of catching Clinton in perjury to attain the prosecution he first tried to achieve through investigations into Whitewater. While this fact is undoubtedly true, I argue that the highly explicit nature of the *Starr Report*, which goes well beyond the imperative to establish a sexual relationship between President Clinton and Monica Lewinsky, raises as many questions about Starr's motives as it does about Clinton's behavior. Kenneth Starr seems to be operating on a "mythic level"; that is, to him and those who share his ideology, it is not the president's affair itself that is crucial, but rather what this affair and the public's relatively laissez-faire attitude about it suggests about American values, especially family values. As Doctorow himself put it, "All you need is a sinner and a suit. If you happen to be a prosecutor with a righteous bent, you can transform what morally offends you into a criminal offense" ("Talk" 29).

While the virulent anti-communism depicted in *The Book of Daniel* has clear historical and social causes, the root of the current focus on the president's sexual conduct is less clear. It might be related to anxiety about "family values," an unease with this country's shifting social mores and expanding definition of what constitutes a family, with the increased number of blended families resembling those in *Ragtime, The Book of Daniel*, and *Welcome to Hard Times*. It might be a sense of foreboding at the impending millennium, a fear that is perhaps inherent in people facing uncertainty, as *Welcome to Hard Times, The Book of Daniel*, and *Big as Life* suggest. Whatever the cause, Daniel's troubling question of his parents' legal case might be applied here: if the law cannot protect individual freedom during politically charged times, then what protection does the law actually offer?

Often the first question to be asked in a crisis is what are its short- and long-term causes. Repeatedly, Doctorow's novels imply that history and origins are crucial in determining the evolution of both individuals and societies. As Henry Claridge argues, the self-reliant, autonomous individual is not plausible for Doctorow, for characters are historically determined and identity is socially constructed (11). For many Doctorow characters, these identities are constructed along class lines. Undoubtedly, one factor that colors response to President Clinton is his somewhat unconventional background for a President. Arthur Miller refers to Toni Morrison's description of Clinton as ". . . our first black President, the first to come from the broken home, the alcoholic mother, the under-the-bridge shadows of our ranking systems" (A31). Like Billy Bathgate and a number of American protagonists such as Huck Finn, Clinton was a fatherless boy.[1] The young Bill Clinton always dreamed of being president; a frequent, if far-fetched, dream for many American children; but this dream is especially unattainable for a working-class youth. Hence, Clinton seems to embody so many of the questions about America's social hierarchy expressed in Doctorow's work: the importance of class origins, the promise and accompanying pitfalls of upward mobility. He, like Billy Bathgate, was brought up by a mother struggling to provide for him. Like many Doctorow characters, he is someone whom society neglected to nurture.

Bill Clinton's predicament and character are but a small part of the political lens that Doctorow's fiction, like the inverted mirror in *Billy Bathgate*, represents. His books' accurate representation of contemporary political and social attitudes indicates not only that Doctorow has keen perceptions but also, more importantly, that he is able to artistically depict and complicate these conflicts. In much contemporary political discourse a black and white interpretation of events dominates. Ideologues' claims of unfiltered access to truth make Doctorow's skepticism of truth claims for history particularly noteworthy. Often we are told there is one way to interpret events, yet the information that we have on current issues in some ways resembles the various stories told in *World's Fair* or like the fragmented, remembered tale that is *The Waterworks*. To begin to understand, we must, like Daniel, filter through the various truths, to the multiplicity of voices bearing witness to events.

Writers such as Arthur Miller and Toni Morrison, as well as Doctorow himself, have commented on the Clinton sex scandal perhaps because they want to "bear witness" to what is happening in their society. Later, some authors probably will imaginatively render this episode. In doing so they would likely acknowledge that although we know a great deal about the president's affair with Monica Lewinsky, there are many interpretations of the episode and many views as to how much weight to put upon such a transgression. Some might suggest that there is an element of Sherwood Anderson's grotesque in the current situation, that regardless of the accurate perception that the president lapsed in having an affair, the independent prosecutor "[took] one of the truths to himself, called it his truth, and tried to live his life by it." As a result, "he became a grotesque and the truth became a lie" (4–5). To avoid the grotesque, one must recognize that one truth exists along with many others, that each truth must be acknowledged and considered. This is the value of the postmodern elements in Doctorow's work expressed most explicitly in the essay "False Documents" and subtly suggested in the complexities of characters such as Daniel Isaacson or Joe Korzeniowski.

Despite the dangers of reaching authoritarian, "grotesque," claims for Truth we can still make some claims to limited local truth. For example, there is no debate that the president did have an affair with Ms. Lewinsky and that he did lie. What is crucial is that people acknowledge both the variety of interpretation and the necessity of finding and asserting limited truths. Variety does not lead to indeterminacy. If, as Fredric Jameson claims, we are inside the culture of postmodernism to the point where either easy repudiation or celebration is impossible (*Postmodernism* 62), it becomes increasingly necessary to find ways to balance the insights of this movement with the possibility of affirming local truths. Doctorow's fiction does so by utilizing postmodern techniques to highlight what cannot be known and, sometimes surprisingly, underscore what can be. Throughout his books there are illustrations of what people can and do know juxtaposed with what they may not. Rochelle surmises the outcome of her trial while Daniel cannot determine his parents' guilt or innocence. The Bad Man's harm is obvious, but his motivations are hidden. Anti-Semitism is a palpable threat in *World's Fair*. While Doctorow's novels recognize the "absolute multiplicity" of voices, they also recognize that some voices will resonate more than others. In the words of Alan Wilde in "Strange Displacements . . .", reality is presented as "neither objectively knowable nor as totally opaque. Assent is limited, local, and qualified, but assent is possible" (182). These are the elements of successful midfiction that characterize Doctorow's work and may characterize an informed political outlook after reading his work.

As I have argued, it is the tension between postmodern indeterminacy and the need to assert truths, as well as the tension between a desire to write socially relevant work and a desire to retain some artistic detachment, that has fueled Doctorow's imagination. This desire to represent society while maintaining some detachment from it takes many forms. Currently the musical based on *Ragtime* is enjoying great popularity and indeed successfully conveying the novel's stories in a form resembling that book's pace and prose style. During a panel discussion, "The Making of *Ragtime*," Doctorow noted its success, especially compared with the film *Ragtime*.[2] Doctorow speculated that the medium is ill-suited to the sweeping romance.[3] Film-viewers, perhaps, have a sense of actually being in the location of the film, even if that location were to be, say, in outer space; while theater-goers are more able to suspend disbelief because the medium is inherently less realistic. While his remarks are certainly debatable, they reflect an artist's continual search to find new ways to express ideas in an aesthetically pleasing and challenging manner. Subtly, they echo Doctorow's concern that art should reflect social issues and that politics should belong to the people. For Doctorow, this has often meant experimental, postmodern techniques coupled with a strong plot line. His collaboration with filmmakers and drama producers further indicates his continuing efforts to negotiate with popular culture, as his protagonist Edgar in *World's Fair* does. As this novel suggests, commodification is an issue and a danger for an artist, yet an artist who wants to comment on his age will find it necessary to engage the popular media, even if he/she, like many intellectuals is suspicious of them.[4] The effort to balance desire for a wide audience with commitment to excellent work is another feature of the skeptical commitment that I see as central to Doctorow's philosophy. This commitment involves realizing, as Tateh did, that in a capitalist society an artist who wants to communicate a vision must find a medium that is accessible to the populace and appropriate to his art. And while doing so, he/she must take care that the resultant art does not placate the public, but rather disturb them into recognizing their complicity. If, as Barbara Foley argues, the problem with the political fiction of the 1930s was that it was not radical enough, we might surmise that the Depression-era proletarian novel was too afraid of experimentation, too afraid of breaking boundaries. These are risks Doctorow continually takes.

The Waterworks depicts McIlvaine successfully investigating an unscrupulous scientist supported by wealthy men and bringing this man to justice. It also represents the power and corruption of Boss Tweed and his eventual demise. Today, it seems people are hungry for a hero like McIlvaine: one who will search out truth (not Truth) and successfully challenge the corrupt. While artists' solitary natures often make it unlikely they will be activists, they may be able to stimulate others to be. They may be the ones who represent the complexities of our contemporary problems, especially some that we are most reluctant to face, such as class inequities whose continuance violates the American ideology of equal opportunity and meritocracy. The first step may be for some artists to "bear witness" by acknowledging and imaginatively representing our lives and thus activate our sense of complicity in our society. Repeatedly, Doctorow has taken this step. As more and more writers do so—and the names of Maxine Hong Kingston, Barbara Kingsolver, and Toni Morrison come to mind—they may create not only an imaginative rendering of our situation, but also an imaginative alternative to it. The genre of American political fiction will thus continue to develop and expand in unforeseen ways.

In his seminal essay "False Documents," Doctorow distinguishes between two kinds of power, the power of the regime and the power of freedom. The power of regime is the modern sensibility that could be defined as realism. In Doctorow's definition, realism is something akin to being realistic and its language reflects, "the business of getting on and producing for ourselves what we construe as satisfaction of our needs—and doing it with the standards of measure, market studies, contracts . . . headlines" (in Trenner 17). In opposition, the regime of freedom has "a regime of language that derives its strength from what we are supposed to be and a language of freedom whose power consists in what we threaten to become" (in Trenner 17). This is the language of the carnies in *Loon Lake*, and Billy Bathgate's mother, voices with what Foucault calls "subjugated" or discredited knowledge. It is the language of Jonathan pondering his alienation as a white middle-aged author. It is the language of McIlvaine pondering a moment of freedom on his friends' wedding day. Ultimately, it is the artist's language that not only reveals what we are, but peels away layers of myths and distorted truths to show how we evolved and, sometimes, offer a vision of how we might be different. Successfully and imaginatively using this language might be the first act of praxis.

Notes

1. See Minako Baba for a discussion of this point.
2. The film was generally faulted for its overemphasis on the Coalhouse Walker subplot, as well as its failure to capture the period's history. See, for example, Vincent Canby "Film *Ragtime*," Pauline Kael, "The Current Cinema," and Barbara Quart "*Ragtime* Without a Melody."
3. As, I would argue, the conventions of realism with its attendant focus on character development would be unsuitable for this novel.
4. Doctorow has said that he was somewhat reluctant to collaborate on the musical because he never had an affinity for the genre.

Works Cited

Alter, Robert. "The American Political Novel." *The New York Times Book Review* 10 August 1980: 3.

Anderson, Sherwood. *Winesburg, Ohio*. New York: Random House, 1947. Rpt 1919.

Appleby, Joyce, et al. *Telling the Truth about History*. New York: W. W. Norton, 1994.

Arnold, Marilyn. "History as Fate in E. L. Doctorow's Tale of a Midwestern Town." Trenner, 207–16.

Atwood, Margaret. "E. L. Doctorow: Writing by His Own Rules." *Book World* 10 28 Sept. 1980: 1+.

Baba, Minako. "The Young Gangster as Mythic Hero in E. L. Doctorow's *Billy Bathgate*." *MELUS* 18 (summer 1993): 33–46.

Bakhtin, M. M. *The Dialogic Imagination: Four Essays*. Trans. Caryl Emerson and Michael Holquist, ed. Michael Holquist. Austin: U of Texas P, 1981.

Barthes, Roland, "Myth Today," in *Mythologies*. Trans. Annette Lanvers. New York: Farrar, Strauss & Giroux, 1972.

Bauman, Zygmunt. "Postmodernity, or Living with Ambivalence." Natoli and Hutcheon 9–24.

Bawer, Bruce. "The Human Dimension." *Nation* 17 (Nov. 1984): 515–19.

Bell, Daniel. *The End of Ideology: On the Exhaustion of Political Ideas in the Fifties*. New York: Free P, 1960.

Bell, Pearl K. "Guilt on Trial." *New Leader* 28 (June 1971): 17–19.

———. "Singing the Same Old Song," *Commentary* 70 (Oct. 1980): 70–73.

Berryman, Charles. "*Ragtime* in Retrospect." *South Atlantic Quarterly* 81 (winter 1982): 30–42.

Bertens, Hans. "The Postmodern *Weltanschauung* and its Relation to Modernism: An Introductory Survey." Natoli and Hutcheon 25–70.

Bevilacqua, Winifred Farrant "Narration and History in E. L. Doctorow." *Studies in Scandinavia* 22 (1990): 94–106.

"Birth of the Blues." Rev. of *Ragtime. Economist* 24 Jan. 1976: 108.

Bluestein, Gene. "Time Capsule." *Progressive* 50 (Mar. 1986): 42–43.

Bourdieu, Pierre. *Distinction: A Social Critique of the Judgment of Taste*. Trans. Richard Nice. Cambridge, MA: Routledge & Kegan, 1984.

Brooks, Cleanth. *The Well-Wrought Urn*. New York: Reynolds & Hitchcock, 1947.

Budick, Emily Miller. *Fiction and Historical Consciousness: The American Romance Tradition*. New Haven: Yale UP, 1989.

———. "Sacvan Bercovitch, Stanley Cavell, and the Romance Theory of American Fiction." *PMLA* 107 (Jan 1992): 78–91.

Burgess, Anthony. "Doctorow's 'Hit' Is a Miss." *Saturday Review* 7 (Sept. 1980): 66–67.

Caesar, Terry P. "Motherhood and Postmodernism." *American Literary History* 17 (spring 1995): 120–40.

Campbell, Josie. "Coalhouse Walker and the Model T Ford: Legerdemain in *Ragtime*." *Journal of Popular Culture* 13 (fall 1979): 302–9.

Canby, Vincent. "Film *Ragtime* Evokes Real and Fictional Pasts." *The New York Times* 20 Nov 1981: C10.

Cantinella, Joseph. Rev. of *The Book of Daniel. Saturday Review* 17 July 1971: 32+.

Cantor, Jay. *The Space Between: Literature and Politics*. Baltimore: Johns Hopkins UP, 1981.

Chaloupka, William. "Cynical Nature: Politics and Culture after the Demise of the Natural." *Alternatives* 18 (spring 1993): 141–69.

Chase, Richard Volney. *The American Novel and Its Tradition*. Garden City, NY: Doubleday, 1957.

Claridge, Henry. "Writing on the Margins: E. L. Doctorow and American History." *The New American Writing: Essays in American Literature Since 1970*. Graham Clarke, Ed. New York: St. Martin's P, 1990: 9–28.

Clayton, John. "Radical Jewish Humanism: The Vision of E. L. Doctorow" Trenner 109–19.

Clerc, Charles. "Dutch Schultz's Last Words Revisited." *Journal of Modern Literature* 18 (fall 1993): 463–65.

Clinton, Hillary Rodham. *It Takes a Village: And Other Lessons Children Teach Us*. New York: Simon & Schuster, 1995.

Coale, Samuel Chase. *In Hawthorne's Shadow: The American Romance from Melville to Mailer*. Lexington: UP of Kentucky, 1985.

Coiner, Constance. *Better Red: The Writing and Resistance of Tillie Olsen and Meridel Le Seuer*. Urbana: U of Illinois P, 1995.

Collingwood, R. G. *Essays in the Philosophy of History*. Ed. William Debbins. Austin: UP of Texas, 1965.

Cook, Blanche Wiesen. "The Rosenberg Case and the Crimes of a Century." Garber and Walkowitz 23-29.

Cooper, Barbara. "The Artist as Historian in the Novels of E.L. Doctorow." *The Emporia State Research Studies* 29 (fall 1980).

Crane, Stephen. *The Responsibilities of the Novelist and Other Essays*. New York: Doubleday, 1903.

Crews, Frederick. "The New Americanists." *The New York Review of Books* 24 Sept. 1992: 32-34.

Dekker, George. *The American Historical Romance*. Cambridge: Cambridge UP, 1987.

———. "Once More: Hawthorne and the Geneology of the American Romance." *ESQ: A Journal of the American Renaissance* 35 (1989): 69-83.

Dickstein, Morris. "Depression Culture: The Dream of Mobility." Mullen and Linkon 225-41.

Diedrich, Maria. "E. L. Doctorow's Coalhouse Walker: Fact in Fiction." Friedl and Schulz 113-23.

Doctorow, E. L. "The Beliefs of Writers" *Jack London* 103-16.

———. "The Bomb Culture: It's a Cold World Out There, Class of 1983." *Nation* 237 2 July 1983: 6-7.

———. "The Bomb Lives!" *Playboy* 21 (March 1974): 114+.

———. "The Character of Presidents" *Jack London* 91-102.

———. "False Documents" Trenner 16-27 (rpt. in *Jack London* 149-64).

———. "For the Artist's Sake." Trenner 13-15.

———. "A Gangsterdom of the Spirit" *Nation* 2 Oct 1989: 229-54 (rpt. as "Commencement" in *Jack London* 81-90).

———. *Jack London, Hemingway, and the Constitution: Selected Essays*. New York: Random House, 1993.

———. "Mythologizing the Bomb." *Nation* 4-21 Aug 1995: 149+.

———. "The Nineteenth New York." *Jack London* 139-47.

———. "An Open Letter to the President." *Nation* 7-14 Jan 1991: 1+.

———. "Orwell's 1984." *Jack London* 51-69.

———. "Politics and the Mode of Fiction" Trenner 48–56.

———. "Ronald Reagan" *Jack London* 71–80.

———. "The Songs of Billy Bathgate." *New American Review 2* (1968): 54–69.

———. "Talk of the Town." *The New Yorker* 12 Oct 1998: 29–30.

Eagleton, Terry. *The Illusions of Postmodernism*. Oxford: Basil Blackwell, 1996.

Eckstein, Barbara J. *The Language of Fiction: Reading Politics as Paradox*. Philadelphia: U Penn P, 1990.

Eder, Richard. "Siege Perilous in the Court of Dutch Schultz." *Los Angeles Times Book Review* 5 Mar 1989: 3.

Emblidge, David. "Marching Backwards into the Future: Progress as Illusion in Doctorow's Novels." *Southwest Review* 62 (autumn 1977): 397–409.

Empson, William. *Seven Types of Ambiguity*. 3rd ed. London: Chatto & Windus, 1953.

Engall, John. "Hawthorne and Two Types of American Romance." *South Atlantic Review* 57 (Jan. 1992): 33–51.

Estrin, Barbara L. "Surviving McCarthyism: E.L. Doctorow's *The Book of Daniel*" Trenner 196–206.

Fender, Stephen. "The Novelist as Liar." *Times Literary Supplement* 27 May 1994: 21.

Foley, Barbara. *Radical Representations: Politics and Form in U.S. Proletarian Fiction, 1929–1941*. Durham: Duke UP, 1993.

Foucault, Michel. "Lecture 1: 7 January 1976." *Power/Knowledge: Selected Interviews and Other Writings*. Ed. Colin Gordon. New York: Pantheon, 1980: 78–92.

Fowler, Douglas. *Understanding E. L. Doctorow*. Columbia: U of South Carolina P, 1992.

Freedman, Melvin. "Boy in Gangland." *Progressive* 53 (Aug. 1989): 39.

Fremont-Smith, Eliot. "*Ragtime* Jackpot: How to Make a Million Bucks in Just One Day." *Village Voice* 25 Aug. 1975: 35–36.

Friedl, Herwig. "Power and Degradation: Patterns of Historical Consciousness in the Novels of E. L. Doctorow." Friedl & Schulz 19–44.

Friedl, Herwig and Dieter Schulz, eds. *E. L. Doctorow: A Democracy of Perception*. Essen, Germany: Blaue Eule, 1988.

Friedman, Ellen G. "Where Are the Missing Contents? (Post)Modernism, Gender, and the Canon." *PMLA* 108 (March 1993): 240–52.

Frietag, Michael. Insert interview in Tyler, Anne "American Boy": 46.

Garber, Marjorie and Rebecca L. Walkowitz, eds. *Secret Agents: The Rosenberg Case, McCarthyism, and the Fifties*. New York: Routledge, 1995.

Gentry, Marshall Bruce. "*Ragtime* as Auto Biography." *Kansas Quarterly* 21 (Fall 1989): 105–12.

———. "'Ventriloquists' Conversations: The Struggle for Gender Dialogue in E.L. Doctorow and Phillip Roth." *Contemporary Literature* 34 (fall 1993): 512–37.

Glueck, Grace. "A Solid Gold Jubilee for Random House." *The New York Times* 10 Aug 1975: 10.

Gore, George. "Read 'Em Cowboy." *The American Scholar* 50 (summer 1981): 389–400.

Graeber, Laurel. Insert in Simon Schama, "New York, Gaslight Necropolis": 31.

Graff, Gerald. "Co-Optation." Veeser 168–81.

Gross, David S. "Tales of Obscene Power: Money and Culture, Modernism and History in the Fiction of E.L. Doctorow." Trenner 120–50.

Gulenson, Eleanor, M.D. "The Effect of Paternal Deprivation on the Capacity to Moderate Aggression." *New Literary History* 26 (spring 1995): 443–54.

Hardy, J. P. Introduction. *Johnson's Lives of the Poets: A Selection*. By Samuel Johnson, Ed. J. P. Hardy. Oxford: Clarendon P., 1971.

Harpham, Geoffrey Galt. "E. L. Doctorow and the Technology of Narrative." *PMLA* 100 (Jan. 1985): 81–95.

Harris, Calvin E. "Alienation as a Multidimensional Theme in Political Fiction." *Nature, Society, and Thought* 1 (fall 1987): 37–46.

Harter, Carol and James R. Thompson, *E. L. Doctorow*. Boston: Twayne, 1990.

Hartman, Joan E. "The Philosophical Bases of Literary Criticism." *New Literary History* 19 (autumn 1987): 105–16.

Henry, Matthew A. "Problematized Narratives: History as Fiction in E. L. Doctorow's *Billy Bathgate*." *Critique* 39 (fall 1997): 32–40.

Hilfer, Tony. *The Crime Novel: A Deviant Genre*. Austin: UP of Texas, 1990.

Hutcheon, Linda. "Beginning to Theorize the Postmodernism." Natoli and Hutcheon 243–72.

———. "Historiographic Metafiction." O'Donnell and Davis 3–4.

———. *The Politics of Postmodernism*. London: Routledge, 1989.

Iannone, Carol. "E.L. Doctorow's 'Jewish' Radicalism." *Commentary* 81 (March 1986): 53–56.

Jameson, Fredric. *The Political Unconscious: Narrative as Socially Symbolic Act*. Ithaca: Cornell UP, 1981.

———. *Postmodernism, or the Cultural Logic of Late Capitalism*. Durham: Duke UP, 1991.

Johnson, Diane. "Waiting for Righty." *New York Review of Books.* 6 Nov 1980: 18–20.

Kael, Pauline. "The Current Cinema." *The New Yorker* 23 Nov 1981: 176–85.

Kammen, Michael. "The Problem of American Exceptionalism: A Reconsideration." *American Quarterly* 45 (March 1993): 1–43.

Kaverny, Roz. "Dim Lights, Big City." *New Statesmen and Society.* 17 June 1994: 40

Keesey, Douglas. "The Ideology of Detection in Pynchon and DeLillo." *Pynchon Notes* 32–33 (spring-fall 1993): 44–59.

Kermode, Frank. "Those Were the Days." *New Review* 2 (1976): 57–59.

King, Richard. "Two Lights That Failed." *Virginia Quarterly Review* 57 (spring 1981): 341–50.

Kleist, Heinreich von. *The Marquise of O and Other Stories.* Trans and intro. David Luke & Nigel Reeves. rpt 1980, 1982. Middlesex, England: Penguin, 1978. "Michael Kohlhaas" 114–213.

Knorr, Walter K. "Doctorow and Kleist: 'Kohlhaas in Ragtime.'" *Modern Fiction Studies* 22 (summer 1976): 224–27.

Koenig, Rhoda. "Billy the Kid." *New York* 20 Feb. 1989: 63–64.

———. Rev. of *World's Fair. New York* 18 25 Nov. 1985: 96–97.

Kolodny, Annette. *The Land before Her: Fantasy and Experience of the American Frontier.* Chapel Hill: U of North Carolina P, 1984.

———. *The Lay of the Land: Metaphor as Experience and History in American Life and Letters.* Chapel Hill: U of North Carolina P, 1975.

———. "Letting Go of Our Grand Obsessions: Notes toward a New History of the American Frontiers." *American Literature* 64 (March 1992): 2–18.

Kramer, Hilton. "Political Romance." *Commentary* 80 (Oct. 1975): 76–80.

Kundera, Milan. "Somewhere Behind." *The Art of the Novel.* New York: Grove P, 1986: 97–117.

La Capra, Dominick. *Rethinking Intellectual History: Texts, Contexts, Language.* Ithaca: Cornell UP, 1983.

Lehan, Richard. "Urban Signs and Urban Literature: Literary Form and Historical Process." *Studies in Historical Change.* Ralph Cohen Ed. Charlottesville: U of Virginia P, 1992: 230–45.

Lehmann-Haupt, Christopher. "No Handwriting on the Wall." *The New York Times.* 8 July 1975: 29.

Lentricchia, Frank. *Criticism and Social Change.* Chicago: U of Chicago P, 1986.

———. "Foucault's Legacy." Veeser 231–42.

Leonard, John. "Bye, Bye Billy." *Nation* 3 April 1989: 454–56.

Levine, Paul. *E. L. Doctorow*. London: Methuen, 1985.

———. "The Writer as Independent Witness." Trenner 57–69.

———. "E. L. Doctorow: The Writer as Survivor." Friedl and Schulz 61–73.

Lewis, R. W. B. *The American Adam: Innocence, Tragedy, and Tradition in the Nineteenth Century*. Chicago: U of Chicago P, 1955.

Li'l Monster et al. "When You're a Crip (or a Blood): Gang Life in Los Angeles." *Harpers* (Mar. 1989): 51–59.

Lipsitz, George. "Swing Low, Sweet Cadillac: White Supremacy, Antiblack Racism, and the New Historicism." *American Literary History* 7 (winter 1995): 700–25.

Lubove, Roy. *The Progressives and the Slums: Tenement House Reform in New York City, 1890–1917*. Pittsburgh: UP of Pittsburgh, 1962.

"The Making of *Ragtime*." Panel discussion with E. L. Doctorow, Garth H. Drabinsky, and Frank Galati. John Lahr, moderator. 92 St. Y Tisch Center for the Arts, 9 Mar.1998.

Maloff, Saul. "The American Dream in Fragments." *Commonweal* 7 Nov 1980: 627–30.

Mandel, Ernest. *Delightful Murder: A Social History of the Crime Novel*. Minneapolis: UP of Minnesota, 1984.

McCaffery, Larry. "A Spirit of Transgression." Trenner 31–47.

McCormick, Richard. *From Realignment to Reform: Political Change in New York State, 1893–1910*. New York: Ithaca P, 1981.

McHale, Brian. *Postmodernist Fiction*. New York: Methuen, 1987.

McInerney, James. "Author, Author: An Interview with Doctorow." *Vogue* 174 (Nov 1984): 152–55.

McWilliams, John. "The Rationale for 'The American Romance.'" Boundary 2 17 (spring 1990): 71–82.

Meindl, Dieter. *American Fiction and the Metaphysics of the Grotesque*. Columbia: U of Missouri P, 1996.

Miller, Arthur. "Salem Revisited." *The New York Times*. 15 Oct.1998: A31.

Milton, John R. *The Novel of the American West*. Lincoln: U of Nebraska P, 1980.

Morris, Christopher. "'Fiction Is a System of Knowledge': An Interview with E. L. Doctorow." *Michigan Quarterly Review* 30 (summer 1991): 439–56.

———. *Models of Misrepresentation: On the Fiction of E. L. Doctorow.* Jackson: U of Mississippi P, 1991.

Mullen, Bill and Sherry Linkon, eds. *Radical Revisions: Rereading 1930s Culture.* Urbana: U of Illinois P, 1996.

Natoli, Joseph and Linda Hutcheon, eds. *A Postmodern Reader.* Albany: SUNY P, 1993.

Nelson, Joyce. "TV, the Bomb, and the Body: Other Cold War Secrets." Garber and Walkowitz 31–45.

Neumeyer, Peter F. "E. L. Doctorow, Kleist, and the Ascendency of Things." *CEA Critic* 39 (May 1977): 17–21

Newman, Katherine. "An Ethnic Literary Scholar Views American Literature." *MELUS* 7 (spring 1980): 3–19.

Nickerson, Edward A. "'Realistic' Crime Fiction: An Anatomy of Evil People." *The Centennial Review* (spring 1981): 101–32.

O'Connell, Shaun. *Remarkable, Unspeakable New York: A Literary History.* Boston: Beacon P, 1995.

O'Donnell, Patrick, and Robert con Davis, eds. *Intertextuality in Contemporary American Fiction.* Baltimore: Johns Hopkins UP, 1989.

Parks, John G. *E. L. Doctorow.* New York: Continuum, 1991.

Pease, Donald. Rev. of *Billy Bathgate. America* 13 May 1989: 458.

———, ed. *National Identities and Post-Americanist Narratives.* Durham: Duke UP, 1994.

Pfiel, Fred. "Icons for Clowns: American Writers Now." *Another Tale to Tell: Politics and Narrative in Postmodern Culture.* New York: Verso, 1990: 15–32.

Prescott, Peter S. "Getting into Dutch." *Newsweek* 13 Feb. 1989: 76.

Quart, Leonard and Barbara. "*Ragtime* Without a Melody." *Literature/Film Quarterly* 10 (1982): 71–74.

Rabinowitz, Paula. *Labor and Desire: Women's Revolutionary Fiction in Depression America.* Chapel Hill: UP of North Carolina, 1991.

Radar, Barbara A. et al. *The Sleuth and the Scholar: Origins, Evolutions, and Current Trends in Detective Fiction.* Westport, CT: Greenwood P, 1988.

Radosh, William and Joyce Milton. *The Rosenberg File: A Search for the Truth.* New York: Holt, Rinehart & Winston, 1983.

Ragtime. Film. Dir. Milos Forman. Prod. Dino De Laurentiis. Screenplay Michael Weaver. Paramount Pictures, 1981.

Ragtime. Musical. Dir. Frank Galati. Book Terence McNally, 1997.

Ransom, John Crowe. *The New Criticism.* Norfolk, CT: New Directions, 1941.

Reich, Wilhelm. *The Mass Psychology of Fascism.* Ed. Mary Higgins and Chester M. Raphael, M.D. New York: Noonday P, 1970.

Richmond, Jane. "To the End of the Night." *Partisan Review* 39 (1972): 627–29.

Rosenberg, Brian. "Historicizing the New Historicism: Understanding the Past in Criticism and Fiction." *Modern Language Quarterly* 50 (Dec. 1989): 375–92.

Rubin, Merle. "Bathgate: Technique Surpasses Tale." *Christian Science Monitor* 22 Mar. 1989: 13.

———. "Doctorow's Nightmarish, 19th Century Metropolis." *Christian Science Monitor* June 1994: 13.

Ryan, Mary P. "Narratives of Democracy, or History without Subjects." *American Literary History* 8 (summer 1996): 311–27.

Said, Edward. *Culture and Imperialism.* New York: Knopf, 1993.

Sanoff, Alvin P. "The Audacious Lure of Evil." *US News and World Report* 6 Mar 1989: 56.

Sante, Luc. "The Cabinet of Doctor Sartorius." *New York Review of Books* 23 June 1994: 10–12.

Schama, Simon. "New York, Gaslight Necropolis." *New York Times Book Review* 19 June 1994: 1+.

Schneir, Walter and Miriam. *Invitation to an Inquest: Reopening the Rosenberg Case.* New York: Pantheon, 1985. 2nd ed.

Sennett, Richard, and Jonathan Cobb. *The Hidden Injuries of Class.* New York: Alfred Knopf, 1972.

Shelton, Frank W. "E.L. Doctorow's *Welcome to Hard Times*: The Western and the American Dream." *Midwest Quarterly* 25 (autumn 1983): 7–17.

———. Rev of *World's Fair.* *National Forum* (summer 1986): 47.

Sheppard, R. Z. "The Artist as a Very Young Critic." *Time* 18 Nov 1985: 100.

Sloterdijk, Peter. *Critique of Cynical Reason.* Trans. Michael Eldred. Minneapolis: U Minn P, 1987.

Smith, Henry Nash. *Virgin Land: The American West as Symbol and Myth.* Cambridge: Harvard UP., 1950.

Solataroff, Ted. "Of Melville, Poe, and Doctorow." *Nation* 6 June 1994: 784–90.

Stade, George. Rev. of *Ragtime. The New York Times Book Review.* 6 July 1975: 1–2.

Starr, Kevin. Rev of *Welcome to Hard Times. New Republic.* 6 Sept. 1975: 25–27.

Staub, Michael E. *Voices of Persuasion: Politics of Representation in 1930s America*. New York: Cambridge UP, 1994.

Strout, Cushing. "Twain, Doctorow, and the Anachronistic Adventures of the Arms Mechanic and the Jazz Pianist." *Making American Tradition: Vision and Revisions from Ben Franklin to Alice Walker*. New Brunswick: Rutgers UP, 1990: 117–32.

Tanner, Stephen. "Rage and Order in Doctorow's Hard Times." *South Dakota Review* 22 (1984): 79–85.

Terdiman, Richard. "Is There a Class in This Class?" Veeser 225–30.

Thomas, Brook. "The New Historicism and Other Old-Fashioned Topics." Veeser 182–203.

Tocqueville, Alexis de. *Democracy in America*. New York: Knopf, 1945.

Tokarczyk, Michelle M. "The City, *The Waterworks*, and Writing." *The Kenyon Review* 17 (winter 1995): 32–37.

———. *E. L. Doctorow: An Annotated Bibliography*. New York: Garland Publishing Co., 1988.

———. "From the Lions' Den: Survivors in E.L. Doctorow's *The Book of Daniel*." *Critique* 29 (fall 1987): 3–15.

———. Rev. of *The Waterworks*. *The Literary Review* 39 (spring 1996): 435–36.

Towers, Robert. "A Brilliant World of Mirrors." *The New York Times Book Review*. 28 Sept 1980: 1+.

Trenner, Richard, ed. *E. L. Doctorow: Essays and Conversations*. Princeton: Ontario Review P, 1983.

Turner, Frederick Jackson. *The Frontier in American History*. rpt. 1920. Huntington, NY: R.E. Krieger Publishing Co., 1970.

Tyler, Anne. "An American Boy in Gangland." *The New York Times Book Review*. 26 Feb 1989: 1+.

Uruburu, Paula. *The Gruesome Doorway: An Analysis of the American Grotesque*. New York: Peter Lang, 1987.

Van Der Haag, Ernest. "History as Facutalized Fiction." Ed. Sidney Hook. *Philosophy and History: A Symposium*. New York: NYU P, 1963.

Veeser, Aram, ed. *The New Historicism*. London: Routledge, 1989.

Veysey, Laurence. "The Anatomy of American History Reconsidered." *American Quarterly* 31 (fall 1979): 455–77.

Vidler, Anthony. "Psychopathologies of Modern Space: Metropolitan Fear from Agorophobia to Estrangement." Ed. Michael Roth, *Rediscovering History: Culture, Politics and the Psyche*. Stanford: Stanford UP, 1994: 11–29.

Vischer, Emily B., and John S. *Stepfamilies: A Guide to Working with Stepparents and Stepchildren.* New York: Brunner/Mazel, Inc., 1975.

Wald, Alan M. "The 1930s Left in U.S. Literature Reconsidered." Mullen and Linkon 13–28.

Waring, Belle. *Dark Blonde.* Louisville: Sarabande Books, 1997.

Weber, Bruce. "The Myth Maker: An Interview with E. L. Doctorow." *The New York Times Magazine* 20 Oct 1985: 24+.

Wellek, Rene and Austin Warren. *Theory of Literature.* New York: Harcourt Brace, 1949.

Wexley, John. *The Judgment of Julius and Ethel Rosenberg.* 2nd ed. New York: Ballantine Books, 1977.

White, Edmund. "Pyrography." *Nation* 30 Nov. 1985: 594–95.

White, Hayden. *Metahistory: The Historical Imagination in Nineteenth Century Europe.* Baltimore: Johns Hopkins UP, 1973.

———. *Tropics of Discourse: Essays in Cultural Criticism.* Baltimore: Johns Hopkins UP, 1978.

Wilde, Alan. "'Strange Displacements of the Ordinary': Elkin, Barthelme, and the Problem of the Excluded Middle." *Boundary 2* 10 (winter 1982): 177–99.

———. *Horizons of Assent: Modernism, Postmodernism, and the Ironic Imagination.* Baltimore: Johns Hopkins UP, 1981.

Wilding, Michael. *Political Fictions.* London: Routledge & Kegan: 1980.

Williams, John E. "Images of Power and the Power of Images: Essays on the Fiction and Nonfiction of E.L. Doctorow." Diss. Ohio University, June 1990.

Williams, Raymond. *Marxism and Determinism.* Oxford: Oxford UP, 1977.

Wills, Garry. "Juggler's Code." *New York Review of Books* 2 Mar.1989: 3–4.

Winkler, Allan M. "*Ragtime* and the United States Before World War I." Friedl and Schulz 105–12.

Wood, Michael. "Light and Lethal American Romance." *Times Literary Supplement* 15 Sept. 1989: 997–98.

Zins, Daniel L. "The Cult of Fact: E. L. Doctorow's *The Book of Daniel*, Robert Coover's *The Public Burning* and the Rosenberg Case." MLA Convention. Chicago. Dec. 1995.

Index

African-Americans, 74, 86, 93, 94, 95, 100–101, 104, 105
American Dream, xiii, 95, 105, 111, 112, 134
Anderson, Sherwood, 6, 30, 122, 144
Anti-Semitism, 39, 41, 76
Anzaldua, Gloria, 62
Appleby, Joyce, et al.
 Telling the Truth About History, 20, 21, 152
Arendt, Hannah, 153
Arnold, Marilyn, 55, 57

Baba, Minako, 134
Bakhtin, M. M., 3, 13, 16
Barthes, Roland, 47
Belenkey, Mary, 34
Bell, Daniel
 The End of Ideology, 77
blended family, 52–54
bourgeois, 15, 135, 146
Brown, Norman O., 121
Budick, Emily Miller, 91–92

Caesar, Terry P.
 "Motherhood and Postmodernism," 139
Cantor, Jay, 113, 146
Chase, Richard, 91
Chodorow, Nancy, 7, 34
Claridge, Henry, 174
class issues, 18, 135, 155

Clayton, John, 2, 39
Clerc, Charles, 141
Clinton, Pres. Bill, 171–175
Communism. *See under* political outlooks
Conrad, Joseph
 Heart of Darkness, 21, 39, 94, 128, 154, 163
Crane, Stephen
 The Blue Hotel, 9, 47
 The Bride Comes to Yellow Sky, 47

death, 38
Dickens, Charles
 Hard Times, 49
Dickstein, Morris, 42
Diogenes, 33
Donne, John
 "For Whom the Bell Tolls," 96, 153
Dos Passos, John, 105

Eagleton, Terry, 80, 166
 The Illusions of Postmodernism, 73
Eckstein, Barbara, S., 12, 17, 19, 35, 57, 71, 83, 113, 135
Eco, Umberto, 141
Emblidge, David, 102
environments
 the Bronx, 73, 74, 134
 New York City, 73, 74, 151, 156

the West, 9, 50-53, 82
essays
  "The Beliefs of Writers," 27
  "False Documents," 175, 177
  "Jack London, Hemingway, and the Constitution, 3
  "An Open Letter to the President," 55
Estrin, Barbara L., 84
exceptionalism, American, 54, 61, 145

feminist theorists, 95-96
fiction
  Big as Life, 10, 67
  Billy Bathgate, xv, 4, 17-18, 19, 133-148, 154
    reviewed, 19-20
  The Book of Daniel, xii, xv, 3, 4, 5, 10-11, 12, 67-86, 111, 116, 123, 141, 165, 166
  "The Leather Man," 6-7, 19, 29-30
  Lives of the Poets, 4, 5, 6, 27-36, 139, 157
  Loon Lake, xii, xiii, 4, 15-17, 19, 111-129, 141, 165
  Ragtime, xii, xvi, 4, 12, 17, 20, 89-106, 172, 176
  The Waterworks, xi, 4, 5, 20-23, 151-167, 172
  Welcome to Hard Times, 3, 4, 9-10, 11, 21, 47-63, 120
  World's Fair, xvi, 4, 6, 15, 21, 36-43
  "The Writer in the Family," xvi
Foley, Barbara,
  Radical Representations, 10, 93, 105, 112, 119, 125
Foucault, Michel, 140, 166, 177
Fowler, Douglas, 68
Friedman, Ellen G.,
  "Where Are the Missing Contents?" 29
Frietag, Michael, 134

gangsters, 133-148

genre, 62-63
  bildungsroman, 1, 98, 113, 116, 117, 133
  counter-western
    "The Blue Hotel" (Crane), 9, 47
  historical fiction, 43, 47
  kùnstlerroman, 8, 36
  metafiction, 90
  political fiction, 103
  proletarian, 93, 98, 111-129
  romance, 92-94, 102, 104, 105
  Romantic, 115
  science fiction, vii, 10, 67
  Western, 5, 9, 50-53
Gentry, Marshall Bruce, 101
Gilded Age, 151, 158
Gilligan, Carol, 7, 34
Goldbeck, Eva, 113, 145
Goldman, Emma, 92, 96, 98, 99, 104
Graff, Gerald, 78, 101
Gross, David S., 47, 55, 114, 121
grotesques, 6, 157, 175

Harpham, Geoffrey G., 116, 127
Harter, Carol
  and James R. Thompson: *E. L. Doctorow,* 6, 116, 152
Hawthorne, Nathaniel, 151
Himes, Chester, 100
historical records
  contingencies, 61
  documentary elements, 60-61, 70, 81
  historical interpretations, 60-61, 70
  worklike elements, 60-61, 70, 112
Holocaust, 9, 39, 56
Howe, Irving, 113
Hutcheon, Linda, 68, 84, 105

isolation, 7

Jameson, Fredric, xi, 78, 175
Jewish immigrant culture, 2, 36

Index

Johnson, Diane, 112
Joplin, Scott, 90
Joyce, James
   "Portrait of the Artist as a Young Man," 5, 8, 36, 127

King, Richard, 128
Kleist, Heinrich von, 102, 103
Kolodny, Annette
   "Letting Go," 62
Kundera, Milan, 69, 173
künsterlerroman, 8, 36

La Capra, Dominick
   Rethinking Intellectual History, 59–60, 70, 81, 90, 122
Lentricchia, Frank, 35, 166
Leonard, John, 136
Levine, Paul, 73, 77, 85, 96
   "The Writer as Independent Witness," 68
Lewinsky, Monica, 175
Lewis, R.W.B.
   The American Adam, 144
Lubove, Ray, 97, 98

McCaffery, Larry, 3, 27
McHale, Brian, 141
midfiction, 11, 152
Miller, Arthur, 174
Milton, John R., 53
Morgan, J. P., 103, 106
Morris, Christopher, 32, 48, 55, 59, 67, 89, 95, 127, 162
   "Fiction Is a System of Knowledge," 32, 139
   "Models," 41, 42, 55
Morrison, Toni, 174

Nesbit, Evelyn, 96, 99, 103–104, 111
Neumeyer, Peter, 101
New Criticism, 2
Newman, Katherine, 35
nineteenth-century American fiction, 113

O'Connell, Shaun, 49, 158
optimism, 166
Ovid
   Metamorphoses, 13, 91

Parks, John G., 58, 111
Pease, Donald, 146
Pfeil, Fred, 33
philosophical outlooks
   Enlightenment, 3, 114
   Skepticism, 92
political outlooks
   American exceptionalism, 54, 61, 145
   capitalism, 98
   communism, 11, 74, 76
   Constitutionalism, 75
   cynical detachment, 5, 33–34, 73
   enlightened false consciousness, 6, 34, 72
   family structure, 147
   grotesque, 146
   Marxism, 6, 113–114, 138
   skepticism, xvi, 56, 92, 159
   skeptical commitment, 4
politics of indirection, xi
postmodernism, xvi, 10, 11, 63, 68, 69, 80, 151–167
poststructuralism, 152
praxis, 8, 20, 27–43, 68, 152, 166, 167
Prescott, Peter S., 133
Puzo, Mario, 135

race issues, 101–102
Ransom, John Crowe, 2
   New Criticism, 2
Reagan administration, 136, 138–139, 144
Reich, Wilhelm, 4, 85
Robeson, Paul, 76
Rosenberg case, xii, 68, 70, 75, 76, 79, 81, 85
Ryan, Mary P., 172

Schama, Simon, 157, 163
Schultz, Dutch, xii, 17–20, 133–148

Sennett, Richard
and Jonathan Cobb: *The Hidden Injuries of Class,* 16, 31, 118
Shelton, Frank R., 50
Simmel, Georg, 156
    "Metropolis and Mental Health," 156
Sloterdijk, Peter, 6, 33–34, 72, 73, 123, 126, 164
spatial pathology, 156
Starr, Kenneth, 175

Thomas, Brook, 59
Thoreau, Henry David, 30, 115
Tokarczyk, Michelle M.
    "The City, *The Waterworks*, and Writing," 151, 161, 164
Tocqueville, Alexis de, 51
Trenner, Richard,
    "Politics and the Mode of Fiction," 4, 114
Turner, Frederick Jackson
    The Frontier in American History, 9, 49–50, 54, 62, 80, 162

Tweed, Boss, xi, 152, 158, 166

union activity
    Lawrenceville, Mass., 90, 125, 126

Waring, Belle
    "It Was My First Nursing Job," 5
wars
    Civil War, 21, 97, 156
    Gulf War, 148
    Vietnam, 71
    World War I, 97
    World War II, 21
Wilde, Alan, 11, 69, 102, 152, 166
Wilding, Michael, 13, 81, 113
Williams, John, 33, 42, 53
Williams, Raymond, 35, 92, 146
    Marxism and Determinism, 61
Winkler, Alan, 103

Zen Buddhism, in *Loon Lake,* 126

OHIO UNIVERSITY

Pleas